Interviews with **John Kenneth Galbraith**

Conversations with Public Intellectuals Series
Douglas Brinkley and David Oshinsky, General Editors

Interviews with

John Kenneth Galbraith

Edited by
James Ronald Stanfield and
Jacqueline Bloom Stanfield

University Press of Mississippi
Jackson

www.upress.state.ms.us

The University Press of Mississippi is a member of the
Association of American University Presses.

Frontis: Photofest

11 10 09 08 07 06 05 04   4 3 2 1

Library of Congress Cataloging-in-Publication Data

Galbraith, John Kenneth, 1908–
    Interviews with John Kenneth Galbraith / edited by James Ronald Stanfield and Jacqueline
Bloom Stanfield.
        p. cm.—(Conversations with public intellectuals series)
    Includes bibliographical references and index.
    ISBN 1-57806-610-7 (cloth : alk.paper)
    1. Galbraith, John Kenneth, 1908– —Interviews. 2. Economists—United States—Interviews.
3. Ambassadors—United States—Interviews. 4. Economics—United States—History—
20 century. 5. United States—Politics and government—1945–1989. I. Stanfield, J. Ron, 1945–
II. Stanfield, Jacqueline Bloom. III. Title. IV. Series.

HB119.G33A3 2004
330'.092—dc22   2003060093

British Library Cataloging-in-Publication Data available

Books by John Kenneth Galbraith

Modern Competition and Business Policy. Oxford: Oxford University Press, 1938.
A Theory of Price Control. Cambridge, MA: Harvard University Press, 1952.
American Capitalism: The Concept of Countervailing Power. Boston: Houghton Mifflin, 1952.
Economics and the Art of Controversy. Rutgers, NJ: Rutgers University Press, 1955.
The Great Crash, 1929. Boston: Houghton Mifflin, 1955.
The Affluent Society. Boston: Houghton Mifflin, 1958.
The Liberal Hour. Boston: Houghton Mifflin, 1960.
Economic Development. Boston: Houghton Mifflin, 1964.
The Scotch. Boston: Houghton Mifflin, 1964.
The New Industrial State. Boston: Houghton Mifflin, 1967 (subsequent editions 1971, 1978, and 1985).
The Triumph. Boston: Houghton Mifflin, 1968 (a novel).
Ambassador's Journal: A Personal Account of the Kennedy Years. Boston: Houghton Mifflin, 1969.
How to Control the Military. Camden City, NY: Doubleday, 1969.
The American Left and Some British Comparisons. London: Fabian Society, 1971.
Economics, Peace, and Laughter, edited by Andrea D. Williams. Boston: Houghton Mifflin, 1971.
Economics and the Public Purpose. Boston: Houghton Mifflin, 1973.
A China Passage. Boston: Houghton Mifflin, 1973.
Money: Whence It Came, Where It Went. Boston: Houghton Mifflin, 1975.
The Age of Uncertainty. Boston: Houghton Mifflin, 1977.
The Galbraith Reader. Cambridge, MA: Harvard Common Press, 1977.
Almost Everyone's Guide to Economics (with Nicole Salinger). Boston: Houghton Mifflin, 1978.
Annals of an Abiding Liberal: Perspectives on the Twentieth Century and the Case for Coming to Terms with It, edited by Andrea D. Williams. Boston: Houghton Mifflin, 1979.
The Nature of Mass Poverty. Cambridge, MA: Harvard University Press, 1979.
A Life in Our Times: Memoir. Boston: Houghton Mifflin, 1981.
The Anatomy of Power. Boston: Houghton Mifflin, 1983.
Reaganomics: Meaning, Means, and Ends. New York: Free Press, 1983.
The Voice of the Poor: Essays in Economic and Political Persuasion. Cambridge, MA: Harvard University Press, 1983.

A View from the Stands: Of People, Politics, Military Power, and the Arts, edited by Andrea D. Williams. Boston: Houghton Mifflin, 1986.

The Culture of Contentment. Boston: Houghton Mifflin, 1987.

Economics in Perspective: A Critical History. Boston: Houghton Mifflin, 1987.

History of Economics: The Past as the Present. London: Hamish Hamilton, 1987.

Capitalism, Communism and Coexistence: From the Bitter Past to a Better Prospect (with Stanislav Menshikov). Boston: Houghton Mifflin, 1988.

A Short History of Financial Euphoria. Knoxville: Whittle Direct Books, 1990.

A Tenured Professor. Boston: Houghton Mifflin, 1990 (a novel).

A Journey through Economic Time: A Firsthand View. Boston: Houghton Mifflin, 1994.

The Good Society: The Humane Agenda. Boston: Houghton Mifflin, 1996.

Letters to Kennedy. Cambridge, MA: Harvard University Press, 1998.

The Socially Concerned Today. Toronto: University of Toronto Press, 1998.

Name-Dropping: From FDR On. Boston: Houghton Mifflin, 1999.

Contents

Introduction xi

Chronology xix

The World Through Galbraith's Eyes 3
Anthony Lewis

The Public Sector Is Still Starved 16
Challenge

The Playboy Interview:
John Kenneth Galbraith 26
Michael Laurence

Conversation with an Inconvenient Economist 75
Challenge

Galbraith and His Critics 95
John McClaughry

John Kenneth Galbraith 105
John F. Baker

Advice to Exxon 110
Downs Matthews

The Anatomy of Power   116
Richard D. Bartel

Galbraith: America Will Feel the Crunch of
Reagan Revolution   130
William Olsen

The Political Asymmetry of Economic Policy   133
Eastern Economic Journal

Conversation   140
Steven Pressman

Communist Economies of Eastern Europe   147
Senate Foreign Relations Committee

John Kenneth Galbraith   153
John Newark

John Kenneth Galbraith Looks Back at the
Reagan-Bush Era   161
Thomas Karier

Conversation with John Kenneth Galbraith   169
Robert MacNeil

The Lion in Winter: The Harvard Prof's Latest Lesson:
How to Age Wisely   175
William A. Davis

John Kenneth Galbraith   180
David C. Colander and Harry Landreth

A Conversation with John Kenneth Galbraith   192
Kimberly Blanton

The Ken Galbraith (and Bill Buckley) Show   196
Lorie Conway

A Gentler, Kinder Approach—the Galbraith Way   202
Hardev Kaur

Galbraith Fears Recession to Trample Poor   206
Leslie Gevirtz

Galbraith Says Capitalism Will Prevail   208
Toru Kunimatsu

The Origins of the Galbraithian System:
Stephen P. Dunn in Conversation with J. K. Galbraith   217
Stephen P. Dunn

On Bush, Greed, and God's Ministers:
John Kenneth Galbraith Speaks Out   238
Sharon Basco

Index   243

Introduction

John Kenneth Galbraith, a leading scholar of the American institutionalist school, is the world's most famous economist in the second half of the twentieth century. Among American economists of any era, he is rivaled only by Thorstein Veblen for the introduction of phrases that have taken on a life of their own in the literate idiom. *Countervailing power, the conventional wisdom, the affluent society, the new industrial state,* and *the technostructure* have become familiar even beyond Galbraith's remarkably wide readership. No other twentieth-century economist, excepting perhaps John Maynard Keynes, can claim so secure a place in the belles-lettres of the English-speaking world.

John Kenneth Galbraith was born in 1908 to a Scotch Canadian family in a rural area of southern Ontario. He was the second of four children born to William and Catherine Galbraith. The Galbraiths like most of their neighbors seem to have been sternly religious and staunchly dedicated to practical knowledge. William Galbraith was a farmer but at various times also ran an insurance agency and taught school; he was also actively engaged in Liberal Party politics at the local level. Kenneth Galbraith recalls having had a happy childhood but there were some bleaker aspects.[1] His mother died when he was fourteen and the family struggled for some time adjusting to the trauma.

After completing a bachelor's degree at the Ontario Agricultural College, Galbraith set out to pursue graduate studies in agricultural economics at the University of California, receiving his Ph.D. in 1934, upon submission of a dissertation on public expenditures in California counties. Berkeley was then a citadel of left-wing economics, housing the likes of Robert Brady, Leo Rogin, and others who supported migrant workers, small farmers, and trade unions.[2] In 1934 Galbraith left Berkeley and began his long—though frequently interrupted—tenure at Harvard University, where he is now an emeritus professor.

Galbraith recalls studying Alfred Marshall and ever after sought to apply Marshall's dictum that economists study "the ordinary business of life." Nonetheless, he came to be a persistent critic of the neoclassical movement that Marshall headed. He also studied Thorstein Veblen, whom he admired and through whose influence he became critical of complacency in economics. In an interview with Stephen P. Dunn, Galbraith notes that Veblen was one of several important "modifying influences" that pulled him away from conventional economics, but to Steven Pressman he also observes that Veblen "brought a critical but nonconstructive judgement to bear on economics." No doubt this "nonconstructive" verdict stems in large part from Galbraith's view that Veblen's central construct, the dichotomy between industrial progress and business status, was a blind alley.[3] This suggests that Veblen did not influence the substance of Galbraith's later work, but one could argue that there is much Veblenian influence in that regard.[4]

Galbraith has often set aside his academic career to devote time to public service and partisan politics. He worked in the Department of Agriculture during the New Deal and in the Office of Price Administration and Civilian Supply during the war. From his wartime work emerged a monograph, *The Theory of Price Control* (1952), which, though not widely influential, contained some of the seminal ideas of his major works. With the cessation of hostilities in Europe, he worked with the Office of Strategic Services, directing research on the effectiveness of the Allies' strategic bombing of Germany. In 1947, Galbraith was one of the liberal founders of the Americans for Democratic Action, an organization he later chaired. After working prominently in the presidential campaigns of Senator Adlai Stevenson and President John F. Kennedy, Galbraith served as U.S. ambassador to India in the early 1960s. A very outspoken critic of U.S. involvement in Viet Nam, he campaigned on behalf of the presidential ambitions of Senators Eugene McCarthy (1968) and George McGovern (1972). Later he was to work in the campaigns of Congressman Morris Udall (1976) and Senator Edward Kennedy (1980).

Many of the interviews collected here deal with aspects of his political service and provide him ample opportunity to apply his celebrated wit to those
with whom he disagreed.

The young Galbraith, ever a man of his times, would likely have been
amused by the great American celebration that followed the First World War.
The exuberance of a business culture which had, not for the first nor the last
time, forgotten all the lessons history made available, surely caught his eye.
The second of the great merger waves swept through industrial structure as
the financial markets soared to maniacally speculative heights. The inevitable
financial market crash and the catastrophe of the 1930s must have left an
indelible imprint of just how unregulated the putatively self-regulating market
really was. These themes, and the need for new policy responses and continuous reform to deal with them, became his mantra. The Second World War
powerfully affirmed the ideas of Keynes which Galbraith had already readily
accepted. But Galbraith was soon convinced of the asymmetric and inflationary implications of utilizing aggregate demand policy without complementary attention to structural considerations. Ever after Galbraith emphasized
the illegitimate power of the corporate oligarchy and the ever present threat
that a new period of financial mania would end in panic. Two books in 1952
dealt with corporate power and inflation and a book on the great crash of
1929 followed in 1954.

There is general agreement that three of Galbraith's books lay out most
coherently his thinking on the modern economy. In this central trilogy,
The Affluent Society (1958), *The New Industrial State* (1967), and *Economics and the
Public Purpose* (1973), Galbraith emphasized power, its abuse, its neglect by
conventional economists, and the need for social reform to channel it to the
public interest. Such deeper concerns about the postwar prospect were lost
in yet another great American celebration in the 1950s and 1960s. The celebration spread to conventional economics but its complacency was soon
to be shattered by the instability of the 1970s and the splintering of economics into many competing camps.

The first book of Galbraith's central trilogy, *The Affluent Society*, argues that
the outmoded mentality of more-is-better impedes the further economic
progress that would be possible if contemporary affluence were put to more

reasonable use. Advertising and related salesmanship activities create artificially high demand for the commodities produced by private businesses and lead to a concomitant neglect of public sector goods and services that would contribute far more to the quality of life. This social imbalance and its deleterious effects becomes Galbraith's most powerful argument; it remains today the most powerful indictment of America's priorities. It has never been effectively refuted and little effort has been made to resolve it.

In *The New Industrial State,* Galbraith expands his analysis of the role of power in economic life by elaborating the argument with regard to the social power exercised by the corporate oligarchy in its advertising and related salesmanship activities and in the access it has to major political figures. The social imbalance theme is revised to emphasize the political economy's attendance to the interest of the powerful corporate sector relative to the sector that continues to operate upon the conventional market economic pattern. The imbalance thus becomes less a matter of the public versus the private than of the powerful versus the weak. This strengthens and refocuses the social imbalance argument as well as the countervailing power argument for social reform to empower the weak.

Economics and the Public Purpose, the last work in Galbraith's major trilogy, is in many ways a restatement and clarification of the two earlier books in the trilogy. But the assault on conventional economics becomes more pointed. Galbraith argues that economic ideas should be evaluated by the "test of anxiety," i.e., by their ability to relate to popular concern about the economic system and to resolve or allay this anxiety. Conventional economic thought, with its competitive model and presumptions of scarcity and consumer sovereignty, what Galbraith calls the "imagery of choice," serves to hide the power structure that actually governs the American economy. It is the "convenient social virtue" of conventional economics to serve the powerful by this obscurantism.

Galbraith is a prolific author. In addition to his major trilogy, he has published countless articles and essays and more than two dozen books, including two novels, a coauthored book on Indian painting, memoirs, travelogues, political tracts, and several books in economic and intellectual history. He also collaborated on and narrated a Public Broadcasting System television series, "The Age of Uncertainty." As revealed in the *Playboy* interview, Galbraith became a best-selling author as a result of a conscious resolution to write for a larger audience than academic economists. *The Great Crash* (1954) received some public attention and led to Galbraith's testimony before a Senate committee in 1955, but it was *The Affluent Society* that made good on Galbraith's pledge to reach a larger audience. This best-seller established Galbraith's status as a very public intellectual.

The interviews gathered here attest to this status. There are interviews in academic journals, such as the *Eastern Economic Journal*, the *Review of Political Economy*, and the *Journal of Post-Keynesian Economics*, in which Galbraith comments on specific economics topics. The several interviews from *Challenge Magazine* are broadly academic and cover similar themes as the journals. Such interviews deal with power and the dual economic structure of advanced capitalism, the inadequacy of aggregate demand policy alone to deal with the wage-price spiral of corporate capitalism, the resort to disastrous monetary policy when fiscal policy proves to be politically asymmetric, the need for continuous reform of financial regulation to stay abreast of financial innovation, the theory of social imbalance, and the structure of taxes and expenditures.

In interviews with John McClaughry and Steven Pressman, Galbraith discusses the emphasis he has put on the dual structure, an emphasis he considers to be among his most important contributions. One sector of the economy is comprised of large corporations with significant market power, indeed so much that for Galbraith, their relationship to the market is essentially one of administration or planning. The other sector is comprised of small business organizations which are subject to the discipline of the market in pretty much the manner depicted by conventional economics discussion of competition. Given this dual structure, it is important not to separate the microeconomic and macroeconomic effects of policy and to employ a multifaceted approach to stabilization. If aggregate demand policy, that is, fiscal and monetary policies, achieve anything close to macroeconomic balance, the market power of corporations and unions in the

administered sector will be unleashed and set in motion a wage-price inflationary spiral. If resort is made to aggregate demand policy to counter the
inflationary trend, the task is likely to fall to monetary policy. Fiscal policy
is politically asymmetric because government officials find it difficult to
muster the courage to raise taxes and cut expenditures, in contrast to the
politically palatable actions to fight unemployment, increasing expenditures
and cutting taxes. The use of monetary policy falls heavily upon the market
sector, while the administered sector enjoys more favorable financial terms
and has significant retained earnings to draw upon.[5] The use of monetary
policy therefore increases the disparity between the two sectors, exacerbat-
ing not only inequality but also social imbalance. Recessionary budget
restrictions tend to fall upon weaker, less organized claimants to the public
purse. Well-connected, well-organized political forces representing the
administered sector fair better.

In a 1967 interview in *Challenge*, Galbraith expresses his concern about
the effects of taxes and expenditures, fiscal policy, on social imbalance. In
particular, the choice between tax cutting and increasing government expenditures is not neutral in its effects on the quality of life. The shift toward tax-
cutting to expand aggregate demand early on concerned Galbraith since it
meant that less attention would be placed upon increasing expenditures—
expenditures necessary to reduce social imbalance. For this reason he feared
the success of the Kennedy-Johnson tax cut policy would be seized upon by
conservatives to the detriment of wiser fiscal policy in the future. Galbraith's
prescience in this regard could not be more evident or more topical given
the tax cut mantra of prominent Republicans over the past twenty years.

Galbraith's stabilization policy proposals emphasized the use of some
direct intervention on the wage-price structure of the administered sector
alongside the maintenance of high employment by appropriate fiscal policy.
He retained the early Keynesian conviction that monetary policy should
not be used as a tool of counter-cyclical policy. Although he came to doubt
the political feasibility of wage-price controls, he never modified his model
to suggest any other workable stabilization program. Nor did he ever recant
his insistence on the need for progressive income tax policies and rising

government expenditures to improve social balance by offsetting the socially destructive imbalance of power in the social economy.

These interviews frequently deal as well with the intellectual historical concerns of those who influenced Galbraith and as to his thinking at various times in his career and his views of other prominent economists, particularly John Maynard Keynes. In an interview reprinted from *The Coming of Keynesianism to America* (edited by David C. Colander and Harry Landreth), Galbraith comments upon the coming of Keynes to America, referring both to Keynes's ideas and his visits to America to put these ideas forward, as well as to Galbraith's spending a year at Cambridge, England, discussing Keynes with the young economists who were engaged in sorting out Keynes's ideas.

These concerns arise as well in interviews in less academic periodicals, such as the ones in this collection from *In These Times* and *Playboy*, but understandably they are given a more political, less technical economic twist. Moreover they usually range widely to social and political topics beyond the scope of academic economics, such as Galbraith's views of economic policy, political strategy and political figures, his tenure as ambassador to India, his friendship with the Kennedy family, the role of the fine and liberal arts in society, the outlook for the stock market, and, in his conversation with William A. Davis, age-bias. Oddly, despite his interest and work in the fields (*A China Passage, Journey to Poland and Yugoslavia*), Galbraith's views on economic development, comparative economics, and the transitional economies are not frequently called forth by interviewers. Three exceptions included here are the interviews with Anthony Lewis and John Newark and Galbraith's testimony before the Senate Foreign Relations Committee.

In these interviews, as in Galbraith's works, the reader will find perhaps the wittiest, most articulate public intellectual of his time. Widely read, widely influential, widely recognized, Galbraith has clearly achieved celebrity status. But the editors hope that the reader of these interviews and Galbraith's works comes away with something more, something more important. Galbraith's institutionally oriented approach to economics is crucially important. For, contrary to the prevalent antistate ideology, Galbraith instructs that free societies and market economies do not spontaneously erupt if only one minimizes government. Preservation of freedom and order in a complex society is anything but simple; it requires a framework of formal and informal rules to which government must contribute in many positive ways. Moreover, the rules of the game are never fixed but in constant flux. People try to change them to serve their interests or their passions. Technical and organizational innovations directly and indirectly impact these rules so that continuous social reform, continuous policy experimentation is necessary. Turning the state toward service to the wider public purpose is problematic given the presence of powerful vested interests, and even as he entertains, Galbraith instructs in the institutional economic analysis that is a vital component of our democratic discourse.

Notes

1. Lamson, Peggy, 1991, *Speaking of Galbraith*, Boston: Houghton Mifflin.
2. Galbraith, J. K., 1971, *Economics, Peace, and Laughter*, Boston: Houghton Mifflin, pp. 344–60, and Galbraith, J. K., 1981, *A Life in Our Time*, Chapter 2.
3. Galbraith, J. K., 1979, *Annals of an Abiding Liberal*, Boston: Houghton Mifflin, p. 144.
4. Stanfield, James Ronald, 1996, *John Kenneth Galbraith*, St. Martin's Press: New York, pp. 153–60.
5. Galbraith, J. K., 1957, "Market Structure and Stabilization Policy," *Review of Economics and Statistics*, 39 (May).

Chronology

1908	Born in Iona Station, Ontario, Canada.
1931	Completes bachelor's degree in agricultural economics at Ontario Agricultural College (now the University of Toronto).
1934	Received Ph.D. in agricultural economics at the University of California, Berkeley.
1934–1935	Worked at United States Department of Agriculture.
1936	First hired at Harvard University.
1937	Became American citizen; married Catherine Merriam Atwater.
1937–1938	Social Science Research Fellowship at Cambridge, England.
1938–1941	Harvard University and Princeton University.
1940	Federal Farm Bureau.
1941–1943	Deputy administrator in the Office of Price Administration and Civilian Supply.
1943–1948	Editor at *Fortune Magazine*.
1945–1946	Leave from *Fortune Magazine*; worked with the Office of Strategic Services, as director of the U.S. Strategic Bombing

Survey, directing research on the effectiveness of the Allies' strategic bombing of Germany which culminated in a report titled *The Effects of Strategic Bombing on the Germany War Economy*.

1946   Awarded Presidential Medal of Freedom.

1947   Co-founder of the Americans for Democratic Action, an organization he later chaired.

1948   Came to Harvard permanently, where he is currently the Paul M. Warburg Professor of Economics Emeritus.

1952   Published *A Theory of Price Control* and *American Capitalism: The Concept of Countervailing Power,* worked prominently in the presidential campaign of Senator Adlai Stevenson.

1954   Published *The Great Crash, 1929*.

1958   Published *The Affluent Society,* for which he won the Tamiment Book Award and Sidney Hillman Award.

1960   Economic advisor to Senator John F. Kennedy during Kennedy's presidential campaign.

1961–1963   Served as U.S. Ambassador to India.

1967   Published *The New Industrial State*.

1968   Nominated Senator Eugene McCarthy for president at Democratic Convention.

1969   Published *How to Control the Military*.

1972   President of the American Economic Association.

1973   Published *Economics and the Public Purpose*.

1975   Retired from Harvard.

1976   Worked in campaign of Congressman Morris Udall.

1979   Published *Annals of an Abiding Liberal*.

1980   Worked on presidential campaign of Senator Edward
            Kennedy.

1981   Published *A Life in Our Times: Memoirs.*

1982   Elected to the American Academy of Arts and Letters for
            literature.

1983   Published *The Anatomy of Power.*

1984–1987   President of the combined American Academy and Insti-
            tute of Arts and Letters.

1992   Published *The Culture of Contentment.*

1994   Published *A Journey Through Economic Time: A Firsthand View.*

1996   Published *The Good Society: The Humane Agenda.*

1998   Published *Letters to Kennedy.*

1999   Published *Name-Dropping: From FDR On.*

Interviews with **John Kenneth Galbraith**

The World Through Galbraith's Eyes

Anthony Lewis / 1966

From the *New York Times Magazine*
18 December 1966, p. 25+.
Reprinted by permission.

LEWIS: *You wrote in* The Affluent Society *about the necessity for more spending in the public sector. It seems that in Britain there's a tremendous will to spend more in the public sector, but isn't the difficulty that the pie isn't large enough and that they don't seem to be able to get it large enough?*

GALBRAITH: Of course it isn't really a small pie. The pie has grown steadily and enormously in the last 20 years and even more so in the last hundred years; the wealth of Britain today is immeasurably greater in the aggregate and per capita than it was at the very peak of Victorian power.

One has only to reflect on how intolerable life would be in these small islands if there was not very substantial spending in the public sector. If the cities here were as casually managed as those in the United States—if London traffic were as casually managed as it doubtless is, say, in Indianapolis—they would be intolerable. With a dense population heavy public-sector spending becomes a matter of greater urgency even than with us.

But, of course, Britain does have problems. It seems to me that the problem of economics in Britain is very much like that of sex in the United States: Both countries have an enormous difficulty in keeping it in perspective.

LEWIS: *Just what is wrong with Britain's economy?*

GALBRAITH: First of all, it is very delicately balanced. The British have to import a great deal, which means that they have to export a great deal. It's an open, as distinct from a closed, economy. They have to maintain a very close relationship between their prices and those of other countries. They have to be competitive.

Also England is probably the most egalitarian of the non-Communist countries. This means that a very large part of the population has lower-middle-class consuming tendencies—that is, a strong propensity to spend and not to save. Governments naturally yield to the demands of these people by offering more consumption, with the result that about every two years consumption in Britain gains too much on production. There isn't enough left for export, because the domestic market is too favorable.

So then there's a balance of payments crisis. An atmosphere of crisis develops. Indeed it must develop before the Government is able to take the relatively modest action—limiting wage and price increases, increasing down payments, increasing taxation slightly—that slows the increase in consumption and presently the balance of payments becomes all right again and the process starts over.

This is the reason for my earlier suggestion that the British who gave economics to the world have never been able to get it fully in perspective. Each of these crises has come to the people of Britain as though it were a complete novelty, when in fact every one since World War II has had the same fundamental character. I would fault the present tendency of Labor party politics—as of Democratic politics in the U.S.—for being too tactical, insufficiently concerned with long-run strategy.

LEWIS: *We often hear about the British workman being stodgy and lazy, seeking protection too much in restrictive practices, and the British themselves are in an extremely self-critical mood. Do you think there is something to that?*

GALBRAITH: Absolutely not. Anybody who is intimately associated with workers always is impressed by their dislike for sustained manual labor. As

I recall the days when I did manual farm labor myself, my principal memory is of wanting to do less of it.

I have no doubt whatever that part of the great impetus to mechanization and automation in the United States is the low productivity of the American worker in purely manual terms. Every employer yearns for machines instead. Of course, America also has a greater propensity to save and a larger capital supply, so it overcomes the constitutional laziness of its workers by investing in machinery, whereas the British have to struggle along with more men. Neither the French workers nor the Italian workers are models of productivity and I think that within a few years the Japanese will learn the malingering tendencies of the rest of the world. I think that the desire to escape sustained manual effort can be put down as one of the fundamental human qualities.

LEWIS: *Is there any hope of some general solution to overcome what you say is a very logical tendency not to like production-line work?*
GALBRAITH: I expect the answer lies in the automatic and mechanized enterprise where the worker performs at a console board and/or keeps watch over some dials—this is basically much more pleasant and attractive.

LEWIS: *Apart from Britain's economic problems, how do you regard the modern technological economy in general?*
GALBRAITH: I have just finished a book largely on this subject. So I can be quite eloquent. The central idea in economics has always been that the individual goes into the market and, by purchasing or not purchasing, instructs the productive apparatus. And the productive apparatus, the business enterprises, come into existence in response to this process.

This has been one of the nearly unquestioned assumptions of economics. But when I was working several years ago on *The Affluent Society* I came to the conclusion that this was an assumption which, as the economy matured, could no longer be justified. In particular, there is an increasing tendency for the business firm to create the demand that it satisfies, through product variation, advertising, sales strategy. Certainly the individual still functions in the market, still instructs the productive apparatus. But, increasingly, large organizations go into the market, fix prices, and go on beyond those fixed prices to get the kind of consumer behavior they want. Our view of what a motor car should be like is not something that is inherent—it is given to us by the automobile industry.

The market is also steadily and persistently and progressively undermined by technology. While you can buy simple things in the market, you cannot buy more complex ones—you must plan. You can buy unskilled labor in the market, but it is not easy to buy highly specialized electronic engineers; you could buy pack horses in the market, but not space vehicles. With advancing technology the market becomes ever less efficient as an instrument, and its place is taken by one or another form of planning.

Now the planning of the private firm and the planning of the state tend to supplement each other. The private firm can fix minimum prices but it can't fix maximum prices, so increasingly the state comes in with wage and price guidelines. The private firm can do a lot to influence the behavior of the individual consumer, but it can't insure that there's enough purchasing power for everything that's produced, and that's where the state comes in. The private firm is very good at handling the technology of simple products, but it can't underwrite the technology required for modern military purposes, and so the state underwrites that.

In short, in the modern planning structure public and private planning are rather rationally intermeshed.

It seems to me that one of the reasons the French and the Germans have moved ahead so rapidly in these last years is that they've been much more pragmatic about this intermeshing than the British. The French have quite clearly decided that where the Government needs to do things, it will do them. They have never been worried much by philosophical economics, have never been given to these long debates the British and we so much enjoy on the proper role of the public and private sectors.

Increasingly, these distinctions are irrelevant—as a matter of fact, meaningless. Take an aircraft firm in the United States that does 95 percent of its business with the Government, submits to Government supervision of its expenses, gets all its specifications from the Government and works intimately with the Air Force on specifications. To decide that this firm is in the public sector is obviously to make a highly artificial distinction.

LEWIS: *If we are to plan now for this future society you are envisaging—more and more technological, more and more automated, more and more planned through both the public and private sectors—what do you think would be the single most fundamental thing to concentrate on?*

GALBRAITH: I would say education. Trained manpower is now the decisive factor of production. One very important thing to bear in mind is that the education explosion of recent years is not some new enlightenment. It's a response to the needs of modern industrial society. To a much greater extent than we realize, education is a reflection of industrial needs.

In the last century and the early part of this century, when the new industry, the new capitalism, required hundreds of thousands of unlettered proletarians, that is what the educational system provided. Now that it requires specialists—octane engineers and personnel managers and procurement managers and public relations experts—this is increasingly what the educational system is providing.

We should worry about the educational system being shaped in this fashion. Unless we're terribly careful, humane and liberal arts are going to be submerged and we will be too preoccupied with economic goals. This is a serious problem here. It's very easy now to get money for scientific purposes, but it is very much more difficult to get funds for the larger enjoyments of life. There will be no trouble getting public money for the supersonic transport. We will try to save it on support for the arts or the poverty program.

LEWIS: *It seems to me that with all our talk about the great technological future we may tend to overlook the continuing reservoir of poor people in the United States, about which we don't seem very effective in doing anything. We've had a poverty program now for several years, but it does not seem to be living up to the dreams people had about it. What do you think about the direction of the program, and of its possibilities?*

GALBRAITH: I had something to do with drawing up the program and I've been reasonably close to it since, and I've always thought it was much better than its popular billing. My strong impression is that Sargent Shriver has done an imaginative job under very trying circumstances.

It's also my impression that the best of the programs are of enormous value. The idea behind the Job Corps—giving these youngsters a second chance after they missed out the first time and have come to realize the cost to themselves—is superb. In one form or another, it's bound to continue in the educational system. So is Head Start. And the Youth Employment program serves a very important role.

Perhaps it would have been wiser to have shucked off some of the things which were less useful. A certain amount of money, for example, was wasted on rehabilitating small farmers—this is a sink hole. Nothing much is ever accomplished there, nothing visible. And some of the community-action programs got into the hands of incompetent or corrupt local politicians or were ill-conceived. But overall I think the effort showed that we could come to grips with poverty.

It seems to me that two fundamental things went wrong with the poverty program. First, we weren't braced as we should have been for the fact that *whenever* you spend money on behalf of the poor you get into trouble. The Government can go into West Virginia and sink $50- or $70-million into an electronic monitoring apparatus which doesn't work, and this is dismissed as a minor error. But spend $5,000 on some dead-end youngsters and you're really in trouble. Anything done on behalf of the poor arouses the passion of one dismal kind of political critic.

Second, of course, the program fell afoul of the spending pressures of the Vietnam war. This is particularly tragic. The argument here is that although personal incomes after taxes are at an all-time high, and although they're partly there because of Vietnam war spending, we must cut down on help to the poor because of Vietnam. And to some degree this is what has happened.

Sometime or other we're going to deal with this problem of poverty. The anachronism of a country as rich as the United States with a hard core of people as poor as some Americans simply can't continue. And I'm increasingly inclined to think that we'd better become a bit less Calvinist than we have been in the past. The past theory has been that the only

way to cure poverty is to make everybody a productive citizen, a participant in the economy. But the people who are poor in the United States
are those who are *excluded* from participating in the economy—by personal
disqualification or moral disqualification or educational disqualification
or physical disqualification. I'm by no means certain we can or should
make everybody participants. I think that's going to take too long, and
that in the interim maybe what a rich country should do is get everybody
a basic income.

LEWIS: *Do you mean the negative income tax?*
GALBRAITH: Yes! The negative income tax is really a development of this idea
which gives everybody a basic income but doesn't interfere with incentives.
If a worker earns more he will always have some increase in total income.

LEWIS: *But is that going to be enough? Isn't there something else besides money that is lacking? Don't we need something more dynamic than just giving to those in this vicious cycle?*
GALBRAITH: I'm not suggesting that money is a total cure—but let us not
underemphasize its importance. For example, about 30 percent of the children who are in poor families—with incomes under $3,000—have no
visible male parent. The family is headed by a woman. We would greatly
help these families by supplying them with a standard basic income as a
routine matter.

Poverty has, of course, other roots. There is a deeper community problem in Harlem, for example, associated with a sense of racial injustice, of
inequality, unequal application of the law and ineffectively enforced laws,
and no one should doubt it is of great urgency and great importance.

LEWIS: *Do you feel there is a lack of political leadership in this area? Do you think that
the President in particular has become too distracted by Vietnam, so that the moral impulse
one felt he was giving on civil rights and poverty has been allowed to wane?*
GALBRAITH: I have no doubt that this has been one of the great tragedies
of the Vietnam conflict. There are a good many reasons for regretting our
involvement in Vietnam apart from the neglect of the domestic problems.
But that is one of the great costs—unquestionably.

There is also—and this is curious, you know—a certain state of mind which worries enormously about the problems of liberty and democracy in Saigon but which reacts with total equanimity to similar problems in Harlem or in Birmingham. I am struck by how few of the passionate defenders of Marshal Ky's somewhat guided democracy have ever opened their mouths on civil rights or in support of the poverty program.

LEWIS: *Would you be willing to say a word in general about President Johnson compared with President Kennedy, especially in their reaction to Vietnam? Do you think Kennedy would have been able to stick more resolutely to these domestic questions and provide a better kind of leadership?*
GALBRAITH: Well, I think I knew the drift of President Kennedy's thinking on these general matters. I went to Salgon for him in 1961. And I could readily concoct an argument—as many have—that because he was unwilling to become involved in Laos when many people said that the whole state of the free world turned on moving troops into Vientiane, he wouldn't have gone into Vietnam. He was certainly very much worried about our commitment in Vietnam, and there was nothing willing, nothing avid, about this involvement—it was most unwelcome to him. But I wouldn't really like to make a guess. Nor do I like comparing the two Presidents.

I would say one thing: I don't think anybody could ever doubt that the legislative program President Johnson shoved through in the two years following the death of President Kennedy was an enormous achievement. No one would have respected that achievement more than President Kennedy.

The men I regret, in my less compassionate moments, are those who advised both Presidents that a few soldiers and a few planes would quickly straighten the Vietnamese out. I went to Saigon in 1961 because Kennedy had a recommendation that a division of troops should be sent in—disguised, as I recall, as flood-control workers. I think he hoped that I would advise against it and I certainly obliged.

Arthur Schiesinger used to say that foreign policy is the only field of endeavor where a man gets promoted for being wrong. Eventually the men who agreed that a little intervention would provide quick therapy got their way. They have moved ahead rapidly. So have their military needs. Now they are urging the country to avoid unnecessary criticism of the war effort. Well, one must be large-minded—and never petulant.

LEWIS: *Can you isolate the qualities President Kennedy had that made the world react so strongly to him—and that still produce a tremendous sense of respect and admiration for him now, three years later?*
GALBRAITH: I'm sure that youth had something to do with it—after all, most people in the world are young. My sense of that in 1960 was striking. I'd been accustomed to going to Washington and finding myself among my own generation or men who were older. Within three or four weeks I suddenly found myself surrounded by people who were 10 to 20 years younger and who were saying: Galbraith, he's getting rather fragile, handle him rather carefully. This wasn't entirely pleasant to the people of my generation, but I'm sure it was enormously welcome to people all around the world of the Kennedy generation.

Also it was quite clear that Kennedy had taken the full measure of the dangers, the terrors, of the nuclear age, and was determined to do something about it. Nothing was more central to his thought. I heard him say not once, but several times, that the only problem that he thought about every day, that was never off his mind, was the problem of nuclear catastrophe.

The sense that he was bringing the power of the United States to bear fully on that question was also very important in winning the response he did. Moreover, in some perceptible fashion this terror did lessen during his years. In 1960, we need to remind ourselves, the problem of fallout, the problem of strontium in the milk, got daily headlines in the newspapers. Now it is something that has receded from people's thoughts.

Finally, Kennedy broke with the clichés of politics, which people throughout the country were much more tired of than we imagined. Kennedy deeply disliked the kind of banal oratory that you hear hours on end at a national convention; he disliked the arm-waving, roistering politician trying to ingratiate himself with an imagined proletariat; and he disliked the person who debases himself in an effort to prove that he is a popular figure (although it must be conceded that there are a certain number of Democrats who find this rather easy because the debasing doesn't have to go very far). His break with an outworn style of politics was an enormous source of support and affection and reward.

It is striking how little the lesson has been learned. Just wait for the next Democratic National Convention.

LEWIS: *Do you agree with Walter Lippman that there is a tendency for the countries of the West now to become more inward-looking and think less about cooperation with each other in great international ventures? Or is this merely a reflection of the decline of the American influence in Europe?*

GALBRAITH: There's always been some impression in the State Department that we had influence in Europe because we were loved or because of our superior political system or because of our superior national character. In fact, we had influence in Europe when our help was needed and when Europe was subject to the cohesive influence of fear of the Soviets. And as Europe has ceased to need our help and as the fear of the Soviets has receded, our influence has diminished. I would attribute more of the tendencies that Lippmann mentions to this than to any recurrence of xenophobia. I don't think there's a great deal of that.

LEWIS: *But are these factors that you mention going to kill the dream of a larger Europe? Will they impede all the efforts toward organization of the West that we've made since the war?*

GALBRAITH: By no means. The idea of Europe is here to stay. It is beyond doubt that the old national units of Europe are technologically and economically obsolete, so that a much greater amount of international cooperation is inevitable. The new feature, and the feature we must recognize, is that it's not going to come about under American leadership any more.

We all got a rather biased view of the possibilities of American foreign policy from the immediate post–World War II experience when Europe badly needed American economic help and feared the forward policy of Russia. These two factors combined to give an almost unique impetus to American foreign policy, and it was pushed by very able people—Dean Acheson, Averell Harriman, Paul Hoffman, John J. McCloy—and we have been living on that capital ever since. But that era in American foreign policy is not only coming to an end, it *has come* to an end, and the great mistake of American foreign policy in these last 10 years has been the effort to keep it alive. Our reverses on the Multilateral Force, on the Kennedy grand design, on the effort to get Britain into the Common Market—all followed from this effort to recapture the glory of this earlier period.

As to the Common Market, it does not make a great deal of difference whether we urge Britain to go in or not. Britain will decide this issue on her side and France and the Continental countries on their side, and it's the better part of wisdom for us to realize that we will have very little to do with it.

Instead of lecturing Europe we must confine policy to matters on which we are ourselves involved. Thus if Britain does not make it into the Common Market, I am attracted by the idea of having another look at an association between ourselves and the Canadians and the British if it were sensibly approached. If we're determined and there is enough merit in it to be part of our foreign policy, it is in this direction that we should be looking.

LEWIS: *What about in the direction of East-West relations?*
GALBRAITH: There is a great deal of room here for a creative American policy, but one of the first things we have to do is escape from a kind of schizophrenia which presently characterizes our policies.

President Johnson, in my view, has taken much greater steps than he's been credited with in lowering the tension between ourselves and the Soviet Union and Eastern Europe. He's dropped that prefabricated section that used to be put into every Presidential speech about how we are engaged in a death struggle with the Communist menace but if we are vigilant and we never let down our guard we will, of course, win out over the forces of darkness in the end and without a reduction in our standard of living. He's also taken a variety of steps in addition to sending Gronouski to Poland to indicate our desire to bring Eastern Europe closer to the Western community.

But we've still got to reconcile this part of the policy with the talk about strengthening NATO and sharing nuclear capacity and the other clichés of the State Department and the Pentagon. This is our schizophrenia: We combine the mystique of the cold war with the new policy of bridge-building to Eastern Europe and with seeking Soviet help in Vietnam or encouraging Soviet efforts in settling the India-Pakistan conflict. Nobody seems yet to have faced up to the fact there is a very substantial degree of inconsistency between a policy that assumes conflict and a policy that assumes accommodation—and sometime or other we're going to have to sort that out.

LEWIS: *Might this depend not only on us but particularly on the Germans and their ability to come out of their current political turmoil to a more moderate direction on relations with the East?*
GALBRAITH: Yes, although I think that perhaps we have difficulty in keeping the German problem in perspective. I find it difficult to react to these so-called neo-Nazi gains in Bavaria, somewhere in the range of 5 to 8 percent. My impression is that in any Western country including our own you can get between 5 and 10 percent of the people at any given time to vote against law, decency, and constitutional order and in favor of the most prevalent current form of insanity. The more remarkable feature about Germany is the number of people who in fact consistently vote for the Christian Democrats and the Socialists.

I would think the rather more important thing is to see whether we can't find a modus vivendi for living with the divided-Germany problem. In the next few decades Germany isn't going to be reunited, and I wonder why we have to deny the existence of East Germany quite as systematically as we do.

LEWIS: *What reading do you have of the European Communists' willingness to deal with us, their outward-lookingness, these days?*
GALBRAITH: One major lesson of the period since World War II is that we must not overestimate the cohesive power of Communism and we must not underestimate the cohesive power of Europe. My instinct is to think that the tendency of Eastern European countries is toward Europe and that there is a growing economic pragmatism on both sides in Europe.

The nature of technology—the nature of the large organization that sustains technology and the nature of planning that technology requires—has an imperative of its own, and this is causing a greater convergence in all industrial societies. In the Eastern European societies it's leading to a decentralization of power from the state to the firm; in the Western European industrial societies it's leading to a kind of *ad hoc* planning. In fewer years than we imagine this will produce a rather indistinguishable melange of planning and market influences.

The overwhelming fact is that if you have to make steel on a large scale you have to have a massive technical complex, and there will be a certain similarity in the organization, and in the related social organization. Whether that steel complex is in Novosibirsk or in Nova Huta, Poland, or in Gary, Ind.

LEWIS: *Are you suggesting that as the two societies converge, the Communist society will necessarily introduce greater political and cultural freedom?*
GALBRAITH: I'm saying precisely that. The requirements of deep scientific perception and deep technical specialization cannot be reconciled with intellectual regimentation. They inevitably lead to intellectual curiosity and to a measure of intellectual liberalism. And on our side the requirements of large organization impose a measure of discipline, a measure of subordination of the individual to the organization, which is very much less than the individualism that has been popularly identified with the Western economy.

The Public Sector Is Still Starved

Challenge / 1967

Copyright © 1967 by Challenge
Communications, Inc. From *Challenge*,
vol. 15, no. 3 (January–February 1967),
pp. 18–21. Reprinted with permission of
M. E. Sharpe, Inc.

Q: *Mr. Galbraith, when you decried the starvation of our public sector in* The Affluent Society *almost nine years ago, there was a rather conservative Administration in Washington. Since that time we have had the New Frontier and the Great Society. Has this changed your view any?*

A: Much has been done. But we still face the problem of maintaining some kind of balance in resource allocation between the private and public sectors. The drift of economic ideas and evidence now strongly supports the notion that our public sector is under nourished. There is awareness that, with increasing population and urbanization, the demands on the public sector are becoming more urgent—more urgent than one would have guessed even in 1958. And it is more and more obvious that the problem of unemployment and poverty is a problem of manpower quality and thus a problem of the public sector—or the starvation of the public sector.

Q: *In other words, the problems you pointed out nine years ago are even greater today.*

A: Yes, that is right. But they are better recognized, I think.

Q: *What about the New Frontier and the Great Society. Didn't they come to grips with the question of resource allocation?*

A: Yes, they did. But, without question, the intensity of the problem has increased much more rapidly than the recognition of the problem. I had two principal objectives in the book. One was to destroy, if I possibly could, the atavistic doctrine that showed signs of gaining considerable strength after the war—the notion that public services are a menace to liberty and are some-how inferior to private services. This nonsense reached its apex (one hopes) in the nomination of Sen. Barry Goldwater, or before. In any case, I think this battle has been largely won. I don't think the American people are now in danger of buying the notion that public services are a menace to liberty.

Q: *What was your second objective in* The Affluent Society?

A: I was coming to that. It was to move the Keynesian discussion one step—but a fairly large step—further along. The Keynesian discussion at that time showed a strong tendency of getting into a kind of sterile, quantitative mood in which the volume of undifferentiated production and the amount of unemployment were the only tests of achievement. This is a battle which, of course, is not quite won yet. But I think we are making progress.

Q: *Wasn't it implicit in the Kennedy-Johnson tax cut of 1964 that the private sector was superior to the public sector?*

A: I don't know that this was implicit, but what Robert Lekachman has called "commercial Keynesianism" certainly came to the fore at that time. In the discussions that preceded the tax cut, the only test of performance was the potential increase in gross national product and the potential decrease in unemployment. Everything was measured quantitatively. What this would do to the allocation of resources didn't matter. I had hopes at the time that although that battle was lost, we wouldn't lose the war. Now I venture to think that we are winning—that the importance of the public sector alloca-tion is becoming evident.

Q: *Of course, Walter Heller and Company argued that, yes, you may be right about increased public expenditures being preferable to a tax cut, but this route is politically impossible. And since something had to be done to solve the fiscal drag problem, a tax cut was the only practical solution.*

A: Yes, but though all excellent men, they were looking at the problem in too narrowly economic terms. How do we get higher public expenditure? Well, there is a lot of history on this. Whenever the unemployment rate has risen appreciably, this has provided a case for larger public expenditures. Meanwhile, our thorniest unemployment problem, which is basically concerned with upgrading the labor force, through education and retraining, can only be solved through the public sector. Gardner Ackley has now recognized this publicly. This was the argument that Charles Killingsworth and I advanced during the discussions that preceded the tax cut. The counterargument was that in World War II we got down to minimal unemployment; even the unskilled found jobs. But in World War II there was a system of price and wage controls that helped keep the economy from boiling over. And nobody was desirous of instituting such controls in 1963 and 1964.

Q: *You feel, then, that President Kennedy misjudged the political temper of Congress.*
A: A tax cut was easier to put across than more spending, that I agree. And some unemployment would be eliminated more rapidly with a tax cut. I believed that we needed to eliminate it in a socially desirable way, and in a way that tackled hard-core unemployment, and that the only way to do this was by keeping up the pressure for public expenditures. Another argument I advanced at the time was that if we cut taxes, it would be a difficult action to reverse, if we ever had to reverse it. But I wasn't deeply committed to that argument. No more than anyone else did I foresee the Vietnam war. I enjoy praising my own foresight, but I mustn't overdo it. Very few do this sort of thing gracefully. A further argument which I did advance much more energetically on a matter which worried me much more was that when the conservatives found out that Keynes could be had by tax cuts, they would embrace the faith with too much fervor. If that happened, it would become permanently more difficult to implement Keynes through the expenditure route.

Q: *The 89th Congress, to most observers, was one of the most productive since the New Deal. Do you still feel that the public sector is starved after the massive legislation that came out of the 89th?*

A: Without any question—as I have said. The problems associated with the public sector—population growth, urbanization, etc.—are increasing more rapidly than the solutions. Or than anyone forecasted. No one, and certainly not I, saw how very quickly the problems of the cities would multiply. And while the legislation that came out of the 89th was a step in the right direction, there is a great deal more that has to be done if we are to speak with any meaning of a Great Society.

Q: *Just because money is spent through the public sector doesn't make it well spent; it depends on how it is spent.*
A: That is right. You can have very large defense outlays and great starvation in the public sector. To some extent, the large Vietnam expenditures have, in fact, been charged against the civilian sector.

Q: *Do you think because of Vietnam the nondefense public sector could become more starved in 1967 and 1968 than it was in the 1950s?*
A: There is a very real danger that this will happen. The Vietnam burden plays into the hands of one kind of conservative. It is those who do not quite have the moral courage to come out and say, "Let's cut Head Start, let's cut the Youth Corps, let's cut back on school construction." But they can, without bad conscience, say, "We have a war on our hands, so we must postpone this kind of civilian expenditure." It's an outrageous argument, because personal income, after taxes, is at an all-time high. It is at an all-time high, in part, as the result of the stimulation of the Vietnam war. So what they are saying is, because we are getting rich with the help of Vietnam, we must cut down spending for the poor.

Q: *These same conservatives don't seem to be particularly bothered by heavy defense expenditures.*
A: This is a very important distinction. Big expenditures on the south side of the Potomac are not socialism. Defense expenditures underwrite a whole range of technological activity, which otherwise would be too costly and too risky to be brought within the planning activities of the private corporation. Schools, hospitals and welfare expenditures work on aggregate demand just as well as defense expenditures, but they are

not carriers of research and development funds that underwrite new technology.

Q: *While Eisenhower didn't find it too difficult politically to hold down public expenditures, the expectations of minority groups and the poor have certainly been raised during the past decade. Don't you think Johnson will find it difficult to hold the line in the mid-1960s?*
A: I think it will be progressively more difficult to starve the public sector because the problems, for the reasons that I mentioned, are much more urgent. The needs of the cities are multiplying far faster than local revenues. Walter Heller, as on so many matters, has performed a great service in drawing attention to a basic defect in the American federal system. With growth and urbanization, the federal government gets the revenues, but the cities get the problems. But Walter is wrong, I have now concluded, in suggesting that federal revenues be redistributed to the states; it must be to the cities. The states are not as urgently in need of revenue as the cities, and we would waste too much money filtering it to the cities through the states. The 1930s were the years of the great rural crisis when a great many of the problems associated with rural America, including income maintenance and farm price supports, rural education, farm-to-market roads, among others, were taken over by the federal government. Thus, in large, measure, the most pressing problems of rural America were nationalized. Now, the 1960s are the years of the great urban crisis. The obvious answer is a redirection of federal revenue to the areas of present crisis. The reapportionment decisions of the federal courts should help this along.

Q: *Do you think that President Johnson can build a Great Society here and fight a war in Southeast Asia without raising taxes?*
A: I have never been a friend of the Vietnam conflict, as you perhaps know. I have been opposed to our expanding involvement there ever since President Kennedy sent me to Saigon in 1961. But I cannot claim to have been very persuasive. The dangers of getting bogged down in that quagmire seemed obvious enough, but apparently not to those who must make the decisions. As long as we are there, it certainly is going to be more difficult to give our nondefense public services the kind of money they require.

Men who are capable of worrying about communism and insurrection in a basically bad social structure in South Vietnam—one that encourages a good deal of dissatisfaction—are not so good at worrying about social unrest in the United States. They are the more ardent about saving liberty and democracy the further it is away.

Q: *What about the question of a tax increase to pay for Vietnam and even the limited amount of civilian expenditures the President will undoubtedly propose?*
A: I think that the President will soon ask for a tax increase. But here we run into an interesting and very important psychological problem that has never been fully explored. Action for fiscal restraint is very different from action for fiscal expansion. The need for fiscal expansion is suggested by objective circumstances that are measurable, such as the volume of unemployment and the rate of growth. But when it comes to restraint, this is not so. And there are always some soft indicators that suggest that the economy might be slowing down. Hence, there is always a great temptation for a politically conscious President to postpone action, especially when it involves the nasty business of raising taxes. We were walking the sunny side of the Keynesian street at the time of the 1964 tax cut. It is the chilly side we are now on.

Q: *Do you think recessions are a thing of the past for the United States?*
A: This is an open-end question. To say no is to exclude every unforeseen circumstance—and that is scientifically unwise. And it is also tactically unwise. To deny that depressions are possible is the kind of reckless forecast that people have a peculiar capacity for remembering. The most distinguished, interesting and certainly the most ingenious American economist of the early decades of this century was Irving Fisher. And it is one of the great tragedies of Irving Fisher's life that he is remembered principally for saying, in late October 1929, that stocks had reached a new high plateau from which they would proceed to go up. This was, as I recall, a day or so before Black Thursday. He was never able to escape it for the rest of his life. One can easily devise some models for depression. I think that the most probable one again would be a situation associated with the stock market. It is part of the legend that the 1929 stock market crash was a fiduciary phenomenon

that had no further consequences, no income consequences. This is non-sense. The stock market crash was the single most deflationary influence in the early days of the depression. And it had a direct and visible effect on all kinds of hiring and purchasing. Sales of radios, which were a luxury item at that time, dropped drastically in the last half of 1929. So did the durables.

Q: *Given all the securities regulations that have been instituted since that time, could you imagine another such crash today?*
A: It is possible. Far too many people have been interested in the stock market in these last years. This could extend to another few million innocents. All would be attracted by the fact that the stock they bought yesterday went up today. This would encourage others and continue the rise. These speculators would become uneasy about the market at the same time. This could then start a sell-off of crash proportions. Such a crash could have wide spread deflationary effects, both on consumer spending and on business investment, and it would be very hard for fiscal expansion to come along rapidly enough to offset it. I don't think this is probable, but I don't think it should be entirely ruled out.

Q: *Are there any other circumstances which might set off a depression?*
A: One can also work out a model that would come from unwise use of monetary policy. It is deceptively attractive, for its management is subject to quick and anonymous decision. But monetary policy is also very unpredictable. Nobody, not even William McChesney Martin, with all the assistance of his Maker, knows what the consequences of a given increase in the discount rate will be. One can imagine circumstances in which monetary policy would be used in the absence of fiscal policy to the point where it would bring a sharp contraction in investment. And fiscal policy would not be able to move rapidly enough to offset it.

Q: *Do you think the way we have used monetary policy in the last year is approaching this kind of situation?*
A: I am avoiding prediction. But there is no doubt about the overemphasis on monetary policy in recent months and that it has been unwise.

Q: *What would the alternative have been?*
A: To rely on fiscal policy instead. Economists, or some, have always been unduly fascinated by monetary policy, partly because it has great peda-gogical value. There is a certain mystery about it. It is one of the few areas of our profession which has a seeming association with the mystical, even the supernatural. So, therefore, we rather cherish it. And we talk a great deal about it. The one thing that we have never really reckoned with is its unpredictability. One can tell about the direction, but one cannot tell about the amount. We have been using this policy this past year without any exact knowledge of the point at which we might put such a squeeze on housing investment, or inventories, or on smaller businessmen, or on con-sumers that it would bring a much larger curtailment of spending than we want. In contrast, fiscal policy is far more certain. We know within much narrower limits what the effect of a given tax increase or a given expendi-ture increase will be. And it makes great sense to use the instruments of policy that are certain. What I would do is perfectly clear; and it will eventually be the policy. That is to put interest rates at a moderate level, reflecting some general equity as between the creditor and debtor com-munity. Then fiscal policy in combination with the guidelines will be employed as the major instruments of control.

Q: *Wouldn't this reduce considerably the power of the Federal Reserve?*
A: Ultimately, the Federal Reserve will be a minor instrumentality of the state concerned with accounting and administrative matters, standing in importance somewhere between the Bureau of Printing and Engraving and the Interstate Commerce Commission. The sooner this day comes, the better it will be for all of us. I say this with natural regret because I hold a professorship here at Harvard which is named for a founder of the Federal Reserve System, Paul M. Warburg. So I naturally will participate in this general decline in prestige. But I will face it with such nobility of character as I can muster.

Q: *Monetary policy has not only held a good deal of allure for economists. It has also been attractive to many conservatives. Why?*

A: I suppose they are also attracted by the mysticism. But, in addition, there is a large element of naked self-interest here. It is a great mistake to assume men of substance are lacking in a clear view of their own self-interest. High interest rates are very good for people who have money to lend. As a broad, but I think impeccable, rule, people who lend money have more money than people who borrow money. An active monetary policy means that, recurrently, interest rates will be wonderfully high. Second—and this is also very important—monetary policy is a marvelous ally of big business. Taxation, including the corporate income tax, hits large firms as well as small. It affects General Motors as it affects the small house-builder or the small retailer. Since taxation in this country is generally progressive, it hits unincorporated citizens with money even more. Monetary policy, on the other hand, doesn't much affect large corporations. They are likely to have exempted themselves from dependence on the capital market by establishing sources of internal financing; and they are the favored customers at the bank. And they can run far higher interest costs if they must, so they have minimized their vulnerability to the power of the bankers. Monetary policy does hit the small businessman who generally operates on limited capital and who is much farther down the credit line at the bank. The residential builder is a very good example. So it is obvious why conservatives—Galsworthy's men of property—like monetary policy. And, again, while I never like to be critical of my fellow economists, they have been very, very slow in emphasizing this point. They are men of compassion. They cherish the market and the little man. I would hope that they would not continue to avert their eyes where this discrimination is concerned.

Q: *Getting back to the current situation, do you think that pressures for more federal monies from hard-pressed mayors and governors, and from the poor, could have an important effect on U.S. foreign policy? In other words, could domestic demands for a larger slice of the federal budget force the Administration to ease its policy in Southeast Asia?*
A: In defense of President Johnson, he has so many better reasons for wanting to get out of Vietnam—and I think, he does want to get out of that mess—that these pressures would be marginal, at most.

Q: *Won't this pressure increase if he has to raise taxes?*
A: Maybe a little bit. But I think there is a tendency among those who strongly oppose a tax increase—they are generally conservatives—to skirt the war issue. They usually call for cutting "unnecessary federal expenditures." They do not say, "Oh, God, let's settle this war or else I will have to pay more taxes." It seems rather indecent to react that way—at least publicly.

Q: *Aren't they really thinking that way, nevertheless?*
A: They would be thinking that, but private thoughts don't create political pressure. Such pressure can only come when conservatives who don't like paying the bill for Vietnam start writing their Congressman. And this is highly unlikely. Nobody likes to have his patriotism impugned because he is too cheap to pay the bill.

Q: *Thank you, Mr. Galbraith.*

The Playboy Interview:
John Kenneth Galbraith

Michael Laurence / 1968

Playboy magazine (June 1968), pp. 63+.
Copyright© 1968, 1996 by Playboy.
Reprinted by permission.
All rights reserved.

PLAYBOY: *In moments of candor, even Republicans will admit that the performance of their party in the area that really counts—winning elections—has been less than ideal. Do you think the Republican Party is destined to a permanent minority position?*
GALBRAITH: No, I certainly don't. I think the Republicans have been more fortunate in recent years than the Democrats.

PLAYBOY: *In what way?*
GALBRAITH: Well, economics has been the bane of the Republicans, just as war has been the bane of the Democrats. The Democrats won elections for years by tying the Depression to the tail of Herbert Hoover and to the Republicans. I have little doubt that the Republicans are now going to try to win elections for quite a few years by tying war to the Democrats. The Democrats were in power in World War One; they were in power in World War Two; they were in power in the Korean War and they are in power now. Until Vietnam, there was justification for the Democratic case—they could say they weren't really responsible for the particular wars. They

26

were only in a custodial position and their policy had nothing to do with precipitating those conflicts. But now, with Vietnam, the Republicans have a very good case. And the Democrats will suffer for that for a long while. In 1953 and 1954, President Eisenhower, who was then a good deal less militant than he has become on the matter of Vietnam, was strongly pressed by Secretary Dulles to commit American troops to Vietnam, but Eisenhower very stoutly refused. This was a wisdom that subsequent Democratic Administrations didn't show. I have very little doubt that in one way or the other, the Republicans—inept as they are—will make capital of this. If they run Richard Nixon, of course, they are going to be handicapped, because Nixon was one of the people urging Eisenhower to send troops to Vietnam in 1954. On the issue of the war, Nixon thinks he can beat the Democrats not by taking a wiser position but by extending their errors.

PLAYBOY: *Some cynics have said that the Republicans in the past few elections have revealed a death wish. Every four years they have a fine chance of taking the Presidency and then they pick a candidate who can't possibly win. Is this a valid observation?*
GALBRAITH: Yes, this is undoubtedly a Republican talent—but not exclusively. For example, the Democrats in my own state, Massachusetts, almost always come up with the candidate best calculated to lose. I remember once rehashing the 1960 election with President Kennedy. I suggested that he was the only Democrat who could have won and Nixon the only Republican who could have lost. And I think President Kennedy rather agreed with that assessment. In 1964, there is no question that the Republicans unerringly picked Barry Goldwater, who was the weakest candidate they could have found, a man with an almost eccentric innocence about the great issues of our time. He was laboring until very late in the campaign, for example, under the assumption that old-age pensions are unpopular with old people. I don't have any gift of foresight, but I think there is considerable likelihood of the Republicans' going back to Dick Nixon this autumn; and, with the possible exception of Ronald Reagan, it would be hard to imagine anyone who would be weaker than Nixon. When the Republicans picked him in 1948, Thomas E. Dewey was a one-time loser; but Nixon hasn't won an election on

his own account since he defeated Helen Gahagan Douglas for the United States Senate. That was in 1951.

PLAYBOY: *Who do you think would be the strongest Republican candidate?*
GALBRAITH: Rockefeller. There's no question about that. Rockefeller would be very strong and I think possibly even unbeatable.

PLAYBOY: *In a contest between Johnson and Rockefeller, who would have your vote?*
GALBRAITH: I couldn't answer that right at the moment, but my party regularity is not such that I would be obliged to vote Democratic. To be sure, I would vote only with great regret for somebody other than a Democrat. I have never voted for anybody but a Democrat in a Presidential election and I've very rarely voted for anybody but a Democrat for other offices. But last year, I publicly supported the present Attorney General of Massachusetts, Elliot Richardson, who was a Republican, because he was the better man. And many years ago, when I was living in New York, I supported Jacob Javits, when he first ran for the House of Representatives. In fact, I made a sacrifice greater than that. After I left the city, Javits got my apartment. It was in his district and apartments were very scarce at that time.

Getting back to your question, much would depend on Rockefeller's position on the war. This would be the attitude of a great many liberals. Rockefeller went underground on this issue about three years ago. When he went underground, he was quite a hawk. He was arguing for increased national defense expenditures and he was greatly committed to a bomb-shelter program. I remember seeing Prime Minister Nehru once, after he had a conference with Governor Rockefeller. The Prime Minister said, "Mr. Ambassador, your governor"—he referred to him as *my* governor—"your governor seemed to be enormously involved with bomb shelters. He did nothing but lecture me on bomb shelters. He even gave me a pamphlet on bomb shelters." That was Rockefeller before he became silent on international affairs. If he were to surface as a hawk, I certainly wouldn't vote for him. But if he were to surface with a sensible, conciliatory policy on Vietnam and on other foreign-policy issues, well, I'd have to think about it.

PLAYBOY: *Do you think the war might provoke a left-wing third-party movement in the United States?*
GALBRAITH: No.

PLAYBOY: *If not on the left, do you see any prospect of a right-wing third-party movement sparked by George Wallace?*
GALBRAITH: No. The two-party tradition in the United States is very strong. People think of themselves almost from birth as Republicans or Democrats and then differentiate themselves as liberal Republicans or conservative Democrats, or vice versa. This raises a very large moral barrier against third-party movements. Also, the legal barriers are great. To get a third party on the ballot in all the 50 states, or in anything approaching that number, is quite difficult. Things are loaded in favor of the two-party system.

PLAYBOY: *Do you share the view of those who feel that the effectiveness of the electoral process is threatened by the emergence of movie-star politicians—those candidates who have a previous reputation established in the mass media?*
GALBRAITH: Such as Ronald Reagan?

PLAYBOY: *Or Senator George Murphy, or Shirley Temple Black, or Congressman Robert Mathias, Olympic gold medalist.*
GALBRAITH: No, I don't think so. I think some popular identification of this sort is politically valuable and always has been. I just mentioned Helen Douglas, who was certainly widely known as an actress; but she didn't survive against a relatively unknown Congressman named Nixon. And there is nothing about the showing that Ronald Reagan is making around the country that would indicate his stardom is propelling him into the Presidency. Shirley Temple probably got more votes than if she had been plain Mrs. Black, with no previous fame, but not enough to get her into Congress. So, no. I wouldn't think there is anything more involved here than what everybody knows: that a measure of public notoriety is valuable in politics.

PLAYBOY: *Lack of public notoriety seems to be one of the problems facing Senator Eugene McCarthy. Do you think his candidacy—or Robert Kennedy's—will strengthen the Democratic Party, even assuming defeat at the convention?*

GALBRAITH: Well, there are elements of cliché here. Almost every day somebody comes to see me, to tell me that if there is any opposition to President Johnson within the Democratic Party, this will so split the party that it will improve the chances of the Republicans. Actually, the Democratic Party, in this sense, doesn't exist. The Democratic Party is not a cohesive entity that can be split. It exists, at any given time, as a vast multiplicity of factions. You can't split something that is congenitally fragmented. Are John Stennis and James Eastland united with, say, Wayne Morse? If Gene McCarthy or Bob Kennedy, reflecting as they do an enormous nationwide dissatisfaction with the foreign policy of the Administration, focus that dissatisfaction by running—among other things—as peace candidates, all they do is give expression to a split that exists anyway. Many regular members of the Democratic Party, people who are stringing along with the Administration, aren't happy about its foreign policy. I've been around the country a good deal in the past year, and I can say that the difference between people who have been leaning to McCarthy and Kennedy and the great number of the people who are stringing along with the President is *not* over the war. Both groups oppose the war. The difference is between those who think the war is such a transcendent issue that they will support whoever is opposed to it and those who are going along with the Administration in spite of the war.

PLAYBOY: *The war aside, do you think Senator McCarthy is qualified for the Presidency?*
GALBRAITH: Yes, there's no question about that. He's a highly intelligent and thoughtful man, and in many ways he's been an exemplary Senator.

PLAYBOY: *Yet in the view of the Americans for Democratic Action, which you head, his record has been less than perfect, hasn't it?*
GALBRAITH: Not over the years. People who say this are citing some votes of the Senator during the past session, and some of the issues were quite minor. We score people by their votes, you know; and since McCarthy has been in the Senate, he has been something over 90 percent right by our count.

PLAYBOY: *McCarthy has generated great enthusiasm among critics of the Vietnam war. An earlier Senator McCarthy also took advantage of the emotional climate of war to appeal to millions of Americans. In this case, followers of the late Senator Joseph McCarthy seemed to reason that since Communists were killing our boys in Korea, we had a moral duty to ferret them out on the home front. Do you think recent events—the indictments of William Sloane Coffin and Dr. Benjamin Spock, and General Hershey's repeated attempts to use the draft to curb dissent—indicate the possibility of a McCarthyite resurgence today?*

GALBRAITH: No, I don't. Most people felt the Korean War—unhappy an episode though it was—was necessary. It was a very unpopular war, widely regarded as necessary and widely regarded as having been provoked by the international Communist conspiracy. So, a very small minority of people who had at one time or another—innocently or otherwise—been associated with communism were extremely vulnerable. But they were a small minority, and those who *continued* to criticize the war were an even smaller and more defenseless minority. McCarthyism was directed at this tiny group.

Perhaps for this reason, the critics of the Vietnam war have shown a heroism complex. They feel that they are being peculiarly brave in criticizing the Administration. Well, that's nonsense. There is no bravery involved in identifying yourself with millions of other people. To be specific, as a critic of the Vietnam conflict, there is no community in the United States into which I cannot go and be sure of a sizable and friendly audience. Last spring, I spoke at the most stouthearted military institution in the United States, Texas A & M College, where I had a huge turnout. I hadn't gone down there to talk about the Vietnam conflict, but I had a very friendly reception from people who wanted me to know they agreed with my views on Vietnam. That required no heroism. On the other hand, it requires considerable heroism for Secretary Rusk to go to Harvard to make a speech. There is no university community into which the Secretary of State can go without encountering hostility.

PLAYBOY: *Still, don't you think the draft resisters, as well as Coffin and Spock, who face a possibility of conviction and imprisonment, must be credited with a certain amount of heroism?*

GALBRAITH: Yes. And I'm puzzled why the Administration felt obliged to challenge them. That was the other point I was going to make. Who has suffered on the draft issue? Whose reputation has suffered? Has it been the people who are resisting the draft—or has it been General Hershey? Obviously, Hershey has suffered. Hershey has been, in a way, a tragic figure. Here is an amiable old man—I worked with him years ago—who has been an unspectacular but quite decent administrator. He becomes over-enthusiastic on this one issue and he is now an embarrassment to all concerned. If the Administration could find any graceful way of detaching itself from General Hershey, I think it would.

PLAYBOY: *You once wrote: "We may lay it down as a law that without public criticism, all governments would look much better and be much worse." Considering its salubrious aspect, what major criticism would you have of President Johnson?*
GALBRAITH: My abiding criticism of President Johnson is that he identified himself with a foreign policy—and with the exponents of a foreign policy, notably Secretary Rusk—just at the moment that it became obsolete. Consider the errors in our foreign policy in the past 20 years. First, it relied excessively on the mystique of military power. Second, it had the vision of a unified, international Communist conspiracy, just at the time the Communist world was breaking up and giving way to the stronger force of nationalism. Third, it was rigidly and narrowly anti-Communist. Far too many issues were decided in accordance with whether they seemed to advance or impede the Cold War with what was called the Sino-Soviet bloc. And fourth, it terribly exaggerated the possible American role in bringing about desirable social change in other countries. All of these things were the mistakes of the generation of people who dominated foreign policy in the 20 years following the breakup of the Grand Alliance. And all these mistakes came to a focus in Vietnam. We found ourselves involved with nationalism, not international communism. We exaggerated what military weapons could accomplish; we found we could not reform Vietnamese society. Yet this was the effort with which President Johnson identified himself. I remember—I don't think I'm violating any confidence here or being unduly vain in recalling it—I remember a conversation I had with President Johnson shortly after the death of President Kennedy. We were ranging over the

problems to be faced. I told him that I thought there were no problems on the domestic front that wouldn't yield readily to the kind of social action that was already in process. But I said that if the old generation was able to reassert itself in our foreign policy, there could be nothing but disaster. I had in mind the pressures that had previously been placed upon us to intervene in Laos and the relentless pressures that were then upon us to escalate our intervention in Vietnam. And suggestions kept coming up for military intervention in other parts of the world as well.

PLAYBOY: *But President Johnson inherited Kennedy's State Department. Rusk was a Kennedy appointee, and there haven't been many high-level changes in the State Department since Kennedy staffed it. How would you account for these old pressures reasserting themselves under the Johnson Administration?*

GALBRAITH: As both Theodore Sorensen's and Arthur Schlesinger's books make clear, the great struggle in the Kennedy Administration was not between Republicans and Democrats and it was not between the Executive and the Legislature. It was between the White House and the senior foreign-policy establishment—particularly between the White House and the State Department. The instinct of the older, permanent employees in, say, the Department of Agriculture or the Department of the Interior, is generally progressive. These bureaus can get set in their ways, but they respond to leadership. The instinct of the State Department, however, was overwhelmingly to the older generation attitudes, to John Foster Dulles's view of the world. They saw the problem of foreign policy simplistically, as a conflict between communism and the free world. Everything was forced into that dichotomy. This was a continuing point of conflict all through the Kennedy Administration. It came up with those who wanted—as I said—to send troops to Indochina. General Taylor and Walt Rostow came back from Vietnam in 1961 with a proposal to put a division of combat troops in there. Kennedy said no. The conflict came up with all the negotiations we were involved in Europe. It came up with those who didn't want to make any concessions that might lead, for example, to the test ban. And it came up in Latin America. The point is that in each of these cases, Kennedy

had to reject powerful and well-entrenched attitudes within the State Department itself; and for the most part, he succeeded. President Johnson has not
succeeded.

My second criticism of President Johnson would be briefer: He is a very
shrewd tactician but a poor strategist. He is good at handling today's and
tomorrow's business but poor at defining objectives and moving consciously
and deliberately toward those objectives.

PLAYBOY: *Would you elaborate?*
GALBRAITH: Vietnam provides many examples. Last autumn, the President
brought General Westmoreland and Ambassador Bunker back to sell the
country and the Congress on the notion that we were winning in Vietnam.
It was quite a successful tactic. Even the polls showed improvement. But
as part of a longer-run strategy of promoting confidence in our foreign policy, given the fact that we weren't winning, it was a terrible mistake. The
Tet offensive came along and disposed of the victory.

PLAYBOY: *Wasn't much of President Johnson's style, as well as his attitude toward the issues,
forged in the New Deal?*
GALBRAITH: No question about that. And it was very much my own case.

PLAYBOY: *Do you think, in Johnson's case, that some of his ideas and approaches are
obsolete?*
GALBRAITH: That's a somewhat harsh statement. I would be rather cautious
before agreeing. I might be indicting myself, too. On some matters about
which I have been very much concerned—the problem of our environment,
the protection of roadsides, the preservation of some of the natural charm
of the American community—President Johnson has been very much in the
vanguard, and so has Mrs. Johnson. Or they were, until this miserable war
intervened. On the other hand, I think the President is probably open to a
measure of criticism for his last State of the Union message, a criticism that
was leveled at him quite generally: his excessive preoccupation with increasing national prosperity as the sole test of social performance. I'm not saying that increasing prosperity isn't important, but it's clear that this is not

a remedy for the distress in our cities. And it's clear that the problem of the cities grows from a very bad sense of priorities on the part of the Federal Government.

PLAYBOY: *Some critics have said that Kennedy planted and all Johnson has done is harvest. Do you think Johnson's reputation for success in obtaining progressive social legislation is deserved?*
GALBRAITH: President Kennedy certainly put quite a good deal of legislation on the table. But I never doubted that President Johnson was a better manager of Congress than President Kennedy. President Kennedy saw the Congress as a coequal branch of the Government, in strict constitutional terms. President Johnson sees it as a challenge, as something to be managed. This has achieved results.

PLAYBOY: *Nonetheless, do you regard Kennedy as a great President?*
GALBRAITH: Yes. At least I regard him as having been a very great man. He was subject, of course, to the limitations of three brief years. Most of the people who made a mark in the Presidency, from Washington on, had eight years. Roosevelt had more than 12.

PLAYBOY: *What do you think was President Kennedy's most important achievement in domestic affairs?*
GALBRAITH: The one that he's commonly credited with: the final development of modern economic policy. It was under the Kennedy Administration that we finally got away from the clichés of the balanced budget and came to see the Federal Government as an affirmative instrument for maintaining the level of employment. This has become an accepted fact. But I would add that in a more general sense, Kennedy brought an air of excitement to Washington that, in turn, drew an extraordinarily talented group of people there from all over the country, lifting very markedly the tone and quality of the Federal Executive. On reflection, I might even say that this intangible achievement was his monument. There are also some other Kennedy accomplishments that even the historians tend to overlook. For example, the farm problem disappeared under Kennedy. He appointed a very talented

man as Secretary of Agriculture and gave him a free hand. Secretary Freeman, in turn, had a great capacity for dealing with Congress. Until the Kennedy Administration, everybody assumed that the farm-policy problem was chronic and insoluble. Now, of course, we haven't heard much about it for years. It's curious how little we miss the problems that we cease to hear about.

PLAYBOY: *The mood of excitement you say Kennedy brought to Washington seems to have disappeared. Do you think this is because Kennedy himself is no longer on the scene?*
GALBRAITH: No. I think the war is the cause. Had it not been for the war, the sense of excitement generated by the legislative measures that President Johnson put through in 1964 and 1965 would have continued. I was very closely associated with the poverty program in its early years, first in the drafting of the legislation and then on the advisory committee that was established to oversee it. There was a great sense of excitement in the Office of Economic Opportunity in those early years under President Johnson. It began to dissipate when it became common knowledge that there wasn't going to be any important increase in appropriations. Instead of an all-out war on poverty, it became clear that the program's claim on the budget was wholly subordinate to military requirements. People began to drift away, first a few at a time and then in large numbers. One always has to keep in mind— and this also is something that is not very well understood—that liberals in the United States are summer soldiers. They go to Washington when the going is good, when there's an Administration they like, when there's a feeling of excitement. But when the excitement diminishes, they go back to the universities, or to journalism, or to the law. On the whole, conservatives are more stable. One sees this particularly in the State Department. The liberals come in for short periods of time—as I did—but the stuffier men have much greater stability.

PLAYBOY: *What would you say was Kennedy's greatest accomplishment in foreign affairs?*
GALBRAITH: The nuclear test ban.

PLAYBOY: *Not his handling of the Cuban crisis?*
GALBRAITH: No. That required sensible restraint. The wild men had to be kept down. But that was no great test of capacity. And the Soviets were

quite cooperative, after all. I think the test ban was Kennedy's greatest achievement. And again, it's an indication of how little we miss problems that are no longer with us. Up until the negotiation of the test-ban agreement, there was scarcely a week, and often not a day, when there wasn't a story in the *New York Times* about fallout levels, about strontium 90 in our milk, about radiation poisoning the atmosphere. Now I suppose one could go through the *Times* index for the past year and find only a handful of such entries, mostly concerning the Chinese explosions. This oppressive problem has almost disappeared from our consciousness. When I went to India, I found that one of the subjects that came up most frequently in conversation was what right the Americans and the Russians have to poison the atmosphere that all the world must use. The alarm in the non-scientific community was very much greater than it was in the United States. Once I took Jerome Wiesner, then the President's Scientific Advisor, out to India for the specific purpose of putting the thing in perspective. He held what must have been one of the longest press conferences in history, answering in meticulous detail all the questions of the Indian newspapermen about what the actual dangers from fallout were. He didn't minimize the dangers, of course; he was one of the architects of the test ban. But he managed to persuade the Indians that they weren't in imminent danger of destruction from radioactive air.

PLAYBOY: *About your association with India, Newsweek once wrote: "As U.S. Ambassador from 1961 to 1968, Galbraith allegedly conducted himself in a manner befitting a rajah, dealt too directly with Prime Minister Nehru, dashed off a volume of hot-lined cables that kept international wires smoking, and often disregarded diplomatic protocol to take problems directly to friend and boss John F. Kennedy." Would you plead guilty?*
GALBRAITH: No, I wouldn't. I might take up the indictment step by step. I'm quite certain that my behavior *was not* parallel with that of the rajahs. The rajahs are now a rather depressed and saddened caste in India, whereas I tried to conduct myself with slightly more style. I certainly dealt directly with Prime Minister Nehru. He was, in addition to being prime minister, a personal friend of some years standing. He was also the foreign minister, the person with whom I had to work. About hot-lined cables, I often

found that a sharply worded communication to the State Department produced more results than the passive-voiced, soft and enfeebled prose that
is customary in diplomacy. And I always maintained the fiction that I had
a very close association with President Kennedy. This was extremely valuable in getting action out of the State Department. It gave me a measure of
leverage. But if anybody in the State Department had ever stopped to pon-
der the matter, they would have known that I wasn't really close to Kennedy
at all. If the President had more than one official communication every
six months from his ambassador in India, he would quickly have tired of
such pestering and told me to deal with the Secretary of State. So I carefully rationed my communications with the President, as any experienced
bureaucrat—which I am—knows he must do.

PLAYBOY: *Still, you accumulated quite a sheaf of correspondence with Kennedy, didn't you?*
GALBRAITH: Yes, unofficially. When I went to India, President Kennedy said
one day, in a joking way, "Why don't you drop me a letter every once in a
while and tell me what you do?" He said, "I've always been a bit uncertain,
ever since my father was an ambassador, just what the job entails." Since I
had for years been in a degree of communication with the President, every
fortnight or so I'd send him a letter—a personal letter rather than an official
communiqué—describing what was happening. I described the more interesting or amusing or embarrassing experiences of being an ambassador,
sometimes commenting on matters in the U.S., and giving a great deal of
attention to the thing that worried me tremendously at that time: our deep-
ening involvement in Indochina. Someday I'm going to publish these letters. The time is now approaching when I think I can do so without seeming to be engaged in any undue exploitation of my position in India or my
past association with the President.

PLAYBOY: *Why did you resign from your ambassadorial post?*
GALBRAITH: President Kennedy asked me to go there initially for two years,
in the hope that this would give some impression of the aims and goals of
the Kennedy Administration to the people in that part of the world. Then
we'd extended it, after the Chinese attack on India; this was a period of

uncertainty, so I stayed on. When calm returned after the war, I came home. I certainly didn't consider myself a professional diplomat—a point of view that was shared in some degree by the State Department. I had *The New Industrial State* hanging over my head and I was very anxious to finish it.

PLAYBOY: *Did you find you could live comfortably on an ambassadorial salary?*
GALBRAITH: Handsomely. Over the years, the financial difficulties of ambassadors have been somewhat exaggerated. I'm not speaking of Paris or London, but there's no doubt that my financial situation in New Delhi was infinitely easier than that of my Harvard colleagues who went to Washington. I had a salary of some $27,000 a year; transportation was paid for me and my family; there was a house, a staff, an automobile and an educational allowance for my children; and a very substantial entertainment allowance, certainly sufficient for the entertainment we did. We could have done less without any damage to the United States. But every time I returned to Washington, my friends looked at me in the gloomiest fashion and asked: "Ken, are you going broke out there?" My answer always was: "Don't talk to me, talk to Archibald Cox or Arthur Schlesinger or Abe Chayes, the other Harvard people who came to Washington. They're the ones who are in danger of going broke."

PLAYBOY: *The comment has been made—most recently, in an amiable way, by David Halberstam in an article about you in Harper's—that the Kennedy people were disturbed at the ease with which you made the transition from J.F.K. to Johnson after the President was assassinated. Is this so?*
GALBRAITH: I've been asked about this before. Actually, I was the source of the remark myself, because I kept very careful notes about that whole weekend. Right after the assassination, President Johnson asked me to help with the message that he was about to give to Congress. He had just taken over and had no available staff. Also, as the new President, he was under terrible pressure. So he asked Ted Sorensen and me to give him a hand. We did. And I must say, in the jarring disorientation of that weekend, I found it therapeutic to have something to do. I reported, in the diary that I kept over that weekend, that I'd heard someone remark: "Well,

that was certainly a rapid change in Ken," or something to that effect. Subsequently, I loaned the diary to William Manchester, who was writing *The Death of a President.* I asked him to check back on any use he made of it. But in the great confusion that surrounded publication of his book, as he later explained to me, he was unable to do so. So some of the material he published caused me a degree of embarrassment. The comment was a frivolous one that I certainly would never have published myself. But I don't think many people took it seriously. I never did. As a matter of fact, I doubt that over the weekend I did any more to ease the transition than, say, Robert Kennedy himself.

PLAYBOY: *Were you otherwise involved in the controversy over Manchester's book?*
GALBRAITH: No. I had earlier looked over, for Senator Robert Kennedy and Mrs. Jacqueline Kennedy, a couple of the other Kennedy books, which made some small use of private papers: a book by Pierre Salinger and a book by the former Undersecretary of the Navy, Paul Fay. But I don't think I qualified myself as a particularly meticulous reviewer. At any rate, I had no role in the Manchester book, though I did come to Mrs. Kennedy's defense when I thought she was somewhat unfairly accused of censorship.

PLAYBOY: *You once observed that censorship reflects "the deep conviction of people who do not read concerning the persuasive power of books on those who do." Do you think any form of censorship is justified in the U.S. today?*
GALBRAITH: I oppose all censorship. I am, of course, especially suspicious of censorship having to do with public affairs. I know from my own experience as a public official, particularly during the years when I was running price controls, that every time I made a mistake, I immediately yearned for secrecy. No doubt there are some things that have to be kept secret, in the operation of the Government, but this is better done by instilling confidence in public employees than by censorship.

PLAYBOY: *Speaking of books and their effect on others, we recently saw you quoted as saying that the writings of the late Ian Fleming had an important influence on American foreign policy. Were you speaking facetiously?*

GALBRAITH: Yes, in a way, but there has always been a Bond mystique within the CIA: the notion of the highly organized, highly masculine adventurer who can bring off perfectly fabulous coups. These people must be watched 24 hours a day. Indeed, if at all possible, they shouldn't be hired. It's undoubtedly unfair, though, to attribute their inclinations to too many James Bond novels. It's perhaps more plausible to say that Fleming modeled some of Bond's more outrageous operations on the things these self-styled super-agents imagine—in their wilder fantasies—that they're accomplishing.

PLAYBOY: *Your new novel,* The Triumph, *skewered the State Department mercilessly, but it was surprisingly benign toward the CIA. Does this reflect your own views?*
GALBRAITH: One must bear in mind that my novel concerns a small South American country with an unattractive climate and a poor *ambiance.* It's less attractive to the Bond type than, say, Laos or South Vietnam, or some of the other exotic parts of the world. And since *The Triumph* aims in all particulars to be true fiction, it was natural that I should play down the role of the CIA. I *did* point to one feature of the CIA, however: its ability, when asked to estimate the outcome of a particular suggestion, to get on both sides of the question and then cloak its ambiguities in secrecy. But I must say one other thing: The CIA, on the whole, has had an unfair billing. There have been some impossible people working for it; but in the main, it has been composed of careful, diligent, hardworking men. My own experience with the CIA is that, given strong leadership, it is responsive, loyal and responsible.

PLAYBOY: *What about the charges we sometimes hear—of CIA subversion, fomenting revolutions, sabotage, even assassination? Do these things go on?*
GALBRAITH: They never went on within my area of responsibility. My feeling is that the CIA has been in some degree a scapegoat for weak ambassadors. A lot of ambassadors who have the orthodox and old-fashioned view of their trade like not to know that there are any intelligence activities going on in their country. When something goes wrong, they can say: "Oh, that's the Agency boys, messing things up as usual." They use the CIA as an excuse for their own indifference. But any Chief of Mission who wants to take full responsibility for what is going on in his area can do so. It would be a good

practice, in general, when things go wrong, to blame the ambassador more frequently and less frequently to blame the CIA. The ambassador has all the authority he needs—if he chooses to exercise it.

PLAYBOY: *If you were Secretary of State, what would you do to rid the Department of the rigor mortis that you depicted in* The Triumph?
GALBRAITH: This is a long story. To begin with, it would be very useful to lower the retirement age. In general, a livelier, more eclectic and more knowledgeable group of people has come into the State Department since World War Two. The Pethwicks [Pethwick is a fossilized State Department obstructionist in Galbraith's novel] of the State Department are the people from good families who were looking for a gentlemanly career in government and set great store in having the *manners* of diplomacy. But they never armed themselves to understand the political problems of their task. They tend to regard all popular movements as Communist inspired. And they have the disposition to believe that people should accept any right-wing government, however despotic or noxious it may be. While there are young fogies in the State Department, there's a much larger number of old fogies. We would all profit from their retirement. But the State Department also suffers from the myth of American omnipotence. We have too many people assuming responsibility for too many things. If one imagines, for instance, that somehow or other the United States can affect all developments in Burma, then one is going to have a large number of Burmese specialists. But if one assumes that our relationship to Burma is marginal, that we can have only a very modest role there, then we're going to have only one man part time on Burma. I'm using Burma as an improbable example here; but during the years when we exaggerated our capacity to guide political and social change, we naturally expanded the number of State Department personnel. The result is a very slow and tedious process of decision-making, leading to the *rigor mortis* you mentioned. We're not going to fire those people; this is something that as a plain political matter never happens. If, implausibly, I were Secretary of State, I would divide the State Department into two parts. I would isolate in one part all the intelligence activities and all of the scholarly pursuits of

the Department. The other part would be a relatively simple field staff drawing on the expertise of that large, scholarly apparatus. I'd hope that the field staff could then be accommodated to a more limited view of American foreign policy.

PLAYBOY: *Do you think the U.S. should have any role as what is commonly called a world policeman?*
GALBRAITH: I've never been guilty of using the phrase "world policeman." To think that it is our function to preserve world law and order, or to prevent communism around the world, is fantastic. There's a certain range of matters—economic support, educational assistance, a back of the hand to dictators—where we can exercise a beneficial role. No question about that. But to the total role that is implied in the notion of being a world policeman, to assume we can put down disorders, stop revolutions, arrest communism wherever it breaks out, is exactly the frame of mind that got us into the current tragedy in Southeast Asia.

PLAYBOY: *President Kennedy visited Southeast Asia in 1951. According to Schlesinger's* A Thousand Days, *Kennedy was very much aware of the extent to which French policy had alienated the Vietnamese nationalists. Schlesinger observed that Kennedy was "always concerned not to enlarge our commitment to such an extent as to change the character of the war." If Kennedy had lived, do you think the situation in Vietnam would be substantially different than it is?*
GALBRAITH: There are always some questions in an interview that one should be reluctant to answer. That shows a decent reserve. I think possibly this is one of them. In discussing this whole difficult problem, it's obvious that I'm in substantial disagreement with the President and with the Secretary of State. But I've also tried to be fair. I think it's somewhat unfair, for anyone who was not privy to President Kennedy's thoughts, to compare what he thinks Kennedy would have done with what President Johnson has, in fact, done. It's unfair to measure President Johnson's record against the assumed record of a man who is now dead. Professor Schlesinger was closer to President Kennedy than I was in these matters, and so was Robert Kennedy. It's quite possible that they could speak with more authority. I've been asked

this question many times and I've always been reluctant to answer. I remain reluctant.

PLAYBOY: *Do you have an answer that satisfies you personally, even if you're unwilling to state it?*
GALBRAITH: No, I honestly don't have an answer. It seems just idle speculation. There are so many objective grounds for being critical of the President and the Secretary of State. There's the overwhelming fact that a large part of our reason for being in Vietnam is that we are now concerned with saving reputations. Military reputations, diplomatic reputations, the reputation of the Administration—all these have become committed in this enterprise. We're not trying to save the Vietnamese; we're trying to save Americans. There are so many honest grounds for criticizing the Administration, on evidence that is available to everybody, that I am very reluctant to resort to anything subjective. Perhaps, if one had a weak case, one might be struggling for some such support as this. But when one has an overpoweringly strong case, one doesn't need it.

PLAYBOY: *You've made that case ever more vocally in recent months. What was your role in the A. D. A.'s rejection of Johnson and its endorsement of Senator McCarthy?*
GALBRAITH: I'm chairman, and I tried to be reasonably impartial as regards the conflicting points of view within the A. D. A. This extends from John Roche, who was one of my predecessors as chairman and who is now intellectual-in-residence in the Johnson Administration and a firm supporter of the President, all the way to Al Lowenstein, who is a vice-chairman of A. D. A. and has been one of the most effective organizers of the opposition to President Johnson.

PLAYBOY: *Did you support the A. D. A. endorsement of McCarthy?*
GALBRAITH: Yes. You support the man you think is right.

PLAYBOY: *And you continued your support after Kennedy entered the race?*
GALBRAITH: Oh, yes. But I am far less interested in the choice between McCarthy and Kennedy than in having a strong alternative contender for the nomination. I would be eminently happy with either as a candidate.

PLAYBOY: *What practical contribution can the A. D. A. make to the Democratic Party in an election year? Is it confined to attempts to influence the Democratic platform, or does it go beyond this?*

GALBRAITH: Far beyond. The A. D. A. is the holding company for the liberals who are closely associated with the political process—the liberals who run for office, who speak and are heard and who have been the hard fiber of the liberal wing of the Democratic Party. Virtually all the liberals who came to Washington in the Kennedy Administration came in from the A. D. A.: Schlesinger; James Loeb, Jr., who was ambassador to Peru and later in Africa; and Hubert Humphrey, who was one of my predecessors as chairman. The A. D. A. has provided the liberal muscle of the Democratic Party.

PLAYBOY: *Many of your A. D. A. colleagues have run for public office. Have you ever considered this yourself?*

GALBRAITH: No, not very seriously. I toyed with the idea a couple of years ago, when a number of Massachusetts Democrats raised the possibility of my running for governor. I hasten to say it was something less than a mass movement. And since I live a good part of the year in Vermont, some of my friends up there once urged me to run for the Senate. On both of these occasions, I allowed myself to reflect on the idea and then I discarded it. First, because of the usual uncertainty of all sensible people as to whether they would stir the enthusiasm of the voters to the extent that, in the secrecy of their souls, they are likely to imagine. The other reason is that politics is a full-time activity; I have always sought an existence where I could do several things that interest me and, in particular, where I could protect a goodly amount of my time for writing.

PLAYBOY: *Your past and present successes as a writer must have rewarded you handsomely. Aren't you well on your way to becoming a millionaire?*

GALBRAITH: I wouldn't think so. The income tax provides good protection against that disaster for anyone who receives his income—as I do—in current form. But that's not very important, because all my life I've had enough income. The difference between too little and enough is much greater than the difference between enough and more than enough. The added advantage of having more than enough is relatively marginal. I'm quite happy as a professor.

PLAYBOY: *Do you have any intention of leaving Harvard?*
GALBRAITH: No. I've had the usual suggestions from time to time. Mostly, however, these have been offers of administrative positions, to head academic institutions. I'm not engulfed with them, because I think people rightly guess that I'm not a natural-born administrator. And I've always turned them down, because I consider teaching the price I have to pay for the freedom to write—the time to write and the research support one gets in an academic community. I've never had even the slightest intention of losing that freedom by becoming a bad administrator.

PLAYBOY: *While you play down your own role as a Presidential advisor, there's no doubt that intellectuals like yourself do have the chance to counsel the President officially. To what extent can such advisors really influence Government policy?*
GALBRAITH: Well, I'm quite impressed by a comment President Truman once made about Bernard Baruch. Truman said, approximately: "I've never been quite certain why Mr. Baruch describes himself as an advisor to Presidents. That isn't a very important job. All Presidents have a lot more advice than they're able to use." But there's another side to your question: the pivotal role in the United States of the person with some knowledge of a particular subject and, even more specifically, the person with some capacity for social innovation. This ability, to figure out how social change can be engineered, is very rare—the capacity to decide how prices are to be regulated in wartime, the capacity to design a new system of social insurance, to figure out how Medicare should be set up to do the most good, or to puzzle out what can be done about the tedious state of American television. In the United States, the business community, the trade unions and even the unattached community of lawyers, writers, and so on, is not socially innovative. The capacity to innovate is confined largely to the scientific and educational communities and to the Federal bureaucracy.

PLAYBOY: *Yet the scientific and educational communities seem singularly alienated from the political process today. How do you explain this?*

GALBRAITH: This group is currently frustrated because it is not enjoying its customary power. In recent years, when the scientists and the liberal academic community have pretty well agreed on a proposition, there's been a very strong tendency for the Government to go along. But the scientific and educational estate today is overwhelmingly opposed to the Vietnam war. There's been some disposition to question this in Washington, but the polls all show it. One cannot live in the educational community and be in any doubt about the size of the opposition. Yet the Administration and the military have—at least until now—shown a high level of indifference to these attitudes. So the alienation you mentioned is the result, on this issue, anyway, of not having the accustomed influence.

PLAYBOY: *Then from whom does the President seek advice? Does he look to what you've somewhat facetiously called the American establishment?*
GALBRAITH: Well, the establishment doesn't really give advice; it usually just confirms the *status quo*. The establishment is the group of people whose ideas, at any given time, are eminently respectable. In language I have otherwise used, they are the people who can be counted on to articulate the conventional wisdom of the moment. When appointed to high office—either by Republicans or, more significantly, by Democrats—they confer an aura of stability and respectability on the community. The establishment, for instance, can be relied on to support the Administration's policies in Vietnam long after sensible men have condemned these policies. Meaningful advice, of course, will come from the socially innovative community that I mentioned, from men like Wilbur Cohen, who is now Secretary of Health, Education and Welfare and was Assistant Secretary for many years. Wilbur was the man who invented, in a way—or who at least developed—most of the ideas associated with Medicare. He combined that with the political skill that enabled him to get it through Congress. When the history of this period is written, if it's written with any accuracy, Wilbur Cohen will be credited with a lot more power to change things than, say, John J. McCloy. McCloy was former Assistant Secretary of War, former head of the World Bank, former American High Commissioner in Germany, major archon on the Council on Foreign Relations and a member of the Warren Commission.

He has shown great distinction in making the case for the *status quo*. A few years ago, he was undeniably chairman of the establishment. But even in this role, he wasn't as significant a figure as Cohen, who is associated with change.

PLAYBOY: *McCloy is getting on in years. Who would you put at the head of the American establishment today? McGeorge Bundy?*
GALBRAITH: A good choice. Mac Bundy is certainly the most prominent contender. However, he is not a completely reliable establishment figure. He has all the qualifications: as head of the Ford Foundation, former Harvard dean, former National Security Advisor to the President, member of a family that has had a very distinguished record of public service. His father, as you know, was the great lieutenant of Henry Stimson, Hoover's Secretary of State. And when he watches himself, Mac shows a certain capacity for the reputable platitudes. But then every once in a while he comes up with an idea of disturbing originality, or he endorses ideas that the community at large is not quite ready to accept, or he stops too long on the wrong policy. This is a mistake. A good establishment man never makes mistakes. Bundy got well out in front on the whole issue of public television. And on Vietnam, he has lagged badly. So he is regarded with some slight trepidation by the true establishment figures.

PLAYBOY: *If Bundy is disqualified, then who really heads the establishment?*
GALBRAITH: Some people believe that I am studying up hard for the job. I imagine that a lot of this interview will have a very statesmanlike sound.

PLAYBOY: *You apparently believe the establishment's influence is minor. But among those who are influential, do you think that power corrupts?*
GALBRAITH: By no means. I think power has a very different effect on different people. For instance, I wouldn't think for a moment that power corrupted President Kennedy. I think he carried it with a great deal of pleasure and a good deal of grace. My impression is that most people react rather responsibly to power; it often brings out a side to their character, a depth of concern, that they hadn't previously displayed. The second part of Lord Acton's

famous dictum, that absolute power corrupts absolutely, may be true. But that the mere possession of power corrupts, I think, is only infrequently the case.

PLAYBOY: *There's also the power that accrues to the economist. Keynes once suggested that we're all "the slaves of some defunct economist." As an economist, do you think our every-day lives are profoundly influenced by economic theory?*
GALBRAITH: Well, something broader than economic theory. There is no question that our lives and our thinking are profoundly influenced by organ-ized social theory. To take one example: People who believe that they have an original commitment to free enterprise and to individualism are almost invariably citing, at second or third remove, the ideas of Jeremy Bentham or Herbert Spencer, in many cases without ever having heard of those two distinguished gentlemen. It's also true that the ideas of economists have become part of the blood stream of our life. Things that we take as original truth are, in fact, the formulations of Adam Smith, John Stuart Mill and Alfred Marshall.

PLAYBOY: *Do you think your own works would fit in here?*
GALBRAITH: I've never been disposed to sacrifice truth to modesty. I think that there are certain ideas from my own books that slightly modify the way people think about economic life.

PLAYBOY: *For instance?*
GALBRAITH: At the end of World War Two, partly as a reaction to the restric-tions and controls of the War, partly as a defensive mechanism against another resurgence of New Deal regulation—which was very much feared by business—we had a great revival of the liturgy of free enterprise. People read F. A. Hayek's *The Road to Serfdom* and similar rescripts against the state. It became a part of popular thinking that there was a conflict between indi-vidual liberty and the function of the state, that the state was a menace to liberty. The result was that people thought they were defending freedom when they kept down taxes and when they limited government spending. Well, I set out quite deliberately, in *The Affluent Society*, to do what I could to

reverse that train of thought. My point—which was not an original one—was that you do not have liberty in the absence of law and order or in the absence of a good educational system, which liberates the mind; that there isn't much advantage in having freedom if you can't breathe the air; that there isn't much advantage in the liberty to go swimming if the water is lethal. In other words, liberty requires that there be a balance between public services and private services, between what is done collectively and what is done individually. Many of these observations now sound rather like clichés—but that's partly because they have become the conventional wisdom since I published the book.

PLAYBOY: *Have you made any other significant contributions to the accepted sense of our time?*

GALBRAITH: Yes, there are some other things. But nobody should ever ask an author what his original contributions are, because this could precipitate quite a long lecture. I wrote a little book right after World War Two, called *A Theory of Price Control*, which I believe to be one of the most careful and original books ever written on the problem of the mobilized economy—the best interpretation of a wartime economy. I think this view was shared by other economists who read it. But the most singular aspect of that experience was that only three or four people ever read the book. It was at this point that I decided that in my future writing, I would seek to involve some part of the lay public. This way, my economic colleagues find themselves in the position of being asked by reporters and students, "Well, what do you think about Galbraith?" At this time, I discovered one other thing: There are very few ideas in economics that cannot be expressed in clear English. If you force yourself to state your ideas simply, you can be damn certain you'll think them out clearly in the process.

PLAYBOY: *Do you think your popularization of economics has made you less respected among your colleagues?*

GALBRAITH: I've never thought for a moment that I had popularized economics. I've always rejected that suggestion. All I've done is sought to write economics, however difficult, in clear English.

PLAYBOY: *Well, do you think your having written economics in clear English has lessened your stature among your colleagues?*

GALBRAITH: Not with anybody whose opinion I would respect. Economics, like all sciences, has its crotchets, its petty jealousies and its minor feuds. I have no doubt that a certain number of people have said from time to time, "Galbraith is unfair by not making use of the normal tendencies to obscurity; he's as guilty as a doctor who writes prescriptions in clear English instead of illegible Latin." But these are the attitudes of inconsequential people, and I've always successfully ignored them.

PLAYBOY: *Some of your other critics, particularly on the political right, have accused you of everything from indiscriminate iconoclasm to near treason. And a New Leftist, reviewing* The New Industrial State, *observed that you are actually a subtle and very powerful defender of the* status quo. *Do you think any of these charges has merit?*

GALBRAITH: I'm not aware that I was ever quite dignified by a charge of near treason, but I have certainly been on the receiving end of a formidable range of criticism. In the case of *The New Industrial State*, there was nothing for which I was more braced, and nothing I more expected. As a matter of fact, I would have been disturbed, and deeply disappointed only if the book had been overlooked. As for the charge of being a defender of the *status quo*, I suspect in some large sense that it's true. I've always been a reformer. I've never had any instinct for revolution. There are countries where I think revolution is therapeutic, where there may be no alternative to revolution. But the history of the United States is mainly one of successful reform. This being so, I have an unabashed commitment to reform. If reform works, revolution becomes unnecessary. So the reformer *is* in some measure a defender of the *status quo*.

PLAYBOY: *One of the fundamental premises of many defenders of the economic status quo is that the Government must balance its budget—just as a household does. But the new economics denies this. Would you explain why deficit spending on the part of the Government is less reprehensible than an individual spending more than he earns?*

GALBRAITH: Well, that is a good question, because the oldest of economic errors is the assumption that a state must be in its fiscal arrangements exactly like a household. In fact, the state should be the reverse of a household. An individual or a family can go into debt in the short run, but there are definite limits to what it can spend beyond what it actually has. The state, by contrast, can easily increase the supply of available wealth by offsetting the vagaries of household spending. To be very specific about it: If individuals and corporations spend less and invest less than their income, then this means that the total income in the economy will fall. When total income— aggregate income—starts to fall, there is a recession, or a depression. The meaning of a recession or a depression is that the community is not producing everything it could. Now, if the state comes in and offsets the private reduction in expenditure, by compensating with its own expenditures and doing useful things—public works, schools, and so forth—this brings the economy back up closer to its potential. It increases the volume of wealth being produced. That's why I say that the state's fiscal operations ideally are the mirror image—or the offset—for the aggregate of what households do. One should never reason that what is right for a household, or what is right for a business enterprise, or what is right even for a city, is therefore the proper course of action for the national Government.

PLAYBOY: *Columnist Henry Hazlitt recently wrote in* Newsweek *that any increases in productivity spurred by deficit spending are actually increases in paper dollars only. They don't add to the real value of our national wealth, he argued, because they produce a correspondingly lower purchasing power. What's your answer to that thinking?*
GALBRAITH: Henry Hazlitt is an estimable man but a very poor guide to economics. If any country had attempted to follow Mr. Hazlitt's prescriptions over the past 30 years, that country would have been in a state of permanent depression. If one has idle capacity and idle manpower, which are the conditions under which you bring the remedies I mentioned into action, the effect of expanding demand is not to raise prices, though it may raise prices somewhat. The primary effect will be to increase the use of productive capacity and to increase the use of manpower. This is the very elementary point that Henry Hazlitt overlooks. He is, however, an excellent representative of a much earlier era of economics.

PLAYBOY: *But the remedies you've just described apply to a situation of idle capacity. How does the new economics work when the economy is not in recession—when things are running close to capacity, as they are today?*

GALBRAITH: It's good to keep this aspect in mind. In the past five or ten years, the past five years certainly, the other side of the problem has been presenting itself. For one reason or another, quite a few countries—most notably, the United Kingdom, but the U.S. also—have been spending beyond our current factory capacity and beyond our readily available labor supply. We have unemployment, but the unemployment involves people who are out of location, or have the wrong skills, or who are insufficiently educated for modern industrial tasks, or who are the subject of racial discrimination, or who are otherwise not readily employable. In this circumstance, there's no question that the remedies I described have to work the other way around. Just as one should be able to spur productivity by increasing the deficit, one should be able to dampen a booming economy by reducing the deficit. And this should be done primarily by taxation. Taxation is by far the most equitable device for limiting purchasing power, limiting income, thereby limiting demand for goods.

PLAYBOY: *Are you in favor of the President's proposed tax surcharge, which is supposedly an inflation remedy?*

GALBRAITH: As a purely technical matter, it's certain that taxes should be increased, for we're in grave danger of inflation if the war continues at its present level. Yet anybody who takes a sensible view of the Vietnam problem is always forced back to the obvious alternative, which is to cut back on the useless and wasteful expenditures of that conflict, which would probably make a tax increase unnecessary.

PLAYBOY: *Does your endorsement of the tax surcharge imply that you think we have a good tax system?*

GALBRAITH: Certainly not. We have a very bad tax system; there's no question about that. It's not the worst in the world; there are many that are worse; but it's far inferior to what it should be. The ideal tax system would be one in which, as the first requirement, any two individuals who have the same increase in wealth in the course of a year pay the same taxes. By this test, we fall far short. It has come to be assumed that anybody who gets an income in the form of a capital gain should have a lower rate of taxation than somebody who gets his income, as you do, in the form of a salary. You *are* paid in the form of a salary, aren't you?

PLAYBOY: *Yes.*

GALBRAITH: My condolences. Other people, who aren't paid salaries—the oil people, for instance—have come to assume that tax exemption is a human right. For them it takes the form of depletion allowances. And it has come to be assumed that people who do a great deal of traveling can live partly on tax-free expense accounts, as against more sedentary people, who stay home and pay taxes. And it has come to be assumed that the very rich should have a partial tax shelter in the form of tax-exempt bonds. The consequence of all this is that people with the same income rarely pay the same taxes. It depends on whether you are one of the favored groups. The first and most important tax reform, as I've said, is for everyone to pay the same taxes on the same annual increase in wealth. I would then rely perhaps a bit more than we do on the income tax and the corporation tax. These are very good taxes. If everyone paid the same tax on the same income, we could get a much larger yield of revenue from much lower tax rates. The reason the income tax is high for some people is that it's so low for others.

PLAYBOY: *How would you counter the argument that there should be some tax incentive to encourage people to take risks, as the oil-depletion provisions supposedly do?*
GALBRAITH: The depletion allowance, for instance, is not for a particularly risky industry. There was a time when it possibly rewarded the small wildcatter who found a well and pumped away at it. Perhaps he deserved something for all the capital he had invested in dry wells. But now, to provide this kind of tax loop-hole for huge companies, which can spread their risk over a large number of operations, is outrageous. The way in which the big oil companies proceed to get oil is no more risky than the way in which big auto companies proceed to get customers. The tax exemption of the oil industry is associated not with the need of the industry but with the fact

that Texas is a very large state and that the Texas Congressional delegation has always stood stalwartly behind the depletion allowance. The defense of depletion is, in Texas history, second only to the defense of the Alamo.

PLAYBOY: *How optimistically would you regard the prospect for tax reform?*
GALBRAITH: This is hard to say. It's something Americans should keep talking about. As more and more people become aware of the great inequities of the present tax system, then there will be more and more pressure to do something about it, and sooner or later one of the political parties will get hold of this as part of its program and some legislation will be introduced. There will be a drawn-out fight, but finally something will be done. It's a long, slow process.

PLAYBOY: *Do you favor the sales tax?*
GALBRAITH: I think that for cities and states, the sales tax is a very valuable adjunct to the revenue system.

PLAYBOY: *But don't many liberals think sales taxes fall most heavily on those least able to pay?*
GALBRAITH: Liberals take a very simplistic view of the sales tax. Take my own state of Massachusetts, where we recently voted a sales tax. It turned out to be a very popular tax. Massachusetts was for many years 48th among all states in the per-capita public revenue it devoted to higher education. Then Alaska and Hawaii came into the Union and we became 50th. One reason is that Massachusetts has quite a number of private institutions, such as Harvard, the one by which I'm employed. But they are also very expensive; so that a Massachusetts boy or girl from a poor family has had a real problem getting a university education. The University of Massachusetts has been able to accommodate only a fraction of the youngsters seeking education there. With the sales tax, we have the hope of considerable expansion both in the quantity and in the quality of public education. Now, while the sales tax falls more heavily on the lower income groups—as regressive taxes do— the rewards from the sales tax, in the form of greater access to higher education, become overwhelmingly available to the people within the lower

income groups. And when anybody in this day and age goes looking for a better job, looking for a way to increase his income, the first requirement is that he get into a college. So while the sales tax is regressive in its tax effect, it is highly progressive in its expenditure effect—under the best circumstances, at least.

PLAYBOY: *Of course, this assumes that all the money raised by sales taxes goes to education or to other areas that directly benefit the less fortunate. Is this usually the case?*
GALBRAITH: Yes. Generally speaking, the sales tax is used by city and state governments, mostly by state governments; and, generally speaking, the services of state governments are most used by people in the lower income brackets. Education, welfare, hospitals, law enforcement, recreation—all these are very large items in local and state budgets. And they are proportionately more important to the poor than to the rich. After all, the well-to-do can find their own forms of recreation. Less-well-to-do people have to rely on public recreation. Mass transportation is also increasingly important as you go down the income scale. Some things, such as air terminals, are, of course, for the comparatively well-to-do.

PLAYBOY: *Speaking of the well-to-do, you've often asserted that one of the great threats to our economy is the possibility that one day, given continued prosperity, Americans will conclude that our economy is depressionproof, that corporate earnings must rise year after year. This assumption, you've said, might produce a speculative upsurge in the stock market that would inevitably end in collapse. After 80-odd months of prosperity, do you see any signs of that?*
GALBRAITH: Yes. I wouldn't want to predict when it will happen, but I think this remains one of the real dangers of our time. One has to say a word or two about the speculative dynamic here. Speculation has a life of its own. If people once get the impression that they can get rich sitting down, that all they have to do is to buy stock and watch it go up, then we will have a great rush of money into the stock market. And this creates its own reality, because one of the consequences of it is that with more buyers, stocks *do* go up. And the fact that they go up brings other people in and so stocks go up even more. Presently, the value of securities becomes unrelated to any future earning power; stocks are valued only by the expectation that

they will keep going up. This is an inherently unstable situation, because, increasingly, people will conclude that since stocks are still going up, they'll stay in for the time being; but if anything happens, they'll get out before the others. So you have a large number of people who are in the market but watching for any indication that they should pull out. And, of course, when the supply of new gulls dries up, as one day it will, the market wavers, starts down, and then you have an enormous number of people dumping their stocks in the hope that they can beat the other fellows out. This occurred in 1929. It occurred in almost classic form not with securities but with land in Florida in the early twenties. The real danger is that the resulting collapse, with its massive effect on private business investment and consumer spending, might be so serious that it would not be possible for Government policy to stop it. We would have a very rapid reduction in private spending and private investment and a very great increase in unemployment. If and when we do have another bad depression, I think this will be the way it will occur.

PLAYBOY: *In* The Great Crash, *you outlined a number of speculative phenomena that led up to the 1929 crash and seem to be recurring today: the proliferating corporate urge to merge, the popularity of semispeculative mutual funds, the near-limitless market valuation of a few largely unproved glamor corporations. Is this only coincidental?*
GALBRAITH: No. I would say that many things in the stock market today grow from the same factors that were at work in 1929. For a long while after 1929, we were protected from a recurrence by memory. People remembered what happened in 1929 and acted with consequent caution. Now it's going on 40 years and memories have dimmed. Those who were burned in 1929 are mostly broken old men, either senile or soon to be dead. We have a new generation of innocents, who think there's a fortune to be made in a mutual fund that advertises the peculiar and unique genius of its management, or who think there is some magic associated with an arcane electronic stock, or who believe there is something about computers that's certain to make them rich. These are people who believe they have an original vision; whereas, in fact, memory has run out on them. People had the same belief in 1929 about radio.

PLAYBOY: *Do you invest in stocks yourself?*

GALBRAITH: Yes, I do, but I never trust my own judgment about an individual company. Whenever I have any money to invest, I very cautiously give the job to a bank. I hope that it is in touch with the behavior of individual companies, as I am not. More important, I'd be *bored* if I had to find out what is happening to the management of General Electric or General Dynamics or General Alert. It's not a subject I want to investigate or something that I want particularly to think about. So I generally indicate to the bank what I would like to have them buy—the general areas that seem to me to be good—but I leave the selection of individual companies exclusively to them.

PLAYBOY: *Many investors nowadays are worried about the soundness of the dollar itself. Do you think the devaluation of the dollar is on the horizon—either immediately or in the long run?*

GALBRAITH: I've never thought so. Certainly if we can be sensible in our foreign policy—and this gets back to Vietnam again—devaluation is not necessary. In any case, the devaluation of the dollar would make much less difference than most people imagine, because if the dollar were devalued tomorrow, it's so uniquely important in the world that all other currencies would go down at the same time. We're talking here in Switzerland. Suppose the dollar were devalued by 25 percent and the Swiss franc were not. This would mean immediately that Swiss watches would go up about 25 percent in the United States. It would mean that Swiss precision machinery sold in the U.S. would go up 25 percent. It would mean that Americans coming to Switzerland would find everything 25 percent more expensive. This is a strain the Swiss couldn't stand. So they would take steps to get the Swiss franc back in its old relation to the dollar. Well, we've picked out the Swiss franc, which is usually counted the most stable currency in the world. If *it* had to adjust, surely the lesser currencies would, too.

PLAYBOY: *Some of those who might be most affected by devaluation, or by inflation generally, are people who must live on fixed incomes—notably pensioners and recipients of Social Security payments. Recently, our whole Social Security system has come under increased criticism from the Left as well as from the Right. Do you think the program is basically sound?*

GALBRAITH: There's always a danger in an interview like this that the subject will assume he's an all-purpose philosopher. Social Security is not something on which I speak with any great competence. I think it's served very well up until now.

PLAYBOY: *Can you speak with more competence about the welfare system?*

GALBRAITH: Yes, I can. I think the welfare system is in very poor condition. Its woeful state leads us to the fascinating alternative of guaranteed incomes as a substitute for the present welfare system. Our current welfare system has, among other things, the worst incentive structure imaginable. To speak technically, it taxes marginal income at 100 percent. If an individual is getting $2500 a year on welfare and then gets a $2500-a-year job, he loses the $2500 welfare. So it's a tax of 100 percent on the increment of income. That kind of tax system gives a strong incentive not to work for extra income. If that tax system were applied to corporate executives in the $50,000 bracket, they would scream that the Government is destroying incentives. Indeed, they're already saying this, though they're taxed at a much more tolerable rate, and the argument has less effect coming from a man making $50,000 a year, because he can very rarely confess to working less than at his peak, no matter what the incentives. But a 100 percent tax rate certainly has an adverse effect on the motivation of welfare recipients. For this reason, we have the curious spectacle of both liberal and conservative economists uniting to discuss the possibility of a guaranteed minimum income, the so-called negative income tax.

PLAYBOY: *Do you favor the negative income tax?*

GALBRAITH: Yes, I do. I favor a guaranteed minimum income for all Americans.

PLAYBOY: *Some critics of the guaranteed minimum income have said it will lead to a society in which many people choose not to work, and you yourself have often indicated that there's more to life than just working. On this subject, Keynes wrote, in 1930, that "it will be those peoples who can keep alive, and cultivate into a fuller perfection, the art of life itself, and do*

*not sell themselves for the means of life, who will be able to enjoy abundance when it comes."
Do you agree?*
GALBRAITH: Yes. I would say this was a very succinct statement of the case
I was making in *The Affluent Society*.

PLAYBOY: *The only large-scale manifestation we've yet seen of any group attempting to
achieve Keynes' dream is the hippie movement. How do you feel about it?*
GALBRAITH: Not particularly censorious. For years, I've imagined that something like this might happen—that a growing number of people would not
be susceptible to the desire for more wealth and more goods, who would say,
"Well, we can get along with very little and have leisure time to cultivate
our garden." So the advent of the hippies doesn't surprise me. It seems to be
a rather natural concomitant of wealth. But I confess to some considerable
misgivings about the association of this movement with drugs. I would be
more reassured if I were certain the hippie interests were literary, aesthetic
and experimental, rather than involving what seems to me, in my Calvinist
way, to be rather contrived and inadequate forms of experience. But this may
be a somewhat limited view. I never really get very much pleasure out of
alcohol, and I don't smoke, so I undoubtedly speak from a very parochial
point of view.

PLAYBOY: *Have you ever smoked marijuana?*
GALBRAITH: No, I never have.

PLAYBOY: *Didn't they smoke it in Berkeley when you went to the University of
California in the thirties?*
GALBRAITH: We had never heard of marijuana then. Social experiment, sex
and alcohol seemed much more plausible forms of excitement in those days,
and much more popular. The counterpart of the hippies when I was at
Berkeley were the Communists.

PLAYBOY: *Did you ever have anything to do with them?*
GALBRAITH: I was always too shy. I had just come down from Canada, I
felt rather provincial and I was afraid the Communists wouldn't have me.

PLAYBOY: *The hippie love ethic embraces a joyful and unconfined view of human sexuality. How do you feel about this aspect of what's popularly called the Sexual Revolution?*
GALBRAITH: I take a rather relaxed view of these matters. Sex is here to stay. Each generation seems to make up its own rules and abides by its own code of behavior. It's hard to go back to the 19th century novels, of which I'm extremely fond, without feeling that there was a certain artificiality and stuffiness about the formal relations between the sexes at that time. Certainly, what would look to the Victorians like the enormous revolution that has occurred since has been an improvement. And if further improvement involves further changes, well, I'm still in a highly permissive mood. But you must relate my views to the fact that I've been married only once and happily for thirty years.

PLAYBOY: *The only youth phenomenon that's been as highly publicized as the hippie movement is the growing dissatisfaction with and resistance to the Selective Service System. What do you think of the draft?*
GALBRAITH: This is something I dealt with briefly in *The New Industrial State.* The draft is archaic, there is no question about it. It's based on two assumptions. There's the archaic conviction that there is something morally good about compelling people to serve their country. And there's the very practical belief—shared by most of the well-to-do—that by drafting people to serve at less than the going wage, you shift some of the cost of defending the country from the well-to-do to the much poorer draftee. But neither of these is a very good reason to support the draft. The moral value of compulsion is dubious and the argument that the costs of defending the country should be borne by those least able to pay is questionable, at least to the less able. Also, no matter what the wealthy might think, it's doubtful if the draft *does* save money for the well-to-do taxpayer, because a draft Army is a short-term service, and, with the technology of modern war, you spend most of your time training people. A large part of the Army at any given time is in training; and about the time the people acquire the necessary skills and competence, their term of service is over and away they go. Also, the *esprit* of a volunteer Army has

always been better. The Marine Corps, for example, likes volunteers, for the reason that their morale is better.

PLAYBOY: *But it's frequently asserted there wouldn't be many Marine Corps volunteers without the threat of the draft.*

GALBRAITH: Perhaps there wouldn't. But if you raise wages for military service to the point where you make it attractive, then it would still be possible for the Marine Corps to skim off, as they like to do, the better material. You would then have a long-service Army of trained professional people, and the lower training costs would go a long way to offset the higher wages. The savings might even offset the higher wages completely. There once was a time when people could argue that you had to have the draft because the danger that was associated with serving in the Army was such that the supply of men was inelastic; you couldn't pay people enough, no matter what you paid. Now, at least for peacetime service, there would be no problem. So what remains the case against this proposal? The fear of the Armed Forces that the volunteer Army would be insufficiently white.

PLAYBOY: *We were about to ask you just that. The current re-enlistment rate for Negroes is about three times that for whites. Doesn't this point to the probability that a volunteer Army would be largely a Negro Army?*

GALBRAITH: It would be disproportionately Negro, but I don't see any great difficulty in this. If the Negroes respond first to higher wages, it's an indication that this is an opportunity that has previously been denied them, and therefore you're not doing them any damage. But if the Army wants a balance between the races, then it has a very easy recourse: Make the pay attractive to whites, too. Raise the standards—educational and otherwise—and you could easily get a balance.

PLAYBOY: *But with a volunteer Army—black or white—don't you lose a very vital link between the civilian sector and the Armed Forces? For instance, if we decide to send mercenary troops to a brush war in Southeast Asia, relatives back home could hardly protest. Whoever is sent would simply be doing his job, for which he is paid handsomely. Do you think there is any validity to this argument?*

GALBRAITH: It would seem to me that if there is a crisis sufficiently urgent to call for the dispatch of troops, it's better to have troops that go willingly and without the complaint of their parents than otherwise. The Pentagon would, I think, welcome this. There is another argument that one often hears today: that the professional Army is undemocratic, that it tends to have its own parochial values, whereas a draft Army more precisely reflects the democratic ethos of the community. This, also, I think is nonsense, the reason being that if there are any dangers of a military mentality developing, it will develop not in the rank and file but in the officer corps. And we already have a professional officer corps.

PLAYBOY: *Do you detect this military mentality within our officer corps?*
GALBRAITH: Well, I have seen in many military men the capacity to think the unthinkable—and even to make it commonplace. I'm always struck, when I go to the Pentagon, by how casually the Air Force generals talk about the possible use of nuclear weapons and how casually they have reduced such weapons to slang. The generals say, "Let's 'nuke' them." I've sat, as many civilians have, in conferences where somebody has pointed to a general and asked, "Well, General, can you guarantee success if we have to move in there?" The general will say, "Well, of course, if we're not restrained from using nuclear weapons, I can." This has always astonished me: the capacity to take massive destruction and make it into a commonplace of everyday life. Incidentally, it's of some importance to distinguish among the Armed Services in this respect. The Air Force is subject to special criticism here.

PLAYBOY: *Why the Air Force?*
GALBRAITH: The Army and the Navy tend to have rather more stable and sensitive reactions to problems. The Air Force is a younger service, with less stable traditions. The accident of personalities also has something to do with it. The Air Force had a succession of leaders like Curtis LeMay and Nat Twining who, to say the least, had a very limited view of the problem of mankind.

PLAYBOY: *But some observers have said that the Army and the other services are trying to pattern themselves on the Air Force success. Is this so?*

GALBRAITH: I hope not, and I don't think so. One must bear in mind that the Army, over the years, has had a considerable capacity to produce people capable of taking leading positions in civilian life. General Brehon Somervell, for example, organized the Work Projects Administration in New York under Franklin Roosevelt. This was one of the most difficult jobs of that period. And there was General Hugh Johnson, who organized the National Recovery Administration for F. D. R.; and General Lucius Clay, who, after completing his career in Europe, had a successful life as an industrialist and was also an effective politician.

PLAYBOY: *Did you neglect General Eisenhower intentionally?*
GALBRAITH: No, I didn't neglect General Eisenhower intentionally; he's an obvious example. However one might criticize General Eisenhower, no one doubts that he's a man with a strongly civilian mentality. I could be even more criticized for overlooking General Marshall. But one of the problems of the Air Force is that being a young service, it has had to make its way against the other services and it has made its way by persistently overstating the effectiveness of the weapon it has. I'm not suggesting that air power is an insignificant weapon, but in all military operations—I'll leave nuclear operations aside—air power is wholly supplementary to ground operations. It was very important in Europe in World War Two that we had control of the air over the battlefields. But the real battles were still fought on the ground. On the whole, Air Force claims about the success of strategic air attacks—strategic bombing, in particular—have been vastly exaggerated. I was one of the group set up by Secretary Stimson to appraise the accomplishments of the Air Force after World War Two. The strategic air attacks, we learned, were far, far less than expectations. This was especially true in Germany. For example, we attacked all the German airframe plants in late February 1944. The plants were *all* hit, but German aircraft production actually increased that February—the very month of the bombing—by a substantial percentage.

PLAYBOY: *Why?*
GALBRAITH: There were several reasons. Most of this manufacturing was done with machine tools. It's quite difficult to destroy a self-contained piece of

such machinery. Short of a direct hit, it won't be damaged, or at least it will be repairable. The Germans simply dug out the machines, where necessary, moved them to other locations—churches and farm buildings, for instance— and resumed business. More important, they threw extra energy into what until then had been a relatively inefficient industry. They put it under better management, cut down on the number of models they were manufacturing and tooled up to make planes that were more immediately relevant to their defense needs. You'll recall that they were fighting a defensive war by then; but until we bombed the plants, they'd been manufacturing bombers, which were relatively useless to them. So, as a consequence of all this, during the very month following the attack, they actually increased their airframe output. This discovery, I may say, proved a shocking disappointment to the Air Force.

PLAYBOY: *Was the case for strategic air attacks overstated in Korea?*
GALBRAITH: Yes, it was. Our first reaction when the North Koreans invaded South Korea was that we would send in the Air Force and stop the invasion that way. But within a few days, we found that the Air Force was wholly ineffective for this purpose. As the conflict extended itself, although we had total control of the air over North Korea, full freedom to fly planes wherever and whenever we wanted, we were never able to keep the North Koreans and the Chinese from supplying their front lines. This is very interesting in light of the more recent Air Force claims that they are able to prevent infiltration or movement from North Vietnam into South Vietnam. Repeatedly, the Air Force has made these claims: "Let us bomb this pass and we will stop all movement down to South Vietnam." "We're interdicting the movement along the Ho Chi Minh trail." "The air attacks are all-important for stopping the movement of men and supplies out of North Vietnam into South Vietnam." "Let us add a few more targets around Hanoi or Haiphong." "Let us bomb the harbor at Haiphong and we'll bring the enemy to its knees." We've had dozens of these promises, all of them ending in failure. Those of us, however, who have studied this matter have been totally unsurprised, because we've been accustomed to this overclaiming by the Air Force

and because we've always known that there is no use of air power—with conventional weapons—that will keep people from marching across the countryside. Nothing. The shocking thing about the Vietnamese war is the way the Air Force continues to make these claims.

PLAYBOY: *Your reasons for opposing the war, and the solution you've proposed to get us out of it, have been widely publicized. You stated your position at some length, in fact, in a speech last summer that became the basis for an article in* Playboy *last December. Has your thinking changed since then?*

GALBRAITH: Not really. I've been concerned to find a solution that relates politically not only to the problems of Vietnam but also to the problems of the United States. One could make a very good case for saying the war was simply a great mistake and that we should pull out altogether. I think I can make that case better than most people, because I've felt that it was a mistake from the beginning. I kept copies of the series of letters I mentioned earlier, fifteen or twenty letters that I sent to President Kennedy during 1961 and 1962. A lot of them concern Vietnam. As early as 1961, I thought we were getting deeper and deeper into something that would eventually turn out to be one of the great tragedies of American history. So, as I say, the case could be made for just pulling out altogether.

PLAYBOY: *But you haven't made this case, have you?*

GALBRAITH: No, because it's not one that is going to appeal to the largest number of Americans. We need a Vietnam position that will be politically more attractive—a solution that won't encounter the American uneasiness about, in GI language, "bugging out." There's also one other problem that I think some of my liberal colleagues have not sufficiently considered. A very large number of people in South Vietnam, some hundreds of thousands, have rallied to our side in the South Vietnamese army, in the Saigon government or in the simple pursuit of profits. There's also a number of people, the Catholics in particular, who would feel endangered if there were a take-over by the Viet Cong. We can't simply write those people off. These are considerations one has to keep in mind. Now, the other consideration, which is extremely important, has to do with our changing view of the conflict.

When we launched this enterprise back in the early sixties, those who were urging the commitment of troops were preoccupied with international communism. The Secretary of State said many times during that period that our ultimate enemy was the Soviet Union; that China was a puppet at the bidding of Moscow; that Hanoi represented merely an ultimate extremity; and that we were concerned with a probe that, if not resisted in Vietnam, would be exercised someplace else. The vision that existed at that time—a point I've stressed throughout this interview because it's so important—was the vision of a unified international Communist conspiracy. If we didn't meet it in Vietnam, we would meet it in Berlin or someplace else. Since that time, of course, this rationale has dissolved. We've also seen that North Vietnam has a stubborn desire to remain independent of both Russia and China— particularly China. The South Vietnamese have welcomed—or at least accepted—American troops; but the North Vietnamese, in spite of great military pressures from us, have not admitted Chinese troops. Increasingly, also, we have learned that what we are concerned with in South Vietnam is an indigenous nationalist movement. The Communists are important in this movement, certainly; they are even paramount; but the movement has strong nationalist roots. If this were just an external probe, something inspired purely by Peking or Moscow or Hanoi, it wouldn't be giving us anything like the trouble we've faced. It's giving us trouble because the Viet Cong has managed to associate itself with the patriotic and national sentiment of a very large proportion of the people there. All this comes down to the fact that we are concerned not with international communism; we are concerned instead with *national* communism—communism with strong nationalist roots. I don't think even the more passionate State Department defenders of our enterprise in Vietnam now entirely deny this. As committed a hawk as Professor Walt Rostow agrees on this point. But elsewhere in the world, in Yugoslavia, we not only tolerate but affirmatively assist national communism. It has also been our policy—and I think a very wise one—to encourage it in countries such as Poland and Romania. Why, then, should we fight it in South Vietnam? This leads to the obvious conclusion that we must work out some kind of compromise that gives security to those in Saigon and elsewhere who would feel threatened by national communism but that allows us to tolerate it as we do in Yugoslavia or Poland or Romania. I don't know what kind of bargain we can strike on behalf of our friends. Our bargaining position has become much weaker in recent months. The important thing is to stop the bombing and ascertain the terms on which Hanoi will negotiate. If we can't strike a bargain, then I would de-escalate the war and confine operations to protecting the urban population centers, until we *can* strike a bargain.

PLAYBOY: *But the Viet Cong momentarily captured much of Saigon—and most of Hué—in the recent Tet attacks. Isn't it possible that guerrilla warfare can be effective even in cities?*
GALBRAITH: Well, we have a lot of men in Vietnam. If we once thought of redeeming the whole country, we can now surely think of protecting a few urban areas as a refuge for our friends. The military will argue against it, but everyone knows that the military argues against any solution that it doesn't particularly like.

PLAYBOY: *Wouldn't withdrawal to the urban areas in South Vietnam preclude rural social reform, which many critics of our current policy, Senator Robert Kennedy among them, have deemed very important?*
GALBRAITH: Pacification is already at a standstill and, frankly, I have very little confidence in our capacity to reform South Vietnam. The government in Saigon is a government with a commitment to the *status quo*—except that there seems to be a general interest in increasing the graft. Among the government's commitments are those to the old, traditional system of landholding. When villages have been pacified in the past, the landlords have returned to collect the rent. Despite many opportunities, there has been no effective land reform. We have even seen land reform in reverse as the landlords came back. This is not because our people there have not seen the importance of social reform or the importance of getting away from the old colonial system. It is because the capacity of the United States to press such reforms, in any country, is very limited. One of the mistakes that my liberal friends have made, one of the mistakes with which I've been associated in the past, has been to imagine that the capacity of the United States

to effect social change in other countries is very much greater than it is. As I mentioned earlier, in the years following World War Two, American liberals had a vision of the revolutionary impact the United States could have on other countries. If American idealism were combined with American energy and a good deal of American money, almost any social change could be brought off. This social change was seen as the great antidote to communism. We *can* press for social improvement. But we can never force social change on a recalcitrant government. Even with all of our power in South Vietnam, we haven't been able to do so, and we won't.

PLAYBOY: *Professor Thomas Thorson, of the University of Toronto, has charged that your Vietnam solution overlooks a very basic point. He says that "the overriding reasons communism is no longer monolithic is American pressure and resistance." "The Chinese," he says, "see the Russians as sell-outs to American power. The Russians see the Chinese as reckless in the face of American power." And he suggests that a victory for non-monolithic communism in Vietnam would engender new Communist unity.*

GALBRAITH: I don't know Professor Thorson. I'm a graduate of the University of Toronto, so I'm naturally a little sorry to see a professor at my old university talking egregious nonsense. The reason Moscow and Peking fell out is that they were both pursuing their own national goals. The national goals of a comparatively developed and industrially advanced country such as the Soviet Union, a country much less wealthy than the United States but certainly one of the "have" nations of the world, are very different from those of a poor and densely populated country such as China. And to suppose that Tito broke away from the Soviet Union because of a different interpretation of American power is equally nonsensical.

PLAYBOY: *Another criticism of your moderate solution was raised by several Playboy readers after the publication of your article in December. They argued that your proposed strategy plays directly into the hands of Mao Tse-tung. Mao won the Chinese mainland by establishing bases in rural areas, eventually encircling—and then conquering—the cities. Mao has predicted that the same strategy will eventually produce Communist victories throughout rural Asia, Africa and Latin America. Do you think your strategy plays into Mao's hands?*

GALBRAITH: I'm not as close a student of the works of Mao as some of your readers seem to be, but I wouldn't consider this a serious objection. If we have to accept the reality that the countryside is going to continue to be under nationalist and Communist control, that reality isn't lessened by the fact that Mao sees the countryside as the best place for revolutionary action.

PLAYBOY: *Do you think—as Arthur Schlesinger does—that the Russians are actually quite grateful for our continuing presence in Asia, in that we're helping them restrain the Chinese?*
GALBRAITH: I think that's an interesting hypothesis. There must be some Russians who are sufficiently sadistic to take pleasure in the enormous drain of manpower and treasure that we're investing in that part of the world for no good purpose. They must also derive a certain pleasure out of the ill will the U.S. is generating all through Europe. I noticed in the paper the other day that our ambassador to Portugal had to cancel a speech because of an anti-Vietnam demonstration—in Portugal, of all places. That's like an Israeli ambassador getting hooted out of the Bronx by anti-Zionists. One major consequence of our enterprise in Vietnam is that not since the Russian Revolution has Soviet policy in Europe looked so good in comparison with that of the Western powers. There must be some Russians grateful for that, too. But I have the impression—and I've talked at length about it with quite responsible Soviet authorities—that they would like to see this war ended. Not so much because we're containing the Chinese but, rather, because they worry, as I do, that the war might get out of hand and that the Russians themselves might somehow get involved.

PLAYBOY: *Do you think that if the war continues to escalate, the Chinese, rather than the Russians, might be drawn in?*
GALBRAITH: The State Department assures us that this danger doesn't exist. But the Far Eastern section of the State Department was equally convinced that the Chinese would not intervene in Korea. This view was expressed at that time—not publicly but certainly privately—by the then–Assistant Secretary of State, Dean Rusk. But the Chinese did intervene in Korea. I think that we should always work on the hypothesis that this danger exists. It's the safest hypothesis. When any military

leader, or any State Department leader, tells you it's "a calculated risk" that the Chinese will not intervene, you should interpret that to mean that he doesn't *know;* he *hopes* they won't. The phrase calculated risk is the military synonym for total ignorance.

PLAYBOY: *Some economists have suggested that U.S. withdrawal from Vietnam might have grave effects on the American economy. Do you agree?*
GALBRAITH: No, I don't think so. I think the economic consequences of peace would be almost completely favorable. In the first place, the budget would be freed very quickly from the 25 or 30 billions of dollars that the war is costing. This would remove an important pressure on spending in the economy. It would, in fact, remove most of the inflationary pressure we're now facing. It wouldn't remove that part of the inflation problem that is associated with the wage-price spiral, but that's another matter. And on the other side, one has to bear in mind that this is, fortunately, a rather old-fashioned war, in which much of the expenditure is on simple things: on pay for soldiers, on clothing, equipment, small arms, ammunition. There isn't even much use of armored vehicles in this war. The most sophisticated weapon we employ, I suppose, is the helicopter. So the claims of this particular conflict are all for things that can very easily be used in the civilian economy. For this reason, I wouldn't think the conversion problem from war to peace would be very serious. If we had a conversion problem that involved, for instance, disestablishing our missile system, the economic effects would be much more serious.

PLAYBOY: *If you were the economic czar of the United States and faced all of the problems that the country faces now—the gold drain, the persistent balance-of-payments problem, the real prospect of inflation—what fiscal or monetary measures would you take?*
GALBRAITH: I don't need to put this strictly in terms of hypothesis. Between 1941 and 1943, I was very close to being in that position. I had ultimate charge of all prices in the United States. My basic lesson from that experience was to learn how rapidly you can lose all of your friends and how extremely unpopular an economic czar is in the United States. It is not a career that I recommend to any of your readers. On the larger issue of

economic policy, we return again to a single point: We must stop the Vietnam war. We are wasting a large share of our resources and a large part of our budget on this manifestly unnecessary enterprise, and we are *not* matching the cost of what we're spending in Vietnam against what we are doing to our balance of payments, against what we're doing to our economic position in Europe, against what we're doing to people who need to travel, against what we're doing to the reputation of America in other parts of the world. We've gotten hooked, almost in the manner of a narcotic, by this war, and it has somehow established a priority on all our resources. If we were to de-escalate the war and recover our perspective, we would very quickly find—as I just mentioned—that we have no uncontrollable inflation problem at all. We would quickly discover that the dollar is buoyant and that we have no serious balance-of-payments problem. That's why I have been strongly urging businessmen, and all Americans who have the interests of the country at heart, to make themselves heard—not against wage-and-price controls, not against curbs on overseas investments, not against travel restrictions but against the Vietnam war, which in a most unnecessary way is making all these things necessary.

PLAYBOY: *James Reston wrote recently that you're "just old enough and big enough and Scotch enough to turn the peace movement into a political movement" if that's what you decide to do. Do you think you have the power to transform the peace movement into an effective political organization?*

GALBRAITH: No. Modesty here is not in conflict with the truth. I have never devoted myself to any subject so much as I have to this. I have traveled and spoken to the point of being tired of my own voice—which is remarkable— and I've been closely in touch with all the opponents of the conflict. I've helped organize, written ads and been a source of a certain amount of ammunition for the Members of Congress who have been fighting the battle there. I have put a good deal of effort and thought into crystallizing the alternatives. And I have urged a certain amount of discipline on my friends who oppose the war. But I certainly wouldn't claim to have succeeded in bringing the anti-Vietnam forces into any sort of discipline. Nor do I think that anybody will do so. This great upsurge of opposition really comes out of individual convictions. Never has there been a cause—I hate to use the word *cause*—that has inspired so many people to individual action.

PLAYBOY: *Do you think your own entreaties have helped spur this action?*
GALBRAITH: Well, I have absolutely no doubt that the processes of persuasion here have been enormously influential. I've added my voice to that of many others. And there's no doubt that the tide for months and years has been moving in this direction. Three years ago, when questions started to be asked about the Vietnam war, there were only two Senators, Wayne Morse and Ernest Gruening, who were really willing to speak out. Now we have— publicly or privately—a clear majority of the Senate and almost all whose I.Q. is clearly positive. Similarly, three years ago, the opposition outside of politics was confined to a relatively small number of people in the universities. Now, of course, the university community is overwhelmingly opposed to the war; there's a very large organization of businessmen who are opposed; and there's a large group of Army people who are speaking out. General Shoup, who was President Kennedy's head of the Marine Corps, who holds the Congressional Medal of Honor, has called the whole justification of the war "unadulterated poppycock." And the polls, week by week, month by month, show a general increase in the opposition. It's always possible for the Administration to drag back General Westmoreland, to call on Ambassador Bunker and to enlist a few senior citizens who support its policies, in order to reassure us—or themselves—that everything is going well. But, of course, when the American people discover once again that we're still not accomplishing anything in Vietnam, that all the reassurances have been so much guff, then the opposition to the war increases all the more. I have no doubt as to the trend.

PLAYBOY: *Would you hazard a guess as to how long the war will continue?*
GALBRAITH: No, but I'll say it's unlikely that we'll continue to fight a war in opposition to a majority of the American people. Once we have a clear majority, we'll see light on this matter—and the war will not last very long after that.

PLAYBOY: *And when the war ends, what will you do?*
GALBRAITH: Oh, just what I'm doing already, though perhaps I'll have a bit more time—and a bit pleasanter a world—in which to write.

PLAYBOY: *Do you get your greatest satisfaction from writing?*
GALBRAITH: Yes, I do. I've found that writing—all writing—is a continuous process of self-liberation. For many years—when I was in my twenties and thirties, perhaps even later than that—I didn't have this sense of liberation, because I didn't fully express myself. Perhaps I was overly cautious, or commendably modest. But if I were living my life over again, I think the only thing I would change would be to exploit this sense of liberation—the pleasure of writing a book like *The Affluent Society* or *The New Industrial State* or a novel like *The Triumph*—at an earlier age. Nothing else but that.

Conversation with an Inconvenient Economist

Challenge / 1973

Copyright © 1973 by M. E. Sharpe, Inc.
From *Challenge* vol. 16, no. 4 (September–
October 1973), pp. 28–37. Reprinted
with permission.

Q: Economics and the Public Purpose *is a book of sweeping intent. It would consign existing economic theory and policy to the museum of antiquities and would replace them with new theory and new policy. These are revolutionary ambitions and yet you describe yourself as a reformer. How do you reconcile these two facts?*
A: The main body of neoclassical or textbook doctrine is in the process of being replaced now; the sun is setting on that whole structure of thought. The notion that the individual is all-powerful, that the modern corporation is an automaton, subordinate to the market, can't survive. It is too drastically in conflict with common sense.

Once it is realized that economics as it is taught is part of the process by which people are persuaded to accept the structure of power in society—a vital part of the conditioning process which disguises that power—then the day of neoclassical economics is over. And that realization is coming—is certain. Already the phrase "neoclassical economics" is pejorative. A very large number of younger economists are in revolt. But I suppose the most compelling indictment is simply that neoclassical economics doesn't come to grips with the practical problems with which society, including the modern state, is faced. It doesn't come to grips with the unevenness in growth—as between, say, the housing industry and the automobile industry; it doesn't come to grips with the growing inequality in income distribution; it doesn't come to grips with the problems of coordination of different sectors of the economy now celebrated by such phrases as the energy crisis; it doesn't come to grips—except in a marginal way through the concept of external diseconomies—with the problems of environmental disharmony. It—notably—does not come to grips with the problem of controls—or even admit of their need. The major problem of modern economic policy is barely mentioned! We simply cannot have an economic theory that is nonfunctional.

It is not my instinct to be unduly modest, but let me say that I'm not authoring a revolution. Rather, I'm taking advantage of one that is already well along. Circumstances are the enemy of neoclassical economics, not Galbraith.

Q: *You speak of the economy as being divided into two parts, a market system and a planning system. Would you explain why you make this division?*
A: This is a vital conceptual technique. It is not meant to imply that there is a sharp dividing line in the economy; but the distinction is indispensable. On the one hand we have agriculture, the service industries, artistically oriented industries, those industries that are not susceptible to large-scale organization. They conform roughly to the textbook image. And there is another world, that of General Motors and General Electric and General Dynamics and General Mills, something very different. One cannot deal with the modern economy until one accepts this dichotomy and examines the relations between its two parts.

Q: *One of the central points that you stress is the uneven development of the market system and planning system. But aren't there many firms in the market system that do well, that use advanced technology, that have respectable profits?*
A: As far as income is concerned, yes. There are returns to local monopoly, to what the classical economists called rare and exceptional talents, to

extra diligence, to good fortune. High incomes, even spectacularly high incomes, can be obtained in the market system. Picasso was not a corporate executive, yet he had a remarkably high income. But, broadly speaking, there is less technology, a lesser technological dynamic in what I've called the market system. Agriculture is technologically progressive, but mostly because it gets technology from the big corporations—International Harvester, Deere—or because it uses socialized technology, technology developed by the state experiment stations or the United States government. Technological change is vastly greater in what I've called the planning system, in the roughly one thousand large corporations that contribute something over half of gross national product.

These corporations command resources. Resource use is not exclusively determined by consumer choice; it is influenced very strongly by producer power: by the power to persuade the consumer to buy; to persuade the state to lend support; to command earnings for reinvestment; to stabilize prices and costs and to plan resource use. It is this whole panoply of power that enables the enterprise to develop, and this development explains why we have an advanced automobile industry and the poor housing industry which I have mentioned. Houses aren't less wanted. That industry has much less power to command resources.

Q: *The steel industry is not notable for its advanced technology. At the same time you can find many small firms in the market system which use high technology and in many cases were founded by engineers, chemists and physicists to apply techniques developed in universities.*

A: I don't want to be rigid in these categories. There can be more and less technologically progressive firms in the planning system. I'm prepared to believe that the steel industry is one of the less progressive. Most of the technological dynamic of small firms, when one examines it, tends to come in one way or another from the planning system or the public sector. Either it is underwritten by large firms or, as you say, it is the overflow of work that has come out of the universities or it is sustained by (say) the Atomic Energy Commission or some other agency of the government.

Q: *Referring to the market system again, you have quite a bit to say about the self-exploitation of the small businessman. Would you comment on that?*

A: Yes. In this book I've examined the various factors which keep the small firm in being. One of these is that the small firm often operates outside the structure of rules that characterize organization. The organization has minimum or maximum requirements in wages, hours, and rate of work. It usually has a union, and a grievance procedure. One of the surviving advantages of the small firm is that it operates outside the rules emanating from the large corporation, the union or the government. The individual entrepreneur and his family can reduce their income, extend their hours of work, and otherwise exploit themselves as a means of survival.

Q: *One more point about the market system. You put considerable emphasis on the arts as part of this realm.*

A: There's an instinct that the last frontier of economic achievement has to do with science. There is, I think, a further frontier that is essentially artistic in character—the world of beauty and taste. The small entrepreneur, the individual, has very great advantages in this world. And many of the firms that survive in the market system have an artistic rather than a technological orientation. If I were a neoclassical economist defending my intellectual and commercial interest in what I know or what I had written in a textbook, I would place very much less emphasis on the inventive skills of the small entrepreneur and much more on his artistic advantages. This is the best prospect for the neoclassical entrepreneur. Agreeing that men of orthodox view must defend their vested interest in existing knowledge, I don't think they do a particularly good job of it, and I'm going to help them out.

Q: *You may just have extended the life of neoclassical economics by ten years. The planning system, if we may now turn our gaze in that direction, is made up of super-large firms in the heavily concentrated part of the economy. Why do you call it the planning system?*

A: When I wrote *The New Industrial State*, I called it the industrial system. I suppose I didn't have the courage to give it the name that it should have.

When one has control of prices or substantial authority over prices; control of costs or substantial influence over costs; when one goes beyond prices to influence the responses of consumers or the state; when one goes back beyond costs to organize supply, one no longer has market determination of resource use. The accepted name for that other kind of determination is planning. This is not the formal planning of the socialist state. It is a more informal and much less fully developed apparatus. But it is planning by organizations with the requisite power. One should call things by their right name.

The term also helps to focus on the planning problems that are developing in modern economic society. The expansion of the air-conditioning industry proceeds more rapidly than the expansion of the electric power industry; the expansion of the automobile industry proceeds more rapidly than the expansion of the oil industry. Therefore, we have problems of coordination among different planning sectors of the economy. Such problems don't arise in the market system; they are endemic to planning. So the use of the term "planning system" has the functional virtue of focusing attention on the kinds of problems that one would expect to emerge.

Q: *This is precisely the point that gives me trouble. You have just said that there's an absence of planning in the planning system, there's a lack of coordination between the firms that produce air conditioning and those that produce electric power, or the ones that produce automobiles and those that provide fuel. Don't the large corporations in the part of the economy that you call the planning system still function in a market? They plan within the firm and they try to plan to function effectively in the market, but the relationships of the thousand or so firms in that system are unplanned and the relationships are still market relationships, are they not?*

A: As we are talking here today, newspaper headlines carry the news of the appointment of a man variously described as an energy czar, or an energy coordinator. Governor Love would not be necessary in a market economy. The planning system that is emerging does not have a system of overall coordination; and that discrepancies in performance exist between different sectors—that the gears do not mesh—I concede, and indeed emphasize. But we must be precise in our terminology. One has a market system when the distribution of resources is impersonally governed by the decisions of individuals, of consumers. One has a planning system when the distribution of resources is increasingly controlled by the decisions of producers. That is the substantive difference; and although we have a planning system, we don't necessarily have a perfect one. The coordination is not perfect—it isn't perfect in the Soviet Union. Nor is the planning complete; market influences are not fully excluded. They are obviously still very important. But we must see the broad structural division between that part of the economy in which resource use is still subject overwhelmingly to market influences and that part which is becoming increasingly subject to the power of the productive apparatus, specifically the great corporation.

Q: *Another major feature of the planning system is that the large corporation is controlled not by management, but by what you call a technostructure. Would you explain what the technostructure is, and how it controls the corporation?*
A: This is not a terribly controversial point. As the corporation develops and matures, power passes from the stockholders to the management, and then it passes down into the bureaucratic apparatus of the corporation. This, in *The New Industrial State,* I termed the technostructure. The reason for this transmigration is that power is associated with knowledge. Knowledge grows out of the intellectual division of labor among those who guide the corporation. The stockholder, not being a participant in this process of organizing and sharing knowledge, becomes powerless. And so to a lesser extent does the senior brass. There are of course certain powers that top management retains—the power of casting personnel, initiating major change, reorganizing the bureaucracy. But the power of substantive decisions passes into the technostructure.

Q: *It strikes me that you give us the technostructure with one hand but take it back with the other. Because if management in fact has the powers that you described, then it has plenary power to manage the corporation. It relies on technical personnel for information, and its decision-making is guided by that information. But if management in fact can do the things that you say it can do, then it really manages, doesn't it? And therefore power lies with management.*

A: I'm tolerably experienced in the polemical aspect of economic discussion. If one doesn't use sharp categories, one is said to have left things unclear. And if one does use sharp categories, one is said to be simplistic. In fact, the locus of power in the corporation is not crystal clear, and not necessarily the same for different categories of decision. When technical matters are at issue, the power of technicians, engineers and scientists is great. If the problem is one of suborning the government, the power of the lawyers and lobbyists will be great. And of course the power of top management to change personnel remains. There is, in short, a diffusion of power within the technostructure which doesn't lend itself to any single very easy characterization. We do know that the tendency is for power to pass down into the technostructure.

Q: You argue that the purpose of the large corporation in the planning system is no longer to maximize profits as it was in a market system, but to pursue growth. But isn't the pursuit of growth indistinguishable from the long-run pursuit of profits?

A: No, I don't really think so. The accepted economics must defend profit maximization. If the firm maximizes profit, then it can be said to be wholly subordinate to the market. If other goals are possible, or if there's a choice of goals, then there's an independent exercise of power by the producing firm.

Growth, I may say, is the most plausible goal. A bureaucracy will seek to expand because this is the way it rewards itself. It rewards itself because growth means more pay, more promotions, more opportunity, more perquisites of office, more power—all of which are important. So growth satisfies the essential condition of self-interest for those who are in power. Profits, remember, go to the stockholder—the man who is losing power.

There are also two other important goals. First of all, there must be a relatively high threshold level of profits to keep the stockholders and creditors quiet, to avoid proxy fights, to avoid takeovers, to minimize recourse to banks, to secure the autonomy of the management and the technostructure. In addition, an increase in the profit level from year to year remains an important test of the efficacy of the management and the technostructure. It is therefore an important justification for their continued autonomy, power and independence. I'm also prepared to argue that technological virtuosity may on occasion be an end in itself. Corporations want to be known as smart outfits, as technologically progressive. However, I'm not disposed to rank that at the same level of importance as the other goals I've mentioned.

Now, a further point. It's a mistake to search for a unique solution to this problem. We are dealing with the order of a thousand corporations, some larger, some smaller, some more powerful, some less powerful, some more technically oriented than others, some extensions of the state, as in the case of General Dynamics or Lockheed. No one should conclude that the goal-structure of all these firms will be the same. Perhaps the market economy does yield a unique solution. It's an error—a very common one—to carry the search for a single solution into the world of the big corporation.

Q: *You speak of the transnational system as an extension of the national planning system, and of the multinational corporation as the main element in this system. Will you elucidate?*

A: The nature of the planning system, as I mentioned earlier, requires that it have control of as many things affecting it as possible: price, cost, supply, consumer response, and the multitude of needed services from the state. This is notably, perhaps even hilariously, inconsistent with the orthodox theory of international trade (the most depraved branch of neoclassical theory), which assumes, by and large, that products are carried to the shore, put on a boat, and sold in second countries for what the market will yield. It's idle to suppose that there would be a high degree of certainty in national trade and a high degree of uncertainty in international trade. In fact, firms follow their products into the second countries, re-create the firm there where it becomes part of the oligopoly equilibrium. And it is able to persuade consumers, and bring influence to bear, as required, on the community and the state. Thus the multinational corpo-ration is the plausible extension of the national corporation; it wins the same kind of security in its transnational environment as it does at home. In addition, it can meet competition by going where the cost of labor is lowest and the conditions of production are most efficient. This elides two of the problems of classical international trade. To summarize: the multinational corporation is simply the means by which the modern corporation minimizes the uncertainties peculiar to international trade.

Q: *You've now described the two parts of the economy: the market system and the plan-ning system. What is the relation between them?*
A: There is endemic inequality between the two systems in power and thus in economic development, technical dynamic, income, and security of income. The terms of trade greatly favor the planning system, which, among other things, has the capacity to take advantage of what I've called the self-exploitative tendencies of the market system. There are also vital differences in the relations to the state. The bureaucracies of the planning system work closely with public bureaucracies, with attendant advantages. Firms in the market system do not have such access—to the Pentagon, for example. They must deal with the legislature, a much more cumbersome way of doing business.

Q: *I would say that the central theme of your book is uneven development between the two systems: unequal power, unequal income, unequal opportunity in almost every respect. The conclusion is that left to itself, the market doesn't work to the benefit of anybody except the powerful. How does this theory of uneven development compare with the theory of social imbalance which you advanced in* The Affluent Society?
A: A very good question. The theory of social imbalance advanced in *The Affluent Society* was a first cut at the problem. Fortunately, no arrangement has yet been worked out to require authors to withdraw books to correct defects. Automobile companies, yes; but not economists. In *The Affluent Society* I saw an imbalance between the services of the state and the produc-tion of commodities and services in the private sector. This notion is still valid. But I did not then see that there are some services of the state—those

that are subject to the power and serve the need of the planning system—which do not suffer from this underdevelopment. Where service is rendered to the planning system, as in the case of highways, or where products of the planning system are purchased, as in the case of weapons, public functions are very powerfully developed. Where the state serves the market system or the public at large—where it relates to weakness—its services are much less fully developed. What I offer here is a more complex view of the theory of social balance. It is now right and not subject to further revision!

Q: *One of the most novel and intriguing parts of* Economics and the Public Purpose *is your treatment of the household, and your reintegration of the household into economic theory. You speak of housewives as a crypto-servant class and you coin a new Galbraithian phrase, "the convenient social virtue."*

A: These are very important matters and point up one of the minor crimes of the accepted economics. Nothing is so featured as the ultimate authority of the individual in society, the ultimate authority of the individual in markets, the ultimate authority of the individual in the political process. Then, after all power has been so admirably reposed in the individual, comes a deft sleight-of-hand: the individual is made coordinate with the household; it is assumed that the preference schedules of a man and wife, indeed, of all members of the household, are the same. And this in turn becomes a fascinating and subtle disguise for the role of women in economic life.

As the standard of living rises and the volume of consumer goods increases, so do the problems in administering consumption. The management of the automobile, the extirpation of the crabgrass, the upkeep of the house, the repair of household furnishings, the cleaning of clothes, the preparation of food, and the competitive display of social talent that is an aspect of refined living—all tend to fall as burdens on the woman—or anyhow, the larger share. So it comes to pass that the person we call the head of the household—the man—enjoys the consumption, and the work associated with consumption falls on the woman. And this makes possible a very much greater increase in consumption (and production) than would be possible were the full burden of administration to fall on the person who enjoys the consumption. All this is concealed by the device, really very engaging, of making the household coordinate with the individual. The marriage bed unites men and women and their preference schedules and their personalities; and one never need look further.

Were it recognized in economic pedagogy that increasing consumption is possible only because of the increasing role of women as administrators of consumption, and were this taught to the several hundred thousand women who study economics each year, there might be a general rejection by women of this role. But, by incorporating women into the household, and then making the household synonymous with the individual, the whole problem is very neatly finessed. One is almost unhappy about letting the light shine in on it.

Q: *Where does the "convenient social virtue" come in?*
A: The convenient social virtue is a very useful idea. Any group with power in the society tends to make virtuous what it finds convenient. It was virtuous behavior in the last century to be very frugal. This was the convenience of those who needed capital accumulation—for saving. It has become virtuous in this century for people to spend freely, to have a good American standard of living. This is the virtue that is convenient to the modern large producer of consumer goods. The convenient social virtue of modern woman is to be a good homemaker or a good manager or a good organizer, or a good wife, which is to say she capably administers the high level of consumption that modern economic society requires. When one gets hold of the relation between economic convenience and virtue it's surprising how often they coincide.

Q: *Now we come to the subject that this entire discussion has been leading up to, what you describe as the general theory of reform. You argue that before any particular mechanism of reform can work, it has to be preceded by what you call the emancipation of belief. You stress that today belief—commonly accepted social and economic opinion—is in the service of the planning system. Before any basic reforms can take place, belief has to be freed from its subservience to the goals of the planning system. You call this the public cognizance. Would you explain why this is central to your doctrine of reform?*

A: It is central because the major instrument for the exercise of power by the planning system is persuasion. One of its simplest forms is advertising. But there are many other forms, including the subtle but very important tendency for what is considered sound public policy to be that policy which best serves the purposes of the great firms in the planning system. One extremely important manifestation of this persuasion is the accepted economics. Its conclusions—the subordination of the firm to the market, for example—are those which disguise the power exercised by the planning system. And power that is disguised is power that is exercised with greater freedom and greater safety than power that is identified. To identify power is to invite people to react against it.

The whole process of persuasion is instrumental to the exercise of power, and it's obvious that nothing much is going to be changed until that fact is recognized. The clearest case of this concerns the state. As I said a moment ago, sound public policy tends to be that policy which best serves the planning system. The purposes of the planning system, in turn, are frequently in conflict with those of the public. A recognition of this fact is absolutely essential to the recapture of the state for public purposes. This is necessary because the state remains the essential instrument of reform.

I refer to the perception of the difference between the public purpose and the corporate purpose as the public cognizance. The public cognizance, in turn, is decisive for political understanding and effective public action.

Q: *When you use the phrase "the public cognizance," who is the public? Are there particular groups, classes, or strata of the public that are likely to recognize that the emancipation of belief is necessary in order for the public to serve its self-interest?*

A: Oh yes. There are in any society groups that exercise leadership, and groups that tend to be acquiescent in the leadership of others. One such leadership group would be the academic, scientific, journalistic, and professional community where ideas of this sort first take hold. People who do not want change, who want to perpetuate the existing myth, always say: "Don't pay any attention to the nonsense of the so-called thinkers. They're always wrong." People who want to stand pat are, as Keynes said, the slaves of the defunct thinkers or those who serve their interest. In fact, most ideas do begin with a relatively small group and spread out from there.

Q: *You refer to the Republican Party as an instrument of the planning system, and part of the Democratic Party as an instrument of the planning system. That leaves half a party, the reform wing of the Democratic Party, as the political group which potentially will accept the public cognizance. Do you think this is sufficient to bring about the kinds of reforms that you propose? Would you like to see other groups—say an American Fabian Society—advocate the program you have outlined?*

A: The Republican Party rather openly identifies the purposes of the planning system with the public interest. So does a considerable part of the Democratic Party without quite realizing it. On the other hand, there is a growing group within the Democratic Party, and perhaps also in the liberal wing of the Republican Party, that does recognize—if not explicitly, then as a matter of political instinct—that there is a conflict between the public purpose and that of the great corporation. And this perception has been growing. It's my hope, indeed my expectation, that the perception of this conflict will become increasingly clear and that the division in our politics will be increasingly between those who insist on the purposes of the planning system and those who identify themselves with the public purpose.

Whether new political organizations will come into being to advance this change I couldn't possibly say. I'd be for something more dynamic than the Fabians now are.

Q: *You have a rather comprehensive strategy for reforming the market and planning systems. What major reorganization would you like to see take place within the market system?*

A: The great strengthening of the bargaining position of the market system vis-à-vis the planning system. This entails measures which arrest the tendency to self-exploitation. The guaranteed minimum income is important here as an alternative to unacceptably low income associated with self-exploitation and the bargaining weakness of the market system in general.

To equalize growth and development between the two systems is a matter of central importance. This has caused me to argue for what I've called the new socialist imperative. This does not seek out the parts of the economy where there is power, which has always been the instinct of the person who is oriented to strong social action. Rather, it seeks out the weak parts and brings the resources of the state to support development. Circumstances have, as usual, already forced the pace. When one looks at the areas of public social action, one doesn't find the government trying to make General Motors more efficient, or General Electric or General Mills. The main area of government activity is in the fields of housing, agriculture, health and the like. We are already putting most of our social energies into shoring up the weak sectors of the economy. Practical reform has anticipated the theoretical argument—as it often does.

Q: *One of the proposals that you offer is that small and weak firms in the market system be encouraged to combine, that the antitrust laws be set aside in these cases, that they form trade associations, that they be encouraged to fix prices and output. Doesn't this have the danger of creating rigidities which would have a negative effect on resource allocation? In another instance you deplore the fact that the American Medical Association acts as a guild to restrict necessary developments. Isn't there the risk that similar guilds in other cases would be self-serving?*

A: You may have somewhat overstated the case that I make. I would not abandon supervision in this area. But as long as we accord ITT the power that it has under the antitrust laws, it's surely wrong to deny small firms dealing with ITT the right to combine to seek improvement in their terms of trade or to try to limit self-exploitation as a form of competition.

Q: *The total of reforms that you suggest for the market system, which include such things as mergers, trade associations, a minimum wage, and increased unionization, would result in higher prices in the market system. One result of this would be unemployment in those fields where people are simply unwilling to pay the prices required for particular goods or services. To remedy this, you propose a guaranteed income as an alternative for those who cannot find employment. As a matter of fact you refer to the market system as the employer of last resort. You consign to a footnote the use of public service employment. Do I understand correctly that you're giving precedence to guaranteed income over public service employment?*

A: No. I would regard that as a most important footnote.

Q: What kinds of action would you say are necessary to reform the planning system?
A: Since the market system is the weakest part of the economy, the one which is subject to discrimination as regards both development and income, this not surprisingly is the major focus of reform. But the other side of the coin is excessive social support for the planning system. This is the result of the particular power that is exercised over the state; it means that public resources which support the planning system must be reallocated systematically to the support of the market system. Highways for the auto industry are a case in point. The weapons industry is another. Space exploration is another case. Outlays for research and development now strongly orient toward the planning system. It's a commonplace that when large firms in the planning system—Lockheed, for example—get into trouble, they turn to the state for support. These are all instances of excessive allocation of public resources to the planning system—all reflections of its ability to make its needs become sound policy.

I also argue that we would reduce and make much more visible the power of some parts of the planning system by taking firms into full public ownership. A particular case here is the big weapons firms. Working capital is supplied by the government; a large fraction of their fixed capital is supplied by the government; their business comes from the government. Yet the fiction is maintained that they are private firms. This fiction allows them to lobby, encourage lobbying by unions, promote political contributions and candidates and otherwise engage in activities that would be forbidden to full public firms. I see public ownership as a device for reducing the power presently deployed by one part of the planning system.

Beyond this, I suppose the day will come when the really mature corporation will be recognized for what it is—a public corporation. We should not imagine that General Motors in its present form is the final word of God and man, although that is a fine example of the reputable view.

Q: *One element in your proposed reform of the planning system is to bring about the euthanasia of the stockholders of mature corporations. You would have the government buy the stock with fixed-interest-bearing bonds. Stockholders would then be denied capital gains, and a major source of income inequality would be eliminated. But the stockholders have no role in your analysis of the modern economy. Why not bring up the low incomes and let the rich alone?*

A: The idea here—it's a suggestion really—is essentially simple. In the fully mature corporation the stockholder performs no function. The holding of stock becomes a device by which the investor gets his revenue in the form of capital gains, as you said, and therefore gets preferential treatment in his income tax. It would be an honest and straight-forward remedy to convert private stockholders into public bondholders and have the capital gains accrue to the state. And the experience in any number of state-owned corporations—Volkswagen in the past, Renault, British Petroleum in large part—indicates that firms that are state owned function with no perceptible difference from firms that are owned by functionless stockholders. As to your final suggestion that the rich should be left alone and the poor be brought up—this is the old liberal formula, and it simply isn't working.

Q: *Would you accept it if it worked?*
A: No. On the whole I'm committed to the idea of a much greater equality of income as an independent social good. Also, I'm forced to this position by the general logic of the analysis, for it associates income with power. The obvious example is in the corporation itself, in which income is associated with the power of the individual in the corporate bureaucracy. But the distribution of income between the market system and the planning system is also associated with power. So if one is seeking to equalize power and the exercise of power, one is seeking *pro tanto* to equalize income.

Q: *There are several kinds of socialism that you propose in* Economics and the Public Purpose. *One is what you call the new socialism, which would put those parts of the market system that function inadequately, such as housing, local transportation, and medical facilities, under public administration. Another is what you call guild socialism, in which you would encourage small firms in the market system to work together, to cooperate. A third is in the case that you describe as bureaucratic symbiosis, where the bureaucracy of the large firm—in particular the military contractor—works hand in hand with a government bureaucracy, such as the Pentagon. In the final case you would convert large mature corporations into public firms by buying out the stockholders. Doesn't this involve a great deal of centralization and bureaucracy and all the dangers that go with centralization and bureaucracy?*

A: No. I would say this just makes visible what now exists. The mature corporation does not become more bureaucratic by having its stock publicly owned. And the present organization for providing medical services, housing services, public transportation and the like involves an intricate combination of public and private organizations. In housing, to use one example, it would be simpler to follow the European model and recognize that construction and maintenance of medium- and lower-cost housing must be a straightforward public operation. Put public corporations in charge. See that they do it well.

As far as allowing smaller firms to combine to regulate prices, good lord, the large corporations already have this power. This doesn't add to bureaucracy; it simply permits the small man to enter into the same defensive arrangements that the large corporation takes for granted. However, if there is a choice between less centralized private power and more centralized public power—power that responds to the public cognizance and interest—one should choose the latter. But I don't think this is really the issue.

Q: *You choose to use the pejorative term socialism to describe a number of the things you would like to do. Wouldn't it have been more tactful to use a euphemism?*

A: Oh, I suppose so. This is something to which I gave more than passing thought. But even in terminology one should try to reflect the reality, to use the plain language that does so. If this is socialism, let it be called that. We're discussing economics, not a party platform.

Q: *One startling proposal in your list of reforms is that you want to give up the goal of full employment. Why do you think this is necessary? Wouldn't it be possible to retain the goal of full employment by using the government as employer of last resort?*
A: I would make use of public service employment. Still, there is a conflict between the goal of full employment and the unsatisfactory terms on which employment takes place in the weak or self-exploitative parts of the market. I would have some unemployment as the price of maintaining the standards of those who are employed. Unemployment with an adequate guaranteed income may be more civilized than employment with an inadequate one.

I remember a year or two ago, at the meetings of the American Economic Association in New Orleans, I was having my shoes shined by an elderly arthritic man at the shoeshine stand across from the hotel. Had he any alternative income, this poor old man would be unemployed. Is this such a bad thing? Instead of having to accept a derogatory form of employment, he would have an alternative. Such unemployment seems to me desirable. It confines the employment of people as shoeshine operators to the number who can be paid a decent wage.

Q: *The capstone of your program of reforms is centralized planning of the planning system. Could you explain how this is to be done?*
A: This brings us to the frontiers of present policy. Because it is a planning system, there is no assured mechanism (as in the market system) for coordination among its different parts. So the automobile industry produces very large automobiles in very large numbers with very large gasoline consumption, in response to its particular planning dynamic. And the petroleum industry produces gasoline subject to environmental constraints, diminishing reserves, international complications, in short, in accordance with a different dynamic. There is nothing in this mechanism—since price does not operate to bring an adjustment—to ensure that the supply of gasoline will any longer equal the needs of the automobile industry. And so while solemn scholars will be resisting the thought of a planning

system in the United States, of all places, an energy czar appointed by Mr. Nixon (not, presumably, the world's foremost advocate of planning even after his education by Mr. Brezhnev) will be trying to bring about the coordination of gasoline requirements and supply. There is a similar discrepancy between the dynamic of the electric power industry and that of the electric appliance industry, including the needs of air conditioning. Soon we will have coordinators here. There is a similar prospect in transportation. Maybe in lumber and paper. Out of all this will one day emerge some overall body for anticipating these disparities among different industries, anticipating them and forestalling them. Then maybe we'll even get around to using the word "planning." Circumstance is making all this quite commonplace. The surprise lies only in its being so inconsistent with conventional economic pedagogy. Shouldn't economics anticipate problems of this sort, or at least be abreast of them?

Q: *Any reader who has followed us this far will realize that you have proposed both sweeping reforms in economic theory and sweeping reforms in the social order. How do you assess the prospects of success?*

A: Let's take the second first. Reform is inevitable, because the problems are real. When automobiles start running out of gasoline or housing is ghastly or medical services unaffordable or the rich become too obscenely rich in relation to the rest, something gets done about it. Social pressures build up, politicians respond, so the kinds of actions which are required get taken. The action may be disguised by the semantics. It will be some time before we get around to talking about planning. It will be longer, no doubt, before we get around to using so obscene a word as socialism. I sometimes use the phrase "social action," which is more benign. Even talk about income redistribution seems to many people still very odd and dangerous. But circumstances are in the saddle, not theory.

As to the change in economics, there is a new generation of economists for whom the term "neoclassical economics" has already become pejorative. It is increasingly difficult to persuade students into belief. Even at Harvard our graduate students are showing an appalling tendency to question the worth of the neoclassical models. Once we spoke of economics as something that described reality. Now we refer to neoclassical economics (or orthodox or accepted economics) as something which serves the purposes of the textbooks, which occupies students and professors but which is not imagined greatly to illuminate life as it is. So there is an indication of change even here. But we must recognize how change occurs in economics. Scholars do not often change their minds. Men remain with their obsolescence—alas. Change comes from the changing of generations. Very few people of Keynes's generation accepted Keynes—if I may be allowed a pretentious reference. It was the next generation that came along and thought his ideas were interesting. I have very little hope of persuading the people of my generation that power and the many things flowing from it must be brought within the framework of economics along the lines that we've been discussing. But that is not important. People of the next generation have already shown that they are open to a new, or anyhow a revised, view of economic life. They will be persuaded; power will become, in one way or another, part of their system, for power exists. I have every hope—indeed, I have every expectation—of persuading those who are younger. With the passage of time, there will be a new orthodoxy—a chilling thought.

Galbraith and His Critics

John McClaughry / 1973

From *Business and Society Review*, vol. 8
(1973), pp. 12–16. Reprinted by
permission of Blackwell Publishing.

In the fall of 1973 John Kenneth Galbraith published the final volume in
a trilogy that began with *The Affluent Society* and *The New Industrial State*.
Economics and the Public Purpose [Houghton Mifflin] is a further application
of Galbraith's thesis that neoclassical economics, with its thousands of
competing producers, iron law of supply and demand, and consumer
sovereignty, seriously distorts our view of the way the real world operates.

Briefly, Galbraith establishes a model composed of the Planning System,
the thousand or so large corporations which control the great bulk of manufacturing in America, and the Market System, the thousands of small enterprises, particularly in such fields as agriculture, construction, and services,
which operate according to the dictates of a market they cannot dominate.

The Planning System is, according to Galbraith, controlled largely by
its Technostructure—the managers, technicians, and experts who make it
run, as opposed to the owners who supply the capital. It has easy access
to the higher levels of government, and influences national economic
policy in the interests of the large corporations. These interests are earning enough of a return to stave off interference by outsiders (including
shareholders), and beyond that, the expansion of the power and influence of the Technostructure itself.

The Market System, by contrast, features tens of thousands of small firms which lack the power to stabilize prices or bend government policy to their aid. It is characterized by the self-exploitation of entrepreneurs who often work long hours at low wages to survive. The most striking characteristic of the Market System, says Galbraith, is its powerlessness relative to the Planning System. To redress this inequality, Galbraith proposes a "New Socialism": "to enhance radically the power and competence of the market system." To do this he proposes the relaxation of antitrust laws for groups of small firms, government price and production regulation, more unionization, extension and increase of the minimum wage, selective tariff protection, and government technical, educational, and capital aid to market system firms.

Needless to say, as with his two previous works, *Economics and the Public Purpose* has inspired a host of commentators and critics. To get Professor Galbraith's response to some of the major criticisms raised, *Business and Society Review/Innovation* interviewed him at his Vermont hill farm.

JOHN MCCLAUGHRY

Contributing Editor

MCCLAUGHRY: *Ever since* Economics and the Public Purpose *appeared, there's been a great wealth of literary productivity about it. Critics have thrown their lances from one direction or another. We're asking you today to respond to the various critics, clear up any misapprehensions that they may hold, and further develop the thesis that you have set forth in your latest work. Not unexpectedly, one of the early critics of your book was Dr. Herbert Stein, Chairman of the Council of Economic Advisors for President Nixon. As I understand Dr. Stein's criticism, his major point is that while you are quite glib and occasionally even amusing in describing what you see as today's economy, your perceptions are rarely if ever based on any solid data or economic fact. How do you respond to that?*
GALBRAITH: Well, I'm afraid I can't clear up Mr. Stein's misapprehensions because I suspect they're occupational rather than substantial. Of course, he's wrong. The basic thrust of the book divides the modern economy into two parts: that of the small number of large corporations, and that of the very many small enterprises. This is a division which is solidly based

on empirical knowledge. I don't think even Dr. Stein would deny it. That there is a difference in performance is manifestly evident, and I don't suppose he would want to deny that either. That there are differences in power also, I don't suppose he would wish to deny. I expect he *might* wish to deny some of the recent empirical evidence of the extent to which the Planning System has bought up the Republican Party and Mr. Nixon, or at least the Committee for the Re-election of the President, but even on that point the empirical evidence is quite adequate. I didn't cite it because I wasn't aware of the full details when I wrote the book. And I think if Dr. Stein had read the book with care, he would have seen, indeed, that I make ample use of the information that bears on the subject.

MCCLAUGHRY: *Dr. Stein suggests that the over-whelming defeat of Senator McGovern in the 1972 election undercuts your thesis that the distribution of income and equality is one of the central issues of our time. Do you agree?*
GALBRAITH: I would think again that that was wishful thinking. The '72 campaign was the first one in which the issue of income distribution was really raised in an efficient fashion, at least in modern times, and on that issue as well as others, Senator McGovern got somewhere close to 30,000,000 votes. This would seem to me hardly the empirical proof on his side that Dr. Stein talks about. It would indicate to me on the contrary that a good many people are deeply concerned with the issue, and that any candidate who doesn't raise it in the future will be ignoring a surprisingly large part of the American electorate.

MCCLAUGHRY: *Dr. Stein observes in his review that "Our author is too delicate to remind us ... of the speed with which Senator McGovern was retreating from the issue in the latter days of the campaign." If the issue of income distribution is as salient to the American public as you suggest, why was it that Senator McGovern seemed to abandon his early efforts at making it a public issue as the campaign went to its conclusion?*
GALBRAITH: I was unaware that Senator McGovern did make any such retreat. Certainly such modifications as he may have made in the idea of income maintenance and guaranteed income were mild as compared with

the headlong retreat of the Nixon Administration from the same idea after Pat Moynihan left Washington.

MCCLAUGHRY: *In your book, in discussing the Market System—the smaller, less powerful and more competitive of the two systems you describe—you offer the idea that much will have to be done to remove some of the element of competition in the name of redressing the inequalities. You seem to concede, as I read the book, that this may in some cases reduce efficiency and productivity. Dr. Stein in his interview pounces upon this point, arguing that your lofty vision of the future of American society relegates productivity to an inferior position. This, he feels, is a grave and serious mistake. Do you think that if your solutions were implemented, productivity in the economy would decrease, and do you think this would be more than compensated for by other advantages?*

GALBRAITH: Well, I have to repeat there are more important things in life than answering Dr. Stein. I confess to thinking that he should be an object of sympathy. His claim to fame in the world will be that he presided over the greatest economic foul-up in modern times without foreseeing it and without even indeed, feeling that he had any personal responsibility for what happened. Maybe part of the explanation is that he was reading or maybe I should say misreading my book when he should have been looking at the oil crisis, or the problem of runaway inflation. And I emphasize misreading because it does not seem to me at all certain that the protection of the bargaining power of the weak is at the expense of productivity. The oldest experiment we have of this kind is in agriculture. For 40 years we have been supporting prices in agriculture, guaranteeing the marginal efficiency, guaranteeing the return to capital and I would share the opinion of I think most agricultural economists that by giving the farmer a guarantee on his investment, letting him know that he could invest without fear of undue loss from adverse price movements, we've enormously enhanced the productivity of agriculture. Of course, again, the empirical evidence for which Dr. Stein begs, bears this out. The productivity gains in agriculture in recent decades have been almost twice those in manufacturing.

MCCLAUGHRY: *In a favorable review in the liberal New Republic magazine, Melville Ulmer nonetheless finds one thing to criticize in your book. That is what he terms your undue reliance on fiscal and monetary policy to cope with the problem of inflation. How do you respond to Mr. Ulmer's critique?*

GALBRAITH: I think I should perhaps slightly rephrase what Professor Ulmer was saying. I don't think he accuses me of excessive reliance on fiscal and monetary policy. I think he recognizes that I also argue for the need for wage and price restraints, that I argue for the need for a comprehensive package. He does criticize me for excessive reliance on general measures to enhance employment when specific and targeted measures, public service employment in the areas of high unemployment for example or for the occupations suffering from high unemployment, or what he stresses and he thinks I insufficiently stress. I confess that I think he's right. I do make the case for public service employment for targeted unemployment. But I do so in passing—even in a footnote—and if I rewrite that section sometime in a subsequent edition, this is something I would want to correct. His point is well taken.

MCCLAUGHRY: *Perhaps the sharpest criticism I have seen of your book comes from a well-known Marxist scholar, Paul Sweezy, writing in the* New York Review of Books. *The general thrust of Mr. Sweezy's attack is that in pinpointing what you have called the Technostructure, the specialists, the management experts in the large corporations who are not necessarily the owners of those corporations, as the prime mover in making government policy bend to serve the interests of the large corporations, you have mislabelled the villain. According to Professor Sweezy the villain is the capitalist owner of the company. In shifting the focus to the Technostructure, you are in effect diverting the liberal or radical attack in such a way as to almost make you a hidden apologist for the capitalistic system. How do you reply to Professor Sweezy's comment?*

GALBRAITH: Well, Paul Sweezy is a very old friend of mine and he's a man whose views I very much respect and which are worthy of respect. It's obvious that our point of view on these matters is different and the difference is not one that we're ever likely to reconcile. I don't think he believes me an apologist for the system. I suppose he does suggest that I am more acquiescent since my hope is for reform as his ultimately is for more revolutionary change. As to the specific point, there is a sharp difference of opinion.

In the evolution of capitalism I see power as passing to organization. I see this as inevitable, given the nature of the productive mechanism, one that characterizes the large enterprise in the Soviet Union as well as the large enterprises in the United States. As public control of the large enterprise in the Soviet Union is weakened by the growth of the bureaucracy of the enterprise, so the capitalist control of the large American firm is weakened by the growth of its bureaucracy. This is the view I hold. Paul Sweezy holds a different view. He believes that in some less easily perceived fashion the power of the capitalist remains. I disagree with him. I do think the evidence is on my side but he would of course hold to the contrary.

MCCLAUGHRY: *You're suggesting then that the classic Marxist view of the capitalist as the root of all evils in a free-enterprise economy has been supplanted by this somewhat amorphous second layer which you call a Technostructure? And thus the Marxist analysis has become outdated?*

GALBRAITH: I wouldn't say that the Technostructure was amorphous or second layer. The bureaucracy of General Motors, Standard Oil Company of New Jersey, IBM—all organizations which have exempted themselves from stockholder or capitalist control—is a very real, specific, and easily identifiable thing. I'm not dealing with any mystical entity here. Perhaps there is some problem in defining its ultimate limits—how far down in the organization it reaches, but that's all. As to the main question, yes, capitalism continued to change after Marx so what were then brilliant insights I see now as in need of modification. I've always ventured the thought that if Marx were alive now, he would be impressed by the power of organization or bureaucracy or what I call the Technostructure. Let me say one further thing about Paul Sweezy's review: that while he sharply differs in his conclusion, his review, which I read with a great deal of care, is one that merits respect. He summarizes my points with a great deal of precision and with a brevity that I would myself on occasion be happy to achieve. Before he comes to his own point of disagreement, he does in the review give the reader every chance to see and agree with the point of view that he's attacking.

MCCLAUGHRY: *You mentioned that if Marx were alive today, he would be impressed with the degree of organization in the economy. Would he also be depressed?*
GALBRAITH: Well, I was using that as a metaphor. I think on the whole he would be perhaps surprised at the way in which the trade unions in the advanced capitalist countries have been brought in and made a part of the corporate enterprise, and he would be surprised and perhaps depressed a bit at the way in which the class conflict, which he saw as the portent of the next great change in the society, has receded.

MCCLAUGHRY: *Do you feel that if Marx were back today, he would regret that the organization of American industry seems now to have blurred what was once a black and white concept of class struggle and polarization? Prominent liberal commentators, such as yourself, now see no real necessity for moving on to a revolution, but instead see a gradual reform movement using various government regulatory measures to correct the ills that have arisen.*
GALBRAITH: Again, this is a line of speculation which I don't find wholly congenial. I should point out that liberals were always suspect to the Marxist, perhaps rightly so. I don't imagine that Marx, were he to return, would be greatly surprised to see them sinning in the way that you suggest. He or more precisely his disciples always suspected the worst of liberals, let's put it that way.

MCCLAUGHRY: *One of the main points of your book as I read it is the need to redress the imbalance between the Planning System and its Technostructure and the small, relatively disorganized and powerless Market System. In the latter, you include such industries as construction, agriculture and service industries. You make a number of suggestions for redressing this imbalance, all operating upon the Market System. Among them are relaxation of antitrust measures as applied to collaboration between small actors in the Market System; price regulation; strengthening of union activity in the Market System; expansion of the minimum wage coverage; careful and selected use of the tariff, and additional governmental investment in technical assistance for the benefit of the Market System. Has this program of support for the Market System produced any applause from those within the Market System?*
GALBRAITH: I think the answer is no, but it has been only a matter of two or three months since the book came out, and even if it were to do so,

one would reasonably expect it to come sometime later on. One doesn't write a book such as this for a vast audience of people on the practical side of agriculture, unfortunately. Maybe that day will come, but it hasn't yet. We should recognize, however, that many of the things that I suggest— minimum prices, relaxation of the antitrust laws, the other steps to redress imbalance—are things that we have been doing for a long while without quite recognizing the reason. Maybe, given the commonplace character of those particular remedies, they're not ones where too much applause is expected or even deserved. Years ago, for example, we relaxed the antitrust laws on agricultural cooperatives. Why? Because we recognized that this was a weak industry that needed market power in any way that it could get it.

MCCLAUGHRY: *In the book you portray many of the firms in this Market System as surviving mainly by self-exploitation of the entrepreneurs and a few employees. If your program for redressing the inequality in power of the Market System were to be adopted, would it not prevent the self-exploitation and thus remove the competitive advantage now enjoyed by these small businesses? Wouldn't it in effect bring them into competitive parity with large businesses, a contest which they would lose?*
GALBRAITH: This would certainly be true to some extent. It's a gradual process but one that could have certain long-run effects. I would say first that I don't associate the survival of the small business only with the opportunity for self-exploitation, for the chance to lower the wage, increase the hours of work, increase the intensity of work, although they're all important. There is also the advantage of the small enterprise in a geo-graphically dispersed business. There are its advantages in artistically oriented enterprises. And there are also very considerable advantages in types of services, so that while self-exploitation has a certain dramatic aspect, it is by no means the only reason for the survival of the small enterprise. On the other hand, if the small businessman, the small self-employed shoeshine operator, had an opportunity instead to have a secure income, there is no question that there would be a retreat from some kinds of work of that sort.

MCCLAUGHRY: *Some critics of your book say that your remedy for the problems of the Market System would in effect be a government welding-together of its dispersed components into another Planning System, then merging that with the Planning System which has already evolved in large industry, and putting it all under government control. In other words, the "new socialism" that you speak of would result in cartellizing, to use Dr. Stein's term, what is presently competitive, taking over that which is presently non-competitive, and putting it all under government auspices. Is this socialism by the back door?*

GALBRAITH: No, I would say there is nothing back door about this. Let's take the case of the health services. There is no question that there is no way they can be made more effective except by a larger role on the part of the government. This has anciently been condemned as socialized medicine. People no longer use that epithet, so great is the dissatisfaction with the present system of medicine, its uncertainty, its extremely high cost, and in many areas of the country its extremely low quality. A very large number of people are willing to say well, if it's socialized medicine, it might be better, and I think it would be. In consequence, I don't shy away from a larger role of the government or from the word socialism. The issue is purely a pragmatic one: Is it working now, or would it work better under public ownership? If I might mention Dr. Stein, he's an ardent defender of private enterprise in the oil industry. Even he would not, I think, however, want to argue that the present conditions of oil supply and oil prices are a very good advertisement for private enterprise in that industry. Even he might concede, if he were not obliged to defend the Administration, that a hands-off policy as regards the oil industry has worked rather badly.

MCCLAUGHRY: *While we're discussing the problems of a large industry such as the oil industry, would you comment on Norton Simon's proposal for consolidation of the United States railroad system into one large AT&T type combine?*

GALBRAITH: I would be very strongly in favor of it, except I think it should be done under full public ownership. These are practical and not ideological questions. We're the only country that has tried having our railroads under private ownership and it hasn't worked.

MCCLAUGHRY: *Now that your book has been out for several months and circulated at least among the critics and the economists, and the academic community, and now that you have had some opportunity for some feedback from a number of sources, what improvements or changes would you now incorporate were you to rewrite it?*

GALBRAITH: I think I would stand on most of it, but one always has a certain range of minor amendments that come to mind. After the two earlier books in the series, *The Affluent Society* and *The New Industrial State*, I accumulated a substantial number of small changes which I used for ultimate revision. I'm not very well satisfied with the chapter in the present book on inequality. A revision would emphasize that in the Market System there is a large amount of inequality associated with scarce professional talents or small-scale monopoly in the supply of particular services. This I was wholly aware of, but for some reason or other forgot to mention. I would want to emphasize much more strongly in another edition the importance of keeping a balance in inflation control between all of the policy instruments. I'm at considerable pains in this edition to point out that one has to have both price control and fiscal policy, and that price control only works in the context of a general equilibrium of aggregate demand and aggregate supply, but I didn't expect that point to be so well demonstrated as it has in this past year. And I think I would give it more prominence in a new edition. But most of the changes that I would want to make are cosmetic. I think I can say that none of my critics has yet seriously persuaded me that I'm wrong. That even includes Mr. Nixon's economists. If they had rallied to my support, I really would have been worried.

John Kenneth Galbraith

John F. Baker / 1975

From *Publishers Weekly*, 18 August 1975,
pp. 10–12. Reprinted by permission of
Publishers Weekly.

John Kenneth Galbraith cannot be easily accommodated at most tables. When *PW* ran him to earth one day recently in the cocktail lounge of the fashionable East Side hotel where he was pausing briefly in his current world travels, it took some time to find a capacious corner in which he could comfortably spread his 6' 8" frame. Having done so, gracefully, and established a bottle of Perrier water at his elbow (the constant journeying has unnerved his stomach), he settled down to talk about himself and his books—the latest of which, *Money: Whence It Came and Where It Went*, is due shortly from Houghton Mifflin, his longtime publisher.

The reason for Galbraith's currently peripatetic state is that he is making one of those massive series for BBC-TV in which a celebrated authority speaks of his subject in a series of carefully chosen settings. Galbraith is to be the guru of an economics series, his predecessors having been Kenneth Clark, in his study of *Civilisation*, Alistair Cooke, in his outline of American history, and Professor Jacob Bronowski, in his scientific survey *The Ascent of Man*. Each of them produced a best-selling book out of the experience, and Galbraith is, of course, hoping to follow in their footsteps.

Already the BBC project has occupied him, on and off, about two years. "First you produce an outline, a basic script in which you present

your themes and characters," he says. "Then there is a lapse of about a year
while the BBC people travel around the world scouting possible locations."
During this lapse he wrote much of *Money*, finishing it early this year, and
now the BBC filming is well under way. "I'm seeing some of the settings
I've talked about all my life," Galbraith says. "Adam Smith's birthplace, and
the country in which he grew up, Karl Marx's hometown in Germany, a
little industrial town Smith saw in a tour of France, absolutely unchanged
since his day. It should give viewers a chance to feel they have relived much
of the economic history of the 18th and 19th centuries—and I must say that
the ingenuity in finding such places has been the BBC's, not mine." And
once the series has been shown (probably next year), Galbraith intends
to rework his narration for the screen into "good, readable form."

The celebrated economist, who has been in his time in charge of economic controls and later of air reconnaissance intelligence in World War II,
a speech-writer and major adviser to Presidents Kennedy and Johnson,
Ambassador to India, longtime Professor of Economics at Harvard, and the
author of several of the most influential economic studies of our time, enjoys
some of his writing a great more than the rest. His own favorites have been
the present volume, his study of 1929, *The Great Crash*, and *The Scotch*, a
reminiscence of his upbringing in a Scottish community in Ontario. "As
long as you have some sort of narrative to work with, as I did in these
books, I find it great fun," he says.

On the other hand, the major works on which he knows his reputation
as an economic thinker will rest, which were, in order of appearance, *The
Affluent Society*, *The New Industrial State* and *Economics and the Public Purpose*, he
has found much tougher going. "However you may want to conceal the
fact," he comments drily, "thinking is very hard work—and here I was
having constantly to work out quite complicated ideas. Oh, there was an
occasional lift during their composition when I felt I had accomplished
something, but I still look back on them as fairly grim tasks."

He is a painstaking craftsman at the typewriter, convinced that revision
and polishing "should only stop when further improvement has become
impossible without a disproportionate amount of further effort." He does

not believe in masterpieces that spring fully fledged from an author's brain: "I deeply suspect that somewhere there must be half a dozen discarded versions of *Paradise Lost.*"

Money began as a long essay on what Galbraith calls "the dilemma of our time—how to stabilize prices without creating an intolerable level of unemployment." Having had what he calls "a lifelong *professional* association with money"—and the italicization in the voice is subtle but unmistakable—he discovered as he began to write, and fill in the necessary background for the lay reader, that there was no satisfactory broad, general history of the subject. And that is what *Money,* despite its excursions into current economic dilemmas, has basically become.

His friend and public scourge William F. Buckley, Jr., might scoff at the notion, but in many ways Galbraith is conservative at heart—and certainly in his publishing habits. He recalls talking to Craig Wylie, then a senior editor at Houghton Mifflin, after the war about economics, and mentioning he was doing a book. "He sent me over a contract and $1000. I was so stunned I accepted immediately and have never changed since."

Galbraith doesn't quite mean that, however. All his major books go to HM, but he has in his time published more academic titles with Harvard University Press, and what he calls "tracts," like one on how to get out of the Vietnam war (an obsession of his for many years), with Doubleday. "I find it is always best in an author's relationship with his publisher to maintain in him a slight sense of uneasiness about your constancy," he declares gravely. "It tends to add interest—and possibly revenue—when drawing up a contract."

As an economist, what is his view of the notion that publishers are not very efficient marketers of their product? "I think perhaps that failure is a necessary counterpart of the small-scale, personal relationships good publishers still have with their authors. If they were to become ruthlessly efficient, I think they would in that process sacrifice most of the features authors want—I wouldn't like them to change in that way, anyway. Informality and closeness are the first essentials between author and publisher."

Galbraith maintains that no one who has once had a best seller can ever thereafter resist peering into bookstores to see if the book is on the shelves, "and of course I'm always appalled when I don't see it there. But I've never complained about this, or about advertising. If a book is good enough, people will get to hear about it somehow."

The first time he ever appeared on the best-seller list, however, Galbraith confesses he was not so philosophical. "It was *The Great Crash*, and it appeared for a wink of an eye, for one, maybe two days, and it was like fire in my blood. I looked everywhere for that red jacket. I was traveling a great deal between New York and Boston at the time, and kept looking in the bookstore at La Guardia airport for it, and never seeing it. Finally I plucked up my courage and asked the proprietor in an offhand way whether she had it—'I think it's called *The Great Crash* or something like that.' She looked at me pityingly. 'Hardly the sort of title you'd sell in an airport, is it?' she said."

Galbraith has, of course, indulged in fiction as well as politics and economics. *The Triumph* was a highly successful novel and he also greatly enjoyed doing a satire, *The McLandress Dimension*, which he wrote under a pseudonym while he was Ambassador to India. ("I knew one was not supposed to write for profit as a government employee, so I wrote to Robert Kennedy, then Attorney General, to inquire whether a pseudonym was acceptable; he apparently found the question so difficult that he never replied.") He also wrote a novel, which he never published, about an election campaign, based on his own experience of working for Adlai Stevenson. "Unhappily I found it was of quite Tolstoyan breadth, and I couldn't keep it all going at once."

There are, he feels, enormous problems with political fiction. "Everyone knows every possible Presidential candidate, and no one really ever believes in a fictional one. And then there is the high rate of obsolescence of political issues." In his view one of the few successful American political novels in recent years was Tom Wicker's *Facing the Lions*—"That really worked; a first-rate job."

Nevertheless, he is going to try again himself, with a study of a politician's success, followed by "the way the curtain comes down the very day he's defeated." That, plus the final text for the BBC book, are next on the agenda, and then perhaps some memoirs.

"You should write memoirs at an age when there are not many left to correct you, and I'm about at that stage now." He has met, as he says, most of the notable figures of the age, and played a role himself, on and off-stage—and is well aware that "the great danger of memoirs is when they are written to enhance the ego of the writer rather than to entertain the reader." The memoirs of a man who can make economics interesting are hardly likely to lack entertainment value. And as Galbraith uncoils himself from his chair and sets off at full stretch down Madison Avenue, *PW*'s interviewer, a mere stripling of 6′ 1″, struggling to match his stride, he gives a sample.

In *The Scotch* he wrote of his notion that tall men are inherently more virtuous than short men because of the prominence their height gives them; they are too obvious to be able to get away with anything. He recalls mentioning this theory once to President de Gaulle, himself a giant. "De Gaulle nodded gravely, in complete agreement with me. Then he added, I swear without the twitch of a muscle: 'But what are we to do with the small men?'"

Advice to Exxon

Downs Matthews / 1978

Copyright © 1978 by M. E. Sharpe, Inc.
From *Challenge*, vol. 21, no. 4
(September–October 1978), pp. 58–59.
Reprinted with permission.

The following interview with John Kenneth Galbraith was conducted by Downs Matthews and appeared in *Exxon USA*, First Quarter, 1978.

EXXON USA: *Dr. Galbraith, Americans express dislike and distrust of large corporations such as Exxon. Can you comment on why this attitude seems to prevail?*
GALBRAITH: It is a natural manifestation. In any society, there is competition for prestige and power, especially for political power. In an industrial society, such as ours, the people who run businesses hold substantial political power. Naturally, this attracts the critical attention of other elements of society—the large trade unions, bureaucrats, professionals, intellectuals, farmers—who want power for themselves and are prepared to compete with the businessman for it. Such a contest will inevitably produce a degree of hostility among the contestants. As a big target, big business attracts rather a lot of critical comment. You have to expect that.

Q: *We in business don't agree that we are as powerful as you suggest.*
A: I know. Your position embraces the classical tradition of the free market, which assumes a market composed of large numbers of small competitors, each essentially neutral politically, and all subject to impersonal market

forces largely beyond their control. This case fluctuates between the implausible and the tedious. No one believes it, because it indicts itself immediately, and this is where many of your problems with the public originate.

Q: *How so?*
A: Well, the theoretical apparatus of the traditional market assumed that you could take any small producer out of the market and it would make no difference to the market as a whole. Obviously, this isn't the market we're looking at today. Take Exxon out of this market and you leave a sizable hole. Also, in such matters as technology, marketing strategy, pricing, labor relations, and production, companies do not work in isolation or ignorance of each other. Of course, managers do not exchange specific price information. That would violate antitrust laws. But managers sense what other large companies are up to, and they make decisions that tend to maintain a balance within the industry that could not be achieved were the classical market a reality. Few people believe the large company to be the powerless automaton of the competitive market that it paints itself as being. When Exxon insists that the corporate world is flat when the public knows it is round, the company lays itself open to the presumption that there is something vaguely illegitimate about a large enterprise. Therefore, almost everybody is against big corporations in principle. On the other hand, everybody is for big corporations in practice, because they are so obviously needed.

Q: *Are you saying that large corporations are necessary to the industrial society of today?*
A: Absolutely. For large tasks, one has to have large organizations. If people want automobiles made in enormous numbers and gasoline supplied to them in enormous quantities and crude petroleum recovered from beneath the North Slope, they must recognize that this cannot be done by little companies employing a handful of people. There must first be a scale of enterprise equal to the job. Second, there must be sufficient stability in price relationships and marketing prospects to permit

planning. This logically leads to greater government involvement and regulation.

Q: *Why must that be so?*
A: You must recognize that an enterprise of your scale cannot function without intimate and continuing association with government. Government provides an enormous number of indispensable services and operates a regulatory apparatus in which it is inevitable that the industry will be heard. The heads of today's companies have access to Washington in a way that the heads of classical enterprises did not. So the only plausible case that can be made is: "Yes, the modern large enterprise has power, and the public has a right to expect that power to be responsibly exercised." All must recognize that the public is going to have a strong voice in defining what "responsible" means. This means that companies must be extremely sensitive to public attitudes. It also means that large companies are going to have to accept a large degree of public regulation as the natural expression of public concern. You are, after all, so important to the public welfare that society cannot afford to be indifferent to your activities.

Q: *Do you propose that bureaucrats in Washington run large companies then?*
A: No. One must make a distinction between regulation and interference with operations. The latter, I concede, is not reasonable nor permissible. It may be wise or unwise, for example, to lay down rules that exclude drilling off of Cape Cod. But such a rule does not interfere with the operating autonomy of Exxon. Specification by civil servants as to when and how and where and how deeply Exxon should drill does interfere with autonomy, is damaging to operating efficiency, is properly to be resisted not only by corporations but by wise legislators and civil servants as well. But there is no alternative to public action in general. We are going to continue to worry about damage to the environment, about unemployment, about inflation. These problems, with the best of goodwill, are not going to be solved by the private sector. They are going to have to be solved by the government. Just because they haven't yet been solved doesn't mean that the government is irrelevant.

Q: *What about rules that go so far as to say that Exxon can be in one business but not in another?*

A: I've never had the slightest enthusiasm for that. Years ago, I came to terms with the big enterprise, and came to regard it as inevitable. The vertical or horizontal extension of corporate expertise is a matter of indifference to me. I can understand how people get worried about your entry into the coal business, but I think most of that concern comes from people who don't know how much coal there is in the world.

Q: *These rules of society's. Who is to enforce them? How do you propose to monitor compliance?*

A: I've been suggesting that the boards of directors of large corporations be replaced by a team of public auditors. No one really believes that the shareholders of a large corporation actually exert any real direction of top management through the board of directors. They don't, and it's implausible to insist that they do. Now, if a corporation wants to resolve its serious problems stemming from adverse public attitudes, it must, above all things, stop trying to sell unsalable myths to a skeptical public. A board of public auditors would provide credibility that is missing today.

Q: *What would a board of auditors do? Who would choose them? Where would they come from?*

A: They would have two basic functions. The first would be to determine if top management is meeting the public's rules. The second would be to recommend replacement in case of failure. I envisage public auditors as a professional class something like the federal judiciary. People would train for these posts. They might be appointed by a cabinet officer, the Secretary of Commerce perhaps. After all, no one should assume that Exxon or IBM or General Motors is the final work of man and God. What comes next?

Q: *If the public is disillusioned with big business, it is also true that the public is equally disillusioned with big government. With the government's wretched record in public planning, how would still more planning, how would still more planning help? Can the federal government deal successfully with such tasks as monitoring the performance of corporations as you suggest?*

A: I would hate to advocate the perfectibility of government. Sure, it will be messy. But the one thing worse than trying to perfect the imperfectible is trying to resist the irresistible. I am absolutely convinced that government planning will increase in the future. The old remedies for economic ills don't work any more. Their cure will require a social contract on which only government can lead. We're not talking about an ideology, but about an absence of alternatives. We're subject, like it or not, to the tyranny of circumstance.

Q: *Given our constitutional right to be obstinate and maybe go our own way, how do you balance the special interests of each of us in achieving the common good? In a constitutional government, you can't issue a fiat saying, you can't do that, or you must do this. What's the answer?*

A: I think we will see a growing reliance on nonmarket bargaining between unions, employers, farmers, white-collar groups, professional groups, in effect to divide what's available. How much for wages and how much for investment; how much for pensions and how much for public services. It will, of course, be under the aegis of government; the Germans, Austrians, and Swiss are already far along on the path to this kind of general social contract. I wouldn't resist it, partly because I don't think there's anything one can do about it. It means some system of wage restraints despite what trade union leaders say. And we aren't going to get such restraint if there's a chance corporations will take advantage of it. So there has to be a counterpart in the form of price restraints. This is the direction we will move in—not because of my advocacy but because of the much more compelling fact that in the modern world of large corporations, strong unions, compelling pressure for public services, we don't have an alternative. It's a pattern you can see throughout the rest of the world. It's not coming, I repeat, because of agitation by college professors or intellectuals, but as the result of desperate governments' not being able to think of another way.

Q: *Returning to the oil industry, have you any advice for Exxon?*
A: I'd like to ask you a question. How can an industry that brings so much intelligence to bear on the technical production and marketing aspects of its affairs be so bad in the case it makes for itself to the public?

Q: *What should we do about the case we make?*
A: Don't assume that you can change the public. Instead, change the case that you make for yourself. Take a look at what worries the public, and then change whatever it is that you are doing that causes the public to worry. Lecturing the public on what it should think is pretty pointless. Even I have had difficulty with it.

The Anatomy of Power

Richard D. Bartel / 1983

Copyright © 1983 by M. E. Sharpe, Inc.
From *Challenge*, vol. 26, no. 3
(July–August 1983), pp. 26–33.
Reprinted with permission.

Q: *For decades you have grappled with the theme of power, from* American Capitalism: The Concept of Countervailing Power *to* The New Industrial State *and to* Economics and the Public Purpose. *Now you are about to publish a book devoted entirely to the analysis of power. I have been looking forward to hearing about it.*
A: *The Anatomy of Power*, as I have ventured to call it, has just gone to press and will be out in October. I have been working on it off and on for three years; it will be published in a relatively short time by modern standards. Even as efficient a firm as M. E. Sharpe should be impressed. When John Stuart Mill finished his autobiography, he took it to the bookseller and had copies in two weeks. Now it would take around two years, and they would ask him to go on the *Today Show* to help sell it.

Q: *In* Economics and the Public Purpose *you wrote that that book was the last in a line including* The Affluent Society *and* The New Industrial State. *Yet* The Anatomy of Power *sounds as if it is a logical continuum from your earlier works.*
A: No, this book is not especially concerned with economics or economic power. I'm concerned with power as Max Weber defined it—the submission of one person or group to the will of another person or group, wherever it

occurs. There is some special concern with economic power, but I have tried to go beyond such concepts to see the common elements in the exercise of power, whether by a politician, a religious leader, a military commander, or a corporation. There is even a footnote somewhere on its exercise by a football coach.

Q: *So this book is a general theory of power?*
A: At one time I thought of calling it. *A General Theory of Power*, but then it occurred to me that some ill-motivated critic would say it was an effort to capture the aura of Keynes and *The General Theory*. So I shifted to calling it *The Anatomy of Power*. A case of pure cowardice. The book looks first at the instruments by which power is exercised—force or the prospect of punishment, which, taking some liberty with the language, I call condign power; the purchase of submission in one form or another, which, in an unoriginal way, I call compensatory power; and what I call conditioned power, which is power that is exercised when someone or some group accepts or is persuaded to accept the will of others in the belief that it is right, virtuous, or proper. Then I go on to look at the sources of power that make these instruments effective.

Q: *When you say "instruments of power," what are they really? What is the form of exercise of condign power?*
A: Punishment of some sort or other. The ability to inflict punishment, as in the case of the whip on the slave, the parents' rod on the child.

Q: *That could also be through the judicial system or through the military?*
A: Both, and much else. I extend the concept on to include the ability to invoke or destroy somebody's standing in the community by verbal attack. Punishment has a wide range of aspects.

As there are three instruments of power, there are also three things that give access to these instruments. Sombart would like this rule of three; he always had three causes, three consequences. One of the sources of power, of course, is personality—the dominant, effective, compelling, sometimes intelligent, personal leader. By physical strength he once had access to punishment. Now personality gives him access to persuasion, to conditioned power. Then, of course, property is a source of power. This is central to economic power; it gives access to compensation.

Q: *And the third, let me guess, is organization, as you argue in* The New Industrial State?

A: Organization is the third source of power and the one which is of greatest modern importance, but which was anciently central to the power of the Church. It gives access primarily to conditioned power, to the ability to persuade. But in association with property it also gives access to compensation, and as manifested in the state, it gives access to condign power. The book might perhaps be described by a deeply perceptive mathematician as a study in the permutations and combinations of the sources and instruments of power. Much of the three years I spent on the book I spent working out those combinations and permutations.

Q: *Again, what exactly do you mean by "compensatory" power?*
A: Buying submission.

Q: *In what sense?*
A: Submitting to a boss in return for wages. Or to a corporation for a salary or bonus. Or to a lobbyist in return for a bribe. There are numerous forms of compensation, the common feature being the purchase of the submission of some person or some group.

Q: *What are some concrete examples of conditioned power?*
A: When a politician makes a speech and persuades an audience that they should submit to his leadership.

Q: *Why conditioning?*
A: Persuading would perhaps have served. A narrower meaning, though.

Q: *Advertising could be an example?*
A: Advertising is an exceptionally prominent example of conditioned power. A singular political development of our time has been the movement from

compensatory power—forthright purchase of political support—to conditioned power, where the politician seeks to persuade through television commercials and through the media generally. Here, of course, property and the resulting ability to buy that persuasion enter in an important way. You see again the role of permutation and combination among the instruments and sources of power.

Q: *What made you come to this subject of power and to approach it in this rather abstract way at this point in your writing?*

A: I don't consider it at all abstract or abstruse. The ideas lend themselves to highly concrete examples. Citing them was a source of much of the pleasure in writing the book—at least so far as writing is ever pleasant. Years ago I concluded that economics divorced from the concept of power was extensively irrelevant. One can understand modern economic behavior only as one sees it not alone as a pursuit of wealth, but also as a pursuit of power. Also one can understand the limits on economic power only as one sees its dialectic—the tendency I've discussed in past times for one exercise of power to be countered and neutralized by another exercise of power. The employer and the trade union. The corporation and the consumer movement. Polluters and environmentalists. One has a very incomplete view of the modern corporation, in particular, if one thinks of it purely as a money-making enterprise. A complete or a more nearly complete view of corporate motivation requires also that there be a theory of power.

Q: *Do you see this book as leading to something else now? A new beginning?*

A: Certainly not. I am content to write one book on the subject. I doubt that readers would want more.

Q: *Does it lead to new strategies for public policy or new strategies of interpreting economic developments today?*

A: Oh, I hope so, yes. I'm always unduly optimistic in such matters.

Q: *How?*

A: I would hope that we now understand better the exercise of corporate power. I would hope devoutly that we would see much more clearly the nature of the modern exercise of military power. Military power combines all of the instruments with two of the three sources of power. It makes massive use of conditioned power—to oppose the Pentagon is to be thought reckless as regards national security, perhaps unpatriotic. It has a massive deployment of compensatory power—to weapons firms, scientists and engineers, the bureaucracy of the Pentagon, the members of the military services themselves. And the military services can enforce their discipline by punishment, by condign power. Going back to the sources of military power, personality isn't important. The military power is exercised by faceless men; no one knows any more the names of the Joint Chiefs of Staff; Secretaries of Defense disappear into a well-earned anonymity when they leave office. But property, in the form of disposable revenue, is a great source of power. The organization of the Pentagon, the armed services, and the weapons firms is the most extensive and disciplined in our time. I would hope that as the result of my treatment of military power we would have a much better view of its nature, how to contend with it.

Q: *But look at the tremendous opportunity to use military power—condign, compensatory, and conditioned power, the sources you mention. How can an opposition which lacks organization cope with that kind of power? Or guide or channel it in the public interest?*
A: A good question. I am not persuaded that it will be easy. But, again, there is the dialectic of power: any exercise of power of this sort tends to build a counter influence. This must be encouraged—a task for all of us. There must be a large constituency operating through the Congress and on the Executive to counter military power. We now see manifestations of the dialectic—in the nuclear freeze movement. There was an earlier manifestation in the opposition to the Vietnam War. It is one of my hopes that as a result of this book we'll understand and use this dialectic a little better.

Q: *Do you think your theory of countervailing power is still as relevant today as it was twenty to thirty years ago?*
A: I do talk about that. It belongs with the dialectic of power to which I just adverted. As I've said, the answer to the power of the employer is the trade union, to the power of the Pentagon the arms control movement, to the

power of the corporation the consumer and the pressure for regulatory support from the state. However, when I dealt with these ideas some thirty years ago, I argued, in effect, that countervailing power led to a generally benign equilibrium. This I no longer believe. Also, at that time, I had not yet explored the subject of power in a truly comprehensive way. At that time, like many economists, I was a captive of the idea of an equilibrium. I've since emancipated myself, an effort, needless to say, that I recommend to all.

Q: *In* Economics and the Public Purpose *you described the U.S. economy as comprised of a market system and a planning system, with concentrated power a formidable aspect of the latter. Since 1973, we have had two oil crises and what probably will come to be called the Great Inflation. Do you think that countervailing power has contributed to the inflationary process in the 1970s? Can countervailing power work in an inflationary environment, especially since you argued that the inflationary process really has its roots and gains momentum in the economy's planning system?*

A: I argued in *American Capitalism,* more presciently than I then knew, that countervailing power did not work in an inflationary context. In that context corporations do not fight the trade unions; the trade unions do not fight the corporations. They coalesce to raise prices, raise wages. The wage-price spiral is the result. What I did not realize in 1952 was how persistently inflation would be a problem of the modern economy. That is another reason why I now take a more reserved view of the idea of countervailing power than I did then.

Q: *But if the inflationary process is essentially rooted in the planning system, and if policies themselves are designed to the advantage of the planning system, then how do we come to grips with the problem of inflation? Conventional restraints will simply plunge the market system into depression and do very little to hold down the process of inflation in the planning system.*

A: That too is a highly valid question. It makes imperative a prices and incomes policy. The alternatives are either persistent wage-price inflation or inflation control that depends, as in these last years, on massive unemployment and much idle plant capacity—on recession as a form of prices and incomes policy.

Q: *But the way the sources of power seem to be organized, do you think that's likely to happen in our system?*
A: Sooner or later, I think.

Q: *Why do you say sooner or later?*
A: Action will come not so much from wisdom but from the nature of the alternatives. Either we have an incomes and prices policy in the highly organized sector by negotiation and government leadership and enforcement or we have one imposed as in these last years by recession or depression. Other industrial countries—Germany, Austria, the Scandinavian countries, free-enterprise Switzerland, Japan—have all, in one fashion or another, come to an incomes policy. The two English-speaking countries are the laggard cases.

Q: *Do you think that conditioned power, to use your terms, is so great that Americans are not willing to give up the mythology that the free market pervades all and can achieve the full employment growth with price stability that we all look for?*
A: I certainly recognize the problem. We have a passionate commitment to equilibrium economics—to the notion that markets clear. In microeconomic theory they do; in macroeconomic reality they most obviously do not. An interesting contradiction. In our microeconomic commitment some important social conditioning is involved. Economics instruction tells many hundreds of thousands of students every year that all corporate power is subordinate to the market. This directs their attention away from the reality, which is that the modern corporation has a very large independent exercise of power. Thus we tranquilize the young and keep them from seeing the actual expression of power in our time—the reality to which they will themselves have to submit.

Q: *How would you respond to the economics student who would look at recent years and say, "But look, the steel industry and automobile industry were eventually subordinate to the marketplace, and are now in the process of contraction and adaptation to global change"? Ultimately aren't they all subject to global markets?*
A: A very bright student. Certainly if you impose enough monetary constraint you can, through unemployment, idle plant capacity, and the threat

of bankruptcy, force down prices and wages, in a sense, reassert market forces. This has been the singular achievement of modern monetary policy. It has also been, you will agree, a very painful exercise.

Q: *But do you attribute the difficulties in the automobile industry simply to monetary restraint?*

A: Of course not; I do not exclude the role of foreign competition. In economics there are no absolutes. But the greatest suffering has been in the so-called credit-sensitive industries or their suppliers; that, also, is where you would expect monetary policy to have the most repressive effect. So I would accord a major role to monetary policy. When the economy was functioning at or near capacity we heard much less—very little—about foreign competition.

Q: *Moving to a different subject, in recent years the conservatives have gone to the American people with the idea that individual freedom is at jeopardy and the reason for that is the gigantic size and continual growth of government. You have posed the idea that there is a danger in all bureaucracies and all large organizations in that they restrict individual freedom. You argued that countervailing power was one way for individuals to offset that concentration of power. Now my question is, if we continually move in our society toward larger organizations in an attempt to balance out ever greater concentrations of power, where will that finally leave the individual, whether it is in the economy or in the political process?*

A: All participants in organizations subordinate their own will to that of the organization; no group of people is more disciplined in the submission of their personal expression to organization goals than corporate executives. They would not dream of speaking out in public in criticism of the purposes of their organization. So it is also in the State Department, the CIA, and the Pentagon. Even in the modern university there is a measure of self-restraint, however much that may be denied. This is the effect of organization. What I do not accept is the way numerous individuals, including some very solemn scholars, react to the idea of liberty. They weep that the liberty of the affluent is being jeopardized by taxes, regulation, the general apparatus of the welfare state. And likewise the liberty of business enterprise. They neglect to consider the way liberty is enlarged by giving people income—by welfare payments, medical care, food stamps, unemployment compensation, old age pensions. It is extraordinary how little in economic discussion we hear of the greatest of liberties, which is having some money to spend. Or how little of the way liberty is circumscribed by poverty.

Q: *Liberty, you are saying, requires a reasonably equitable distribution of income and wealth?*
A: Yes. But I am especially stressing the way liberty is enhanced by the possession of some income.

Q: *So, you still say that the answer lies in organization then, the organization of those who probably are found in what you call the market system, in order to counterbalance the power of those in the planning system?*
A: I don't say that's the only answer. It is certainly a major part of the answer.

Q: *Do you have any hope that we can move in the other direction and dismantle large concentrations of power?*
A: No.

Q: *None whatever?*
A: None whatever. One of the older policy fixations of economics was that large concentrations of corporate power would somehow some day be broken up. This was the case for the anti-trust laws; but even my most passionately archaic friends appear to have given up hope on that. The anti-trust laws inspire none of the affection they did fifty years ago. It has come to be recognized that a recommendation that the anti-trust laws be enforced is the last gasp of the bankrupt policy mind.

Q: *There is no hope of controlling these conglomerations and mergers?*
A: I wouldn't exclude that but I certainly wouldn't expect to do it through the anti-trust laws. We do need to have a close look at the takeover drive, the resulting conglomerates, and the opportunity this gives for manipulating investment and for quick disinvestment in low-paying industries. You do not try to improve their performance; you sell them off. This leads on to the larger issue of a publicly sponsored industrial and investment policy

and to legislation making hostile takeovers more difficult. The anti-trust laws have no useful bearing on these matters.

Q: *You yourself have pointed out that conglomerate mergers themselves often lead to poor performance of the firm that's acquired. Do you think that is one aspect of the stagnation we see in some of our basic industries?*
A: Yes. I am impressed by my colleague Robert Reich's argument that intelligence in the modern conglomerate is devoted to the shuffling of assets rather than to their productive use. When the U.S. Steel Corporation acquired Marathon Oil, it was reducing its commitment to the steel business, shifting management effort and investment to—as it then seemed—the richer prospects of the oil company. If U.S. Steel did not own an oil company, it would be under greater pressure for improved performance in the steel business.

Q: *When a relatively small number of firms, say 500, control two-thirds to three-fourths of the assets of the private economy, by what means could the rest of the system organize itself to bring about a slowdown or a halt to that process of growing concentration?*
A: One cannot be too optimistic. However, I am not totally pessimistic about the democratic process. If the takeovers and the resulting conglomerates lead to neglect and disinvestment in our older industry, this will be of political concern. And there will be demands that something be done about it. I confess that I do not see this as an immediate possibility; but we do, as I've just said, hear talk these days of the need for an industrial policy. There is already some political response.

Q: *But it seems to me that industrial policy could just as easily lead to a greater momentum in the formation of conglomerates. Maybe there wouldn't be disinvestment in the inefficient industries but simply an allocation of scarce capital to those industries that are already running inefficiently.*
A: Your reference to scarcity implies a fixed supply of capital. This is a current cliché that is wholly inconsistent with our large supply of unused economic resources. Still, I would not exclude the possibility of a wrong industrial policy.

Q: *So, you have hope for industrial policy?*
A: If one gives up and says the prospect is hopeless, then one forecloses all thought on the problem. I am in sympathy with what Felix Rohatyn, Robert Reich, and others have been saying on this matter.

Q: *What line of approach would you take to try to bring such a strategy to fruition? Would one propose a specific kind of institution? In Rohatyn's case it would be a financial institution, in another case it would be a planning institution. What route would you think would be best?*
A: I would urge both. I've long felt that we need a high-level planning organization under prestigious public auspices.

Q: *Within the government or outside?*
A: Oh, it has to be done by the government. And it should draw on our best economic, scientific, and engineering resources with an eye also to the expanding role in economic life of the arts. I would also advocate a major financial institution to give investment support to horizon industries and to act against the conglomerate disinvestment of which we have been speaking. We accept that modern industrial trends impair the operation of the market. This being so we must have another mechanism. The only alternative is applied intelligence. We cannot accept the present mythology which causes us to say, "Yes, things are going very badly, but we must not interfere with the market."

Q: *As far as the number of workers and firms are concerned, the majority really operate in what you call the market system, characterized virtually by competition, even though the vast weight of gross national product seems to come from your so-called planning system.*
A: I agree. Small business, agriculture, the service industries, are still in the lesser part of the economy that I refer to as the market system.

Q: *So maybe from the standpoint of these small entities and the masses of participants, the market system is reality, not just a textbook theory?*
A: Yes. But at best it produces around a third of private product. Economists, a dwindling number, I trust, then apply to the whole economy the theory and policy that is more or less relevant to a third of the economy. The answer, obviously, is a bimodal view of the economy—one part that reflects a high

degree of economic concentration, another that conforms more or less to traditional market structure and principles.

Q: *Are there any new developments in the market sector?*
A: There are, if not new, at least widely unrecognized developments. We ignore or greatly underestimate the role of the artistically based industries and the associated importance of design. The visual and performing arts are an increasing part of modern product—a growth industry, much as artists might dislike the designation. And from the artistic tradition come the quality and commercial effectiveness of design. The claim of Italian products on world markets derives not from their superior engineering but from their better design. This in turn reflects the strong Italian artistic base. When we talk about the importance of scientists and engineers, we must also have in mind the modern importance of artists.

Q: *Going back to the market, does the sheer number of participants in the market system explain why it is so difficult to dispel the myth of the classical market—why it remains a popular idea among Americans?*
A: Partly that, yes; the myth of the market depends on its continuing reality in one part of the economy. However, it also depends on the stereotypes of economic instruction. The textbooks are a great support to tradition. They are carefully crafted to reflect the reputable belief. That wins their adoption. And as I said earlier, it would be quite inconvenient were students taught that power rested not with the market but with the great organization. Much better to have them believe that General Electric, General Mills, and General Dynamics have no independent power. Particularly General Dynamics with its interesting relationship to the Pentagon. Some things are better kept out of sight!

Q: *What would be the fruitful lines for young economists to pursue in their research as they think of their professional careers as scholars, wanting to contribute to a better understanding of our system?*
A: Oh, I have no doubt that a young scholar who pays proper attention to his career should get into the mathematical minutiae of equilibrium economics. That is the way he will establish his respectability. And there

he is wise to remain until he gets tenure. More seriously, I would say the greatest area of *useful* performance is in the study of the nature and economic effects of industrial structure, the matter of which we have been speaking. The macroeconomic effects of microeconomic structure. We must never again suppose that macroeconomics and microeconomics are different subjects.

Q: *Why has this line of work not been very interesting for Americans? In the last couple of decades in Europe there has been a greater interest in industrial structure as a focus of study.*
A: Maybe this subject is becoming more central to economic discussion in the United States. More of my young colleagues are, indeed, venturing out from the framework of neoclassical and equilibrium economics. Respectability exacts a heavy price in boredom. And irrelevance.

Q: *Is that what motivated you?*
A: No. But I was helped by beginning academic life with a concern for agricultural economics. In that field we were permitted a certain empirical relevance that the equilibrium theorists were not allowed. The professional price, of course, was heavy. Agricultural economics had the low prestige of what Veblen called exoteric science as compared with the high prestige of economic theory which he called esoteric science.

Q: *Do you think it's possible that as our basic industries achieve great size and their optimal efficiency falls off, they will then contract and the economy will move back to a more competitive system characterized by larger numbers of units of small size?*
A: I see no likelihood of that whatever.

Q: *So you see the formation of conglomerates continuing?*
A: Yes, as a practical matter, I do. I would hope, though, that we would become more aware of the bureaucratic tendency within the large corporation and of the impulse to corporate size for its own sake. Myron Gordon of the University of Toronto has done some interesting work in measuring the cost of the bureaucratic apparatus in modern manufacturing. He has shown that in the ten years for which the most recent data are available, it has commanded an enormously increased share of the income while that

going for materials, for labor, and for profits has diminished. This is some-thing of which we will perhaps become increasingly aware. One is fascinated to read that under the influence of this recession corporations have been shedding personnel and becoming more streamlined and efficient. It leads on to the question: What in the world were those people doing before? Here again power enters the picture as a motivating force. An executive wants a good salary; I don't deny that. But he also wants the prestige that goes with the largest possible number of subordinates. The measure of esteem in a corporation is not what salary the executive gets; the common reference is to how many people he has under him. Thus the bureaucratic dynamic. Thus, too, the thrust for corporate size—the conglomerate drive. To be bigger may not be better, but it is surely a major source of executive and corporate prestige. Better even to be International Harvester than a small, profitable firm in Dedham, Mass.

Q: *Thank you.*

Galbraith: America Will Feel the Crunch of Reagan Revolution

William Olsen / 1987

From the *Tribune*, 6 May 1987,
Business; Ed. 1–6; p. A-23.
Reprinted by permission of the
Union-Tribune Publishing Company.

Declaring the Reagan Revolution over, John Kenneth Galbraith said yesterday the United States will soon begin paying for the mistakes of Ronald Reagan and his administration.

And when the tab comes due, it could produce results similar to the 1929 stock market crash, warned the 78-year-old economist. Galbraith spoke to a packed house at UCSD last night.

In an interview before the speech, Galbraith said, "I wouldn't think the danger is as great as it was in 1929 (for that to happen again.) The economy in 1929 was a very fragile thing—there were no government supports to income, no welfare, no social security program, no bank deposit insurance."

Galbraith, now retired from his professorship at Harvard, is a former editor of *Fortune* magazine and served as ambassador to India during the Kennedy administration.

In the January issue of the *Atlantic Monthly* he wrote an article drawing parallels to today's stock market speculation and the time shortly before

130

the 1929 crash. "I got more reaction to that than anything I've written in years," Galbraith said.

"I've been very careful never to make predictions because people only remember your wrong predictions rather than your right ones. But I wouldn't have any doubt that there's an enormous number of people in the market with a view of getting out if anything happens. So you have a built-in instability and that accounts for these big fluctuations.

"The extraordinary thing is how short people's memory is."

Galbraith, a staunch liberal Democrat, has long been critical of the Reagan administration's economic policies. Some years ago he predicted the policies would cause wild inflation.

"I would still say that (the) danger is very strong, but it hasn't emerged as rapidly as I thought it would. That's partly because ... the Reagan administration has crushed the trade union movement so that the wage price spiral has been much less of a factor in pressing inflation than say it was in the 1970s.

"With the dollar down and the effect this will have on import prices and commodity prices we should not dismiss the danger of another inflationary surge. The danger is that it will have to be dealt with by raising interest rates and tightening on bank lending, which, of course, then could cause the kind of crunch that I mentioned earlier.

"We'll pay for the economic policies of the Reagan administration, there shouldn't be any doubt about that."

Is the Reagan Revolution over, a member of the university audience asked. "Oh, I think so."

Galbraith suggested several ways to end wild stock market speculation. First, he would put "a much stronger barrier against junk bonds" while requiring corporations to give "much earlier notices of takeover attempts."

During World War II, Galbraith was the assistant administrator of pricing controls. He has often suggested to presidents that they institute similar controls, as did Richard Nixon in 1972.

The longer-term solution to such controls, however, is a "closer working relationship between unions and corporations," he said. "The United States and the British are the only ones who still maintain the old labor management conflict in its original form. Japanese, Austrians, Germans, Swiss, Scandavians, have all reached a working relationship between the unions and corporations, but we haven't and we're going to have to do it."

On Third World debt: "Oh, it won't be paid. The only question about the debt is how we disguise it."

Galbraith's views and wit are unlike his fellow economists'. Several times during his talk he produced titters among the audience of more than 600.

"I cherish a certain amount of independence," he said following his talk. "I prefer being right to being fashionable. Alfred Marshall, one of the great economists of the last generation, said there's nothing an economist should fear as much as applause."

Galbraith said he has always considered himself a writer first, anything else second. He has published 22 books, with another due out this autumn called *Economics in Perspective.*

The Political Asymmetry of Economic Policy

Eastern Economic Journal / 1988

From *Eastern Economic Journal*,
April–June 1988, vol. 14, no. 2,
pp. 125–28. Reprinted by permission.

EEJ: *Much of the blame for the recent reversal of the United States economy is being laid on Keynesian debt policy and, by implication, on the Keynesian theoretical system itself. In retrospect, does it now seem that somehow the Keynesian scholars of your generation went wrong in their analyses and policy recommendations?*

GALBRAITH: Economists of my generation were certainly not reluctant to take credit for that remarkably agreeable era in American capitalism from 1945–to approximately 1970. We were very shrewd in selecting the time we chose to practice our profession. And it is probably fair to say that part of the present problem is inherent in the Keynesian system. Few, if any, of the Keynesian scholars of my day anticipated what we may call the *political asymmetry* of the Keynesian system. It was politically easy, even rewarding, to act fiscally against unemployment and deflation. Lower taxes and higher public expenditures were politically agreeable actions. Given the broad tendency toward deflation and unemployment in the industrial countries, such measures were also appropriate. However after 1970, when inflation became a central and compelling concern, the relevant Keynesian action would then have been higher taxes and reduced public expenditures. But these actions were politically unpleasant; here is the political asymmetry that most of us failed to see.

EEJ: *Why couldn't anti-inflationary fiscal policy have been used more effectively instead of working badly?*
GALBRAITH: For one thing, a new and intransigent cause of inflation had become apparent. That was the interaction of wages and prices—prices pulling up wages, wages shoving up prices—something that did not yield easily to the modest restraints of fiscal and monetary policy. Again this was something the Keynesian system did not foresee. What worked well and with political ease against deflation and unemployment worked badly against inflation.

EEJ: *Was there an alternative economic policy that was more attractive politically?*
GALBRAITH: Yes, the political asymmetry of Keynesian budget policy led to monetary policy as a politically more attractive alternative. That was how, in the late seventies and early eighties, we came to enter the world of Professor Milton Friedman, the next most influential economist of our time after John Maynard Keynes.

EEJ: *Why was monetary policy so attractive?*
GALBRAITH: The chief attraction of a monetary policy of firm and intelligent control of the money supply was its promise of a relatively painless end to inflation. Monetarism was thought to have a special magic with only brief adverse effects on investment, housing and consumer spending. It thus escaped wonderfully the political asymmetry of Keynesian fiscal policy.

EEJ: *Are you implying then that monetary policy is socially neutral in its effects?*
GALBRAITH: No, indeed. Monetary policy has a strong tilt in favor of the financially favored. This was, in fact, a major source of support for monetary action. High interest rates reward those with money to lend. As a broad proposition, those who lend money are likely to have more money than those who do not!

EEJ: *But there is no question that monetary policy did succeed in breaking the force of inflation.*

GALBRAITH: That is true. But modern inflation is caused not only by an excess of aggregate demand; it is caused, as I've noted, by the direct pressure of wages on prices and, in turn, the upward pull of prices on wages. This microeconomic process, as we have learned, is not arrested by any slight or modest reduction in demand; it is arrested only by severe cut-backs in plant operations and employment. It also operates with special impact on the mass-employing industries. Trade union power is curtailed only by severe unemployment and only as employer power and the ability to pay higher wages is sharply weakened. Then only are wage increases replaced by wage reductions or "give-backs."

EEJ: *Are you saying that anti-inflationary monetary policy is both anti-business and anti-union?*

GALBRAITH: Exactly! Astringent monetary policy, to repeat, arrests wage/price inflation only by drastically reducing the strength and vitality of the employing firm. One of the great and somber lessons of these last years is that a strong trade union movement requires strong employing industries. And the companion lesson is that monetary policy controls inflation by drastically and even permanently damaging the industrial base of the countries pursuing it. The rust-belt cities of the American Middle West, with their abandoned shops and mills, are a monument to the magic of monetary policy. As are the British Midlands. And, if in lesser measure, the older industrial cities of Europe.

EEJ: *Are you saying that, at the present, there is a particular need for policy measures to address microeconomic problems?*

GALBRAITH:Yes. A large part of the present problem has arisen from new and neglected problems in the market system—in microeconomics. We are suffering from one of the basic Keynesian assumptions: that is the belief that while macroeconomics requires strong and intelligent public action, microeconomics can safely be left to the magic of the market—to the rule of *Laissez-Faire.* There has been a separation of macroeconomics from microeconomics and a tendency to associate all public policy with the first.

EEJ: *Can you point to any specifics, say at the level of the firm, that would help to identify the sources of our new microeconomic problems?*

GALBRAITH: The aging tendencies that are at work in the great corporate structures of the older industrial countries strike me as critical. We have long recognized that, with the passage of time, enfeeblement and eventual senility are a tendency of the human frame. We have not recognized that they are also the tendency of the great corporation. In the older industrial countries, firms suffer from the bureaucratic stasis of age, especially in the mass-production industries. This last manifests itself in a great increase in corporate staff and in a great depth of the layers of command. Managerial status in the modern corporation is regularly measured by the number of subordinates—"How many people does he have under him?" There is also a powerful tendency for intelligence to be measured by what is most companionable to those already there and to approve as wisdom whatever most closely accords with what is already being done. What we see also being played out is one of the longest-running and best-established scenarios in international economic development. It is the advantage that accrues to youth in all mass-production industries. It is the advantage that the United States and Germany once had in relation to Britain; that Japan now has over the United States and that Korea, Taiwan and Brazil are coming to have *vis-à-vis* Japan. Some of this advantage is from younger, better management. Some, no doubt, comes from a labor force that is new to industrial employment. In all countries at all times traditional industry has performed best with labor recently recruited from the ill-paid, demanding toil of rural life. To the first generation in industry, work seems easy, earnings seem abundant and the disciplines of industrial toil a slight thing as compared with the oppression of peasant agriculture and a hostile, demanding nature. This vigor of the younger countries, as I've noted, is a threat Japan now faces. Far more poignant, needless to say, is the threat to the United States and Western Europe.

EEJ: *What are the answers? What sort of policy is appropriate now, especially if inflationary pressures are rekindled?*

GALBRAITH: As to macroeconomic policy the answer is clear. We must see monetarism and the imagined magic of monetary policy, as one of the most grievously destructive policies of modern times. Far better that all countries restrain demand by higher taxes—by responsible fiscal policy—than by high interest rates with their direct, inescapable, immutable effect on capital investment, the very expenditure that is most needed for growth and competitive competence.

EEJ: *In urging fiscal action against inflation when it threatens, does it not become necessary to compromise our social programs?*
GALBRAITH: Social programs have a strong compassionate justification in the modern industrial society. Their contribution to social tranquility is especially important; this is a markedly conservative goal. In the United States, as in Britain, we do have an opportunity for reducing expenditure—and for making capital and qualified manpower available to civilian industry—by getting defense expenditures under control. These, to a marked extent, now serve not defense but the independent power of the military establishment. The experience of Japan and Germany since World War II shows the advantage of using capital and manpower for civilian production. But let me cite the more general rule. Let us, when inflation threatens, always prefer higher taxes to higher interest rates. This, in turn, eases the transfers onto the public debt account. It also encourages investment in new and better plants.

EEJ: *But is the sort of fiscal action you recommend enough to contain inflation?*
GALBRAITH: Probably not. We must not, in the future, rely exclusively on fiscal policy to keep inflation under control. With wage/price interaction as a cause of inflation, that restriction, if it is to be effective, must, as we have seen, be severe. The severity, in turn, is deeply damaging to workers and employing firms alike. Restrictive policy works effectively only as it weakens firms and causes unions to be concerned as to whether the particular company or plant will be kept in operation.

EEJ: *But fiscal policy is surely not an instrument for addressing the problem of wage/price interaction.*

GALBRAITH: Correct! The further answer—the only answer—is a system of agreed restraints between employers and unions. Wages must be negotiated within the framework of existing prices. In one form or another this need is now accepted in most industrial countries—Austria, Germany, Switzerland, Scandinavia and, of course, Japan. It is the English-speaking countries that have lagged in putting such a social contract into effect. In the English-speaking world we strangely still value the destructive enjoyments of old-fashioned class conflict. We are not a model for other countries in this regard.

EEJ: *What other remedies can you envison?*

GALBRAITH: The prospect as regards other lines of remedy is more clouded. Let us recognize the aging tendencies to which even the great enterprises are prone. Perhaps we are doing so; certainly the self-satisfied euphoria that characterized much of the corporate culture of the United States in the aftermath of World War II has dissolved. I am not a partisan of the remedy now being pursued on Wall Street. The sale of failing plants or subsidiaries and profitable ones in their place (rather than working to make them efficient) is a damaging escape. The recent and perhaps still current merger and acquisition mania does not contribute anything to the improved efficiency of industry. On this, again, we are not the example to be followed.

EEJ: *Can you reconcile the fact of our aging corporate firms with the traditional prescription of free trade as the key to efficiency?*

GALBRAITH: I do not rise every morning to make prayerful obeisance to free trade as all theologically reputable economists are required to do. But I am not enthusiastic about tariffs for protecting the less competent firms of the older industrial countries from the younger and more effective producers of the new world. Nor do I respond well to the solution of government bailout—socialism in our time has become the failed children of capitalism. This is a socially costly solution. And it can leave the government saddled with the congenital losers, including those firms that should be lost.

EEJ: *What of the human costs of shutting down the over-age firms and even sectors of the economy?*

GALBRAITH: We can ease the pain of transition. Older workers can be accorded income through early retirement. Job retraining, relocation assistance and temporary tariff protection are all relevant. So are public support to investment in advanced technology and—a much neglected point—strong support to the arts and design. In the latter, the older countries—as Italy and Italian products have so well shown—have a marked advantage and one which serves as an increasingly important part of higher living standards. After things work well, we wish them to look well, and beyond products are enjoyments.

EEJ: *Then one may still be at least somewhat optimistic about economic prospects in the older industrial world?*

GALBRAITH: I for one would be more sanguine were it not for the formula by which we evade the problem and the need to act on it. During these last years, we in the United States have made it a minor act of religious observance to avoid thought and action. We have returned in our faith to the eighteenth-century belief in *Laissez-Faire, Laissez-Passer.* The market is comprehensively benign; God is for free enterprise and will provide. This faith is really a design for evading painful thought and action. It is not the way by which we ensure the future of what some courageously still call capitalism.

Conversation

Steven Pressman / 1989

From *Review of Political Economy*, vol. 1
(November 1989), pp. 381–86.
Reprinted with permission from
Taylor & Francis, Ltd
(http://www.tandf.co.uk/journals).

The following interview took place at John Kenneth Galbraith's
Cambridge, Massachussetts home on 31 March 1989.

PRESSMAN: *Let me start by asking you about some of the influences on your economic
thinking. You have written many times that the difference between good economics and
bad economics is a sense of history. Which historical figures have been most influential
on your thinking?*

GALBRAITH: That would be a considerable list. I suppose if I had to name
a few it would be first of all Alfred Marshall, not because I ever came to
be a faithful follower, but because before you know the problems of classical or neoclassical economics you have to know these strands of economics. I was drilled in Alfred Marshall by Ewaldt Grether of the University
of California. I always considered that one of the most valuable courses
of economic instruction that I ever had. In those years I was also very
much influenced, as were many of my generation, by Thorstein Veblen,
who brought a critical, but nonconstructive, judgement to bear on economics. Then there was the great opening away from the notion of the
full-employment equilibrium economics due to John Maynard Keynes.

When I read the *General Theory* in 1936 I had the impression of lights going on and curtains being drawn back, which I still remember. And going a step further, I have always thought that Marx was far too important, and had far too many insights, to be left to the socialist world.

PRESSMAN: *You said that upon reading Keynes doors opened and lights started to flash. Could you talk some more about those doors and those lights?*
GALBRAITH: One has to recapture the mood of the 1930s, which was one enormously influenced by the great depression. Here was a wealthy country, rich in capital and resources and manpower, and yet impoverished. Until Keynes came along there was first of all—from Shumpeter, Lionel Robbins and others—the assertion that depression was inevitable; one had to accept it. Secondly, there was the instinct that somehow or other one had to adhere to fiscal conservatism, the balanced budget. Thirdly, and most importantly, was the related notion that the state had as its major role either keeping its hands off or assuring the certainty of competition. There was a strong mood in the early 1930s that somehow the problem was the result of monopoly or imperfect competition. Keynes lifted away the curtain and let us see that there was inherent in capitalism the possibility of underemployment equilibrium. And there was inherent in that diagnosis the result that the state could break that equilibrium by public investment, thereby moving the economy towards full employment. Further, there arose the distinction between microeconomics and macroeconomics, a distinction which I did not entirely applaud, but which emphasized the role of the state in maintaining appropriate levels of employment, appropriate levels of growth and responsibility for preventing inflation.

PRESSMAN: *One person missing from your list of influences was John Stuart Mill. I have always been struck by a number of similarities between your work and that of Mill. One thing that stands out is that both of you have written extensively about women and the role of women in the economy. Both of you have also argued against the primacy of production in an economy, with John Stuart Mill arguing for a stationary state. Lastly, both of you would be regarded as the major social critics of your time by many people. Has Mill had any influence on your thinking?*

GALBRAITH: This is a question I have often been asked, and in response to your earlier question my mind was on more contemporary figures, with the exception perhaps of Marx. But I cannot deny I learned a great deal from Smith, Ricardo and certainly from John Stuart Mill. But one must always bear in mind that Mill was in the great sweep of classical economics even though he was on occasion a critic, and even on occasion expressed a good deal of dissatisfaction. Mill was certainly the most brilliant social commentator of his time. But on the other hand it is not as easy, as in the case of Smith, Ricardo and Marx to identify Mill with a particular redirection of economics.

PRESSMAN: *I am going to switch gears a little bit now and talk about some contemporary economic issues and problems. A good place to start is Reaganomics. You have been a frequent critic of Reaganomics. What do you think the major flaws of the Reagan economic policies were?*

GALBRAITH: I was also, to some measure, a critic of the economics before Reagan, and this is a large question. In the most general sense, I would criticize the assumption that the modern economy can be left *passe faire*. I regard the state as having a strong affirmative role. I would also, in an equally general sense, be critical of an assumption implicit in Reaganomics that if something, or some action, was inconvenient it should be avoided. We now witness this with Mr. Bush and his resistance to tax increases. Nothing in the theology of these last eight or nine years has been so strong as the belief that God is a kindly Republican and will always provide. But getting down to more specific matters, during the last eight years we have had a strong reliance on tight monetary policy, high interest rates, and a strong retreat from fiscal policy. The high interest rates, in turn, have had a strongly adverse effect on productive investment, which is now the lowest in a decade. And for a time, these high interest rates bid up the dollar, heavily subsidized imports, heavily penalized exports, lodged foreign manufactured products firmly in our market, and penalized our natural advantage in the export of capital goods and high technology products. These are all consequences from which we are now suffering. I don't have any feeling of great originality on these matters. A very large number of economists who look candidly at the matter tend to come out on roughly the same side.

PRESSMAN: *You criticized the Reagan administration for its running high deficits and talked about the necessity to increase taxes. Yet, earlier, you talked about Keynes opening up the curtain and causing lights to flash for you. We all know that one of Keynes's policies was to run budget deficits to expand the economy. What is different about the deficits of Keynes and the deficits that Reagan has run?*

GALBRAITH: This is a good point. But there is no doubt, as I have said many times, that Keynes must look upon Reagan as one of his more remarkable disciples. I am not against deficits, but I am not for them. I am not for having deficits and then controlling inflation by high, and even murderous, real interest rates. We must always remember that Keynes's deficits were at a time when interest rates were at almost negligible levels. Keynes would have been resistant to having high deficits and then using interest rates to restrain inflation. It was implicit in Keynes's whole thought that at, or near, full employment you balance the budget, or perhaps created a surplus. It was explicit in his thought that you used fiscal policy and not monetary policy as the primary instrument against inflation.

PRESSMAN: *If we need to reduce current budget deficits by raising taxes, as you suggested earlier, what sort of taxes would you propose raising? In specific, I think I remember in* The Affluent Society *you said that sales taxes were a means which you highly recommended to raise government revenues for necessary social spending. Then, in* Economics and the Public Purpose *you seemed to take that back.*

GALBRAITH: No, I have occasionally eaten my words and as Churchill once said "found them an awesome diet"; but this is not one of those occasions. I make a distinction here, a practical distinction, between the Federal Government and the state and local governments. For the Federal Government I regard the income tax, the progressive income tax, as a very important and civilized instrument for, among other things, countering some of the inequality that is inherent in capitalism. But, I have also argued that where state and local governments are involved, the public services that are bought with the sales tax may have a larger social value than the private products that are foregone because of a sales tax. A sales tax can, in terms of its social effects, be progressive. While I also support a state income tax, one recognizes that there are limits to which the state can go on relying on that instrument without having people decide to live someplace else.

PRESSMAN: *At a national level lots of economists have proposed a value-added tax which is, basically, a national state tax. How do you feel about a value-added tax compared to higher income taxes?*

GALBRAITH: I would very much prefer higher income taxes. I have never thought that an income tax was damaging to incentives or innovation. I think this is a cover story that is used to get down taxes on the affluent and had no real effect. Maybe I would not go so far as to say that high marginal rates cause an increase in incentives as people struggle to maintain their after-tax income. But I do remind everyone that our greatest period of stability and economic growth was in the years after the second World War when marginal rates of income tax were very high.

PRESSMAN: *You talked about Reagan's penchant for a* laissez-faire *economics. One of the thrusts of this philosophy was deregulation—deregulation of banking, deregulation of the airline industry, deregulation of the financial industry. Do you see a number of the problems that the U.S. economy is facing now, namely the savings and loan crisis and the problems on Wall Street, as a consequence of this deregulation?*

GALBRAITH: Oh, yes. I regard this as a wholly practical question. One cannot decide as between regulation and deregulation in accordance with some broad ideological principal. One has to examine the circumstances calling for regulation and occasionally calling for deregulation in the particular case. I have no doubt that some easing of regulation on the allocation of airplane routes and also on fares may have been a good thing. But, in both cases, it went much too far and that is one of the reasons that we have converted what was a good airline system in some parts of the country, including parts of the northeast, into a chaotic one. There can be no question whatever that deregulation of the savings and loan industry was one of the great financial fiascos of all time. Banking as an industry in the U.S.A., as in all countries, requires a substantial measure of regulation. This is a practical issue.

PRESSMAN: *For what reason is this regulation needed? Why do you see this regulation on banking and the financial industry as necessary today?*
GALBRAITH: As in the case of the savings and loan industry, to prevent insane and, at times, corrupt action.

PRESSMAN: *I gather you think the same thing is true of the financial industry in general?*
GALBRAITH: Certainly. I have no doubt that we are going to regret, perhaps are already beginning to regret, the damage to the corporate structure that is done as a result of mergers and acquisitions, corporate raiders and the junk bonds.

PRESSMAN: *In one of your latest books,* Economics in Perspective *you wrote in a somewhat negative vein about industrial policy. I found that somewhat surprising and was wondering why you were so negative towards the proposals that people like Robert Reich of Harvard and Lester Thurow of MIT have been advancing. Also, if we were not to use an industrial policy to try to increase our exports, do you have another suggestion as to what to do about the U.S. trade deficit.*
GALBRAITH: I do not get up every morning and make a powerful obeisance to free trade. But I stated in *Economics in Perspective,* and I still believe, that one of the grave and inevitable tendencies of economic life is for simple manufacturing to move from the old countries to the new—as it moved from the U.K. to Germany, on to the U.S.A. and then to Japan, and is now moving on from Japan to Korea, Taiwan and Thailand. I do not see any possibility of arresting that movement. Efforts to do so under the name of industrial policy, I do not accept. There are trade policies that I do approve. I would like to see the government keep a strong investment position, support high technology and encourage that, again, by low interest rates. Of course, this is all contrary to recent policy action. To the extent that this is called industrial policy I am for it.

PRESSMAN: *One final line of inquiry. Last December there was a first at the American Economic Association meetings. The AEA ran two sessions back to back. Both sessions dealt with the Economics of John Kenneth Galbraith. At these sessions a number of distinguished economists got up and spoke about the major contributions of Galbraith. But there was no Galbraith standing up reflecting on what he thought his major contributions were. Would you care to be so immodest now as to reflect on what you think your major contributions have been to the economics profession?*

GALBRAITH: The things that have concerned me most is the bimodel character of the modern economy, and the unwisdom of having an economic instruction that assumes that General Motors, General Electric, and Mitsubishi are of the same order of structure, motivation and institutional character, as are agriculture, handicrafts, artisan activities, and services. I believe that the modern economy needs to be seen in terms of the very different character of the great corporation from the small competitive enterprise, which does conform in a general way to classical and neoclassical market theory. Additionally, and coming back to what I have said before, I do not believe that the modern economy functions, either in its microeconomic or its macroeconomic behaviour, in a socially acceptable fashion, and I accordingly believe that there is a large role for state intervention which cannot be decided by general theory, but involves a pragmatic consideration of the social consequences in the particular case.

Communist Economies of
Eastern Europe

Senate Foreign Relations Committee / 1989

Excerpt from a hearing of the
Senate Foreign Relations Committee,
13 December 1989, chaired by
Senator Claiborne Pell.

SEN. PELL: *And we now turn to the public panel—John Kenneth Galbraith, Paul M. Warburg Professor of Economics Emeritus at Harvard; Jerry Hough, Director of the Center on East-West Trade, Investments and Communications, Duke University; and Jan Vanous, President and Research Director, Planecon, Inc., Washington, D.C. We welcome you all very much indeed. Dr. Galbraith particularly has a familial connection with this committee, of which we're very grateful, and, I believe, another familial connection with the Hill, with another son. And you have, as I understand it, not only background in economics, about which we know, but also, you have written two books on the subject at hand:* Journey to Poland and Yugoslavia, *in '58, and* Capitalism, Communism and Co-Existence, *with Dr. Menshikov, a Soviet economist, in '86. Maybe you would be kind enough to lead off.*

MR. GALBRAITH: Well, thank you, Mr. Chairman. It's a pleasure to be here this morning, a pleasure to be with old friends. I must say that it was a pleasure listening to the Secretary of Agriculture, a formative testimony which did not omit to make clear the difficulty that this administration would have in substituting money for rhetoric, a point that I really think should be made. There is nothing that can be done in Eastern Europe that does not cost money in one way or another, and I would be, I must say, sorry to see institution building, so-called, the sending of consultants, offering of other advice, which is exceptionally economical in our time, made a substitute for the one thing that is really needed in that part of the world. I hope that that will not be taken, Mr. Chairman, as in any way critical of the Secretary's testimony, but I would hope that it would be taken as a somewhat valid reference to our tendency, to the tendency of the administration as regards this great moment of change.

I have had a long, although, as the Chairman says, not always a close association with Polish economic development. I lectured in Poland in Warsaw, Lublin and Krakow in 1958—I believe the first bourgeois economist, as accurately or as inaccurately I'm called, to be invited after the Communists came to power. And I have returned to lecture and learn what I could of the Polish economy since that time.

I might say that I have had a long and rewarding friendship with two of the most distinguished economists of our time, the late Oskar Lange and the late Michael Kalecki, two of the sparkling figures of our profession. Professor Lange returned to Poland from the University of Chicago after World War II, and Michael Kalecki, previously at the University of Cambridge and at the UN, also went back.

This autumn, I went to the universities of Leipzing and Budapest where there were extended discussions of the economic problems and developments in Eastern Europe or, as many there now prefer, Central Europe. I have done the best, Mr. Chairman, to convey the impression that it was my lectures at Leipzig that set off the great changes in that part of the world, but I have had no success in making that particular proposition believed.

I might note, as a mild irrelevancy, that even in my earliest trips to Poland I encountered an undercurrent of comment and humor as regards the economy. One was asked repeatedly if one knew the difference between capitalism and communism. And the reply was always, "Well, I will tell you. Under capitalism, man exploits man, and under communism, it is just the reverse."

(Laughter.)

Developments in Central Europe and in the Soviet Union are being pictured as a sudden, explosive discovery that comprehensive socialism does not work. This is a serious oversimplification. In Poland, in the years immediately following World War II and especially after the regime of Boleslaw Bierut, the Stalinist, there was a time of real hope and of no slight progress. Life was compared with that under the incompetent semifeudal dictatorships that preceded World War II. Much progress was made in rebuilding wartime destruction, and a start was made on creating a heavy industrial base. And with all else, there was a certain sense of exuberance and change.

Poland, also in contrast with other socialist countries, did not put its agriculture under government controls. Independent farmers were left in charge of their land although, unfortunately, under state control as to their prices. The planning and the command structure of socialism in Poland, as was also the case in the Soviet Union, worked reasonably well for building the industrial base—steel, chemicals, coal mining, shipbuilding, and other basic industry. Input/output relationships were known and stable. Orders could go out from the central planning authority, and the resulting response was certain. In the Soviet Union, this system built the second greatest industrial structure in the world, and in Poland and the other Eastern European countries, it was by no means ineffective. The great steel plant of Nowa Huta, near Cracow, became a showpiece of the achievements of these years.

Now, this I come to is a very important point in relation to present policy. The problems with the Polish economy, as those of the Soviet Union, appeared at the next stage. There are four in number.

First, there was the tendency of this system to develop a heavy immobile bureaucracy. Ministries united with the producing enterprises to create a very large and sclerotic structure with the persistent tendency to be over-manned, and with the basic bureaucratic tendency, not unknown in our own country, to identify intelligence with what is already being done. I have mentioned Nowa Huta, and once a seeming monument to social success, it now became overstaffed and technologically stagnant. As I say, this bureaucratic tendency is a basic feature of mature socialism. It also in no small part explains our own problems in steel, automobile, and other industries.

The second problem of the Polish economy and the other countries of the socialist world has been the tendency for unspent money to accumulate in substantial pools. When there is need to equalize the wage system that rewards seeming improvements in productivity or to serve political advantage, the easiest course is to raise wage incomes. This, in turn, causes purchasing power to exceed the supply of available goods at the fixed prices, and the damage is made worse by a policy of holding agricultural prices at low levels for the short-run benefit of the urban population. The consequence has been, of course, the socialist form of inflation, which is not higher prices, but longer and longer lines at the store.

The third problem involves the changing nature of socialist production. As I earlier noted, it works far from badly when building basic industry. However, it does not work well in the provision of consumers' goods. The modern consumers' goods economy has a dismaying variety of goods of many styles and designs. Wants and designs also change, and as in the case of the automobile, products require numerous supporting services. For this vast, unstable, and intricate bill of goods and services, the planning structure does not work. Orders cannot go out from the planning authority for the precision of response that is possible in the case of a steel mill. There is no alternative to some means of direct communication between producer and consumer. And for such direct communication, there is no alternative to the market.

In consequence, in all the socialist countries there has been very great difficulty as these economies have come to the problem of supplying consumers' goods. And, as I say—I'll shorten here—inescapably, the Western Europe and the American standard of living, aided by television and other improved communication, has become the model for those countries.

And the fourth problem, which I'll also summarize, concerns foreign lending. Poland, like Hungary in the 1970s, was the recipient of substantial credits from the West. And here you have what I go on to develop and call, Mr. Chairman, the "whiplash effect." Things are much easier when the money is flowing in and become much more difficult when the time for loan service comes. You move from a very favorable situation to a very difficult situation. This is something which has, of course, also been seen in South America.

I come now—conscious of time—to what should be done. I think the urgent matters are clear. The proposals are not in any way novel. They are for us to come forward, along with the Western European community and Japan, with substantial tangible financial assistance. This should take the form of direct grants—some have already been supplied—along the lines of the Marshall Plan, and it should take the form of the reversal of the whiplash effect, with new loans. At the same time, every possible step should be taken to ease the present debt-service situation. In effect, we can't escape it—there must be a moratorium on debt service. The international banks, the private banks, that have been somewhat involved could still carry these loans on their books. But the countries—Poland and Hungary, in particular—should be given a breathing spell for the difficult period of readjustment. When foolish banks make foolish loans, a high level of repayment should not now be expected.

The administration has accepted the fact that action is needed of the kind I have just mentioned. Unfortunately, the scale of action suggested is far below what is needed or even relevant. President Bush has exercised commendable restraint in commenting on the changes in Eastern Europe. This is not a time for hubris or for celebration. Nevertheless, it was sad when, earlier this year, he visited Hungary and Poland, made speeches of approval as to what was going on and left only a small tip.

There is now a great chance for peace and liberty in this part of the world, which should give thought to the fact that we are spending far less to facilitate this progress than to bail out Mr. Keating and Lincoln Savings, and not even 1 percent of what the whole S&L bailout will cost. My final point—I have mentioned that the failure in the socialist countries concerns food and civilian goods. It should not be expected, accordingly, that our help should go for basic industry although some will certainly be needed there. We should not be reluctant as regards seemingly less substantial consumer needs. The ability to satisfy these needs has become the measure of success or failure in this part of the world. Failure to do so—to repeat—must not be associated. We must not have an association between hardship and the great liberalization process there underway.

One final point, Mr. Chairman—I've spoken of Poland this morning. I would say that the same urgency in much larger scale exists as regards the Soviet Union. This is a matter with which I've been very closely associated in these last months, and I feel that the urgency here—the urgency as regards not associating liberalization there or Eastern Europe with hardship—not associating Mr. Gorbachev with economic hardship—is also very great.

I thank you very much.

John Kenneth Galbraith

John Newark / 1990

From *Aurora Online*, 1990. Reproduced
with permission from Athabasca
University (http://aurora.icaap.org).

John Kenneth Galbraith is perhaps Canada's most well-known intellectual export, known for both his regular puncturing of established
orthodox economic wisdom and the wit with which his attacks are
delivered.

The publication of his books *The Affluent Society, The New Industrial State,*
and *Economics and the Public Purpose* virtually established a Galbraithian
school of thought in the United States. Many of Galbraith's ideas on
the workings of the corporate sector were incorporated into the post-
Keynesian theory that was emerging on both sides of the Atlantic in the
1960s and the 1970s.

Galbraith has published widely and spoken frequently on the problems
facing developing countries, often emphasizing the inappropriateness of
unthinkingly transferring technologies and development strategies produced in the West to the far more different terrain of the Third World.
In this interview, we discuss with Professor Galbraith some of the major
difficulties facing Third World societies.

Dr. John Newark, Assistant Professor of Economics and Chair of the Cen-
tre for Economics, Industrial Relations, and Organizational Studies at
Athabasca University spoke with John Kenneth Galbraith in late 1990.

AURORA: *You have written that, "The tendency of the rich country is to increasing income and the tendency of the poor country is to an equilibrium of poverty." Do you still believe that to be true?*
GALBRAITH: Yes, broadly speaking, this is still true of the poorest of the poor countries. It is certainly true of most of Africa, which has been the great disappointment in the post-Colonial world, and it still is true of a large part of the population of India, Pakistan, and elsewhere in Asia.

AURORA: *Do you think that Latin America, which did experience relatively high rates of growth in the fifties, sixties, and seventies, may be returning to such a state of stagnation in the early 1990s?*
GALBRAITH: Well, Latin America is a mixed situation. The poverty of Argentina, Brazil, even Mexico is not comparable with what one encounters in Africa or much of Asia. But, yes, there is no question that the high rates of growth to which you refer are a thing of the past and to some extent were associated, of course, with a very high level of international borrowing.

AURORA: *What have been the major forces determining this equilibrium of poverty?*
GALBRAITH: In the first place I identify this with primitive agriculture, and two factors have been at work there. One is, of course, population growth. If you were a poor farmer in India, Pakistan, or in much of Africa, you would want as many sons as possible as your social security. They would keep you out of the hot sun and give you some form of subsistence in your old age. So, you have pressure for population growth that is, itself, the result of the extreme economic insecurity. This is something which hasn't been sufficiently emphasized.

Secondly, in some African countries, there has been a deeply misguided effort to keep farm and food prices low in order to benefit an urban proletariat. Whatever advantages this has had in the short run, it has had disastrous effects in the longer run. One has to divide the problem between urban (with some industrial life), and agriculture, with its equilibrium of poverty.

AURORA: *Agricultural economists have certainly spent some time looking at the problems of food production, the problems of small scale agriculture, but would you say that this stands out as one of the major policy failures?*

GALBRAITH: Well, there have been differences. In some parts of India, particularly in the Punjab and generally in the northwest, there have been substantial agricultural successes. The so-called grain revolution carried India into a measure of food self-sufficiency. But in the poor countries as a whole, over much of Africa and Asia and over some of Central America, agricultural development has been extremely disappointing.

AURORA: *One of the stories that emerges from the history of development planning is that there has been such apparently limited learning from policy mistakes, or even successes for that matter. Do you have any thoughts on that?*

GALBRAITH: I think one of the major errors in the whole discussion of economic development has been the tendency to look at the United States or Canada and say this has worked here, and therefore it must work in the poor countries. And we have sought in consequence to transfer from the developed western countries or in the case of the Soviet Union to Mozambique and Ethiopia, the principles and practices of a rather highly developed system.

We forget that in our own path to economic development, we have had a very different set of priorities. We saw the need in the early stages to concentrate on education, on individual farm holdings, and on transportation, and this, in some substantial measure, has been forgotten in the desire to transfer developed structures and developed industry to the poor countries.

AURORA: *Which has been of greater importance, bad advice based on a poor understanding of development processes or reasonable advice ignored when the advice doesn't appear to be in the interests of more powerful political groups in society?*

GALBRAITH: I would attribute something to bad advice, but I would attribute a good deal to other factors, namely illiteracy, political instability, and bad land systems. The later, of course, is particularly important in Central and South America.

AURORA: *You have argued that one of the major difficulties in stimulating development is the accommodation to poverty which is developed in many less developed countries. Could you explain what you mean by accommodation?*

GALBRAITH: The accommodation of poverty is the debilitating influence of poverty which destroys initiative, destroys energy, destroys the search for something better and, therefore, becomes self-perpetuating. No one knows exactly how important that is, but from my own observations, my own sense of the situation, it is something which one must accept.

AURORA: *What factors tend to be key in breaking that accommodation?*

GALBRAITH: I would be quite clear that in all these countries, one has had an emphasis on cultural factors, particularly on education, and the result is an educated and disciplined labour force. Further, there has been stable government, though not always of the most benign sort. Thirdly, it may be that there are some traditional factors in the culture. Those are the three things that I would emphasize.

AURORA: *A reasonable conclusion, I think, to draw from your focus on the equilibrium of poverty is that meaningful change must come from the outside. Is that true?*

GALBRAITH: Absolutely. And one of the significant changes is the longer run prospect for urbanization and the drawing of people from agriculture into industry with a higher productive potential.

But that is something which I would not emphasize at the expense of the other factors that I've mentioned, namely, emphasis on political stability, education, and cultural investment. One must always have in mind one simple fact—there is no literate population in the world that is poor, and there is no illiterate population that is anything but poor.

AURORA: *Migration is very important in the history of the West. Would you not agree that the opportunities for migration tend to be much poorer in the Third World countries today? There are no new continents to discover.*

GALBRAITH: I quite agree that in the last century or the early part of this century, the individual solution for poverty was to move from the poor countries to the rich countries, and I don't think that process is coming completely to an end. It is still true that in the highly industrialized countries the second and third generation of a labour force don't take very kindly to repetitive, systematized industrial labour. And therefore, one has a steady demand for workers from the worst privations of agriculture in other countries. That is what brings a very large number of Yugoslavs to Germany and Northern Africans to France. It brings very, very large numbers of Mexicans and West Indians to the United States. That process, I think, will continue.

AURORA: *I'd like to ask you about three areas of interaction between a poor society and the world economy. These are trade, aid, and capital flows. Concerning trade, a conservative, for example, might agree with the notion of accommodation and proceed to argue that free trade brings a range of new opportunities to a poor country, which acts as a major engine of growth. Do you share this optimistic view of the importance of trade in raising incomes and breaking accommodation?*
GALBRAITH: That is, like so many orthodox views, greatly oversimplified. At a certain stage—that which has been reached by the countries of the Pacific Basin—that is certainly true. But trade opportunity does very, very little for most of the countries of Africa or Central America or Asia.

AURORA: *Why?*
GALBRAITH: This is subsistence agriculture, which produces very little available surplus. These people are beyond the reach of international markets.

AURORA: *Has aid made a difference?*
GALBRAITH: Oh, yes. This is not universal, but I've been a strong supporter of specific aid programs, which encourage grain hybrids, agriculture, and better soil and water management. These have been very successful, particularly in countries such as India and Pakistan.

Aid has also helped create in the more advanced Third World countries the basic infrastructure of electrical generation and transmission, communications, other things of that sort. The aid program, of course, in its various manifestations, has been substantially important for education and for scientific engineering development.

AURORA: *At a time when debts are high and rising in many less developed countries, do you think aid weariness is setting in?*

GALBRAITH: I'm not sure. One factor that is of overriding importance is the transfer of the United States from a surplus producing country to a deficit country. This has certainly had a serious effect on the whole aid morale.

Ill-considered lending in Latin America has also had a bad effect. We have a heavy burden to bear from the wonders of recycling of petroleum revenues of 15 years ago, which was so much praised at the time and which left the Latin American countries with a heavy debt, much of which did not initially finance anything very useful.

AURORA: *The debt crisis in the 1980s has been accompanied by stagnation, falling standards of living, and capital outflows from Third World countries to developing countries. Overall, is development possible or likely in many countries given the existing levels of debt?*

GALBRAITH: The Argentine, Brazilian, Mexican, and Peruvian debts, for example, are not going to be paid. We've been postponing the day of reckoning by lending those countries money with which to pay interest and urging them to cut their standard of living. This cannot go on. We would be in a much, much better position to have a severe write down of those debts.

AURORA: *The debt-related riots in Venezuela showed that the bottom line, the limits to which that kind of adjustment can be pushed, has probably been reached. What is going to happen next?*

GALBRAITH: Venezuela is in many respects the strongest economy in South America. The Venezuelans were being asked to make sacrifices in their standard of living, which would not be acceptable in Canada or the United States. The alternative is to write down and write off the debt, to protect the standard of living and protect democratic government.

AURORA: *Do you hold out much hope for success in either reducing the debt burden or increasing capital flows to try and facilitate growing out of debt?*

GALBRAITH: Growing out of debt is a bit of financial flim-flam, and nobody should take that seriously. It is something that financial magnates invent in order to disguise the problem from the public. The only solution is to bite the bullet.

AURORA: *Do you hold out any prospects for success? The Japanese and the French have floated some plans that move slightly in that direction.*
GALBRAITH: Oh, I think we've moved a little bit in that direction, but one should not minimize the extreme rigidity of the developed financial mind.

AURORA: *What actions, at a minimum, must the West take to begin to lift the brake that debt has placed on development?*
GALBRAITH: I would declare that they write down the debt in the order of 50 to 75 percent. And if that puts one or another of the international banks in trouble, which I doubt, then they should forego dividends for a while. That's one of the penalties for making mistakes. And if they're in real trouble, they'll always be bailed out by the federal reserve and the federal government.

AURORA: *The argument of increasing capital flows in the short run, as you suggested, tends to push off the day of reckoning to the future by just adding to outstanding debt. If that's what we're doing now, what are the implications of continuing that policy for the next five or ten years?*
GALBRAITH: The implications are stagnation in those countries, falling living standards, and a threat to democratic government. There is no doubt as to what the implications are.

AURORA: *Economists have been quick to take credit for the acceleration of growth in the Third World during the postwar era. Now they frequently appear content to blame the current difficulties on "inappropriate" policies and excessive government interference. In the long run, have development economists earned their keep?*
GALBRAITH: My answer has to be favourable because I started the first courses in economic development at Harvard in the very late 1940s. I think this interest has been productive and a range of things have been very useful. I saw them first-hand in India, for example, the help of grain hybrids, fertilizer, and industrial infrastructure.

But the dark side has been an insufficient emphasis on education, cultural investment, and on the absolute importance of stable government. Another negative tendency has been for both the Soviet Union and ourselves to think that we should be concerned primarily with moving developed industrial structures rather than concerning ourselves with the basic needs of agriculture.

And finally, based on the experience of the developed countries, there's the feeling that specific preference should be given to urban society over that of agriculture. I've had occasion to talk about that the last couple of years before the United Nations, and I regard it of particular importance.

John Kenneth Galbraith Looks Back at the Reagan-Bush Era

Thomas Karier / 1992

From *In These Times*, 10–23 June 1992,
pp. 18–19. Reprinted with permission.

John Kenneth Galbraith cut his teeth as an economist designing agricultural programs for the New Deal. His later work included developing wage-price controls during World War II, assessing the impact of allied bombing for the U.S. Strategic Bombing Survey and serving as ambassador to India under President John Kennedy. His widely read books, *The Affluent Society* and *The New Industrial State*, and his principled opposition to the Vietnam War, the arms race, and the supply-side revolution have established him as one of the nation's leading progressive economists. In his new book,. *The Culture of Contentment*, Galbraith looks at how the U.S. has lapsed into a self-serving economic and social stasis. Economist Thomas Karier interviewed Galbraith in Cambridge, Mass., for *In These Times*. Readers should note that this interview took place before the rebellion in Los Angeles.

KARIER: *I thought I would start with some questions on general economic issues. There have been a number of proposals on how to reform taxes. We have a flat tax proposal and a proposal to cut capital gains taxes. What is a better way to go?*
GALBRAITH: I have rarely met a tax-reform proposal that I didn't dislike. The flat tax would be an absolute disaster. One of the civilizing influences of our

time is the progressive income tax. And some of the actual consequences of changing to a flat tax, for example on Social Security, even Jerry Brown came around to admitting would be serious. As far as the proposals for tax reductions in the middle class are concerned, this by-passes the much worse situation of the underclass, which is to some extent dependent on tax revenues.

As far as the capital gains tax is concerned, that is a free ride for the rich. One of the more imaginative exercises in economics has been the effort to show there would be some employment-creating effects from capital gains tax reduction—absolute nonsense. All of this goes back to one disguise or another for making the tax system less progressive.

KARIER: *Another commonly debated issue is that of the huge federal budget deficits. Five years ago people were alarmed about them, but now that they are even bigger, the alarm seems to have subsided. Should people be more concerned?*

GALBRAITH: I have been down to testify two or three times before the Congress on this. The elementary truth is that in the '80s, when the economy was relatively strong, we ran a large deficit when we didn't need it. That means that now when you can think of a lot of things you would like to do with the money—including a strong employment program [to develop] the so-called infrastructure, as well as what would be extremely important major economic support to the states' and cities' localities—you can't call for increased federal borrowing and spending. You can, but the mood of the country and the concern over the deficit have gotten so strong that we can't take action now that would ease the recession. It would take the action which represents a strong commitment to raise taxes and balance the budget, or more toward a balanced budget when we can afford to do so.

KARIER: *You don't hear people talking about raising taxes, at least none of the candidates. But in your book you talk about the importance of raising tax revenue.*

GALBRAITH: I stand for a progressive income tax, and I think the Reagan tax reductions were wrong, especially for the upper 10 percent and certainly the upper 1 percent of income-tax recipients. I would be for correcting that.

KARIER: *Another issue that is playing a key role in this election is health care. It seems to be a serious concern for the uninsured and for everyone now paying higher insurance rates. Is there a clear solution?*

GALBRAITH: I am not an expert on the matter of health economics. This is a highly competitive field, and I have never entered the competition. But I am a Canadian by origin. I have a lot of relatives there and friends, and I've long been led to believe that the Canadian health system, which insures everybody at public expense, is a good one.

KARIER: *Let's turn to the international sphere. With all the changes going on in the Soviet Union and the Eastern bloc countries, there has yet to be a clearly articulated U.S. policy toward the region. What stand should the U.S. take?*

GALBRAITH: I've met with the economists from Eastern Europe, and I have been trying to follow it rather closely. I have had the feeling that the one thing of which we should have been aware was the danger of exchanging a poorly working economic system for none at all, and I think that there has been far too much willingness to specify hardship as somehow having an essentially therapeutic effect.

My urging was always that this be taken somewhat more gradually. Let less important consumer goods and services be released to the market. They were badly provided for under comprehensive socialism, communism. And [ensure] that steps be taken to privatize agriculture, which has never worked well under socialism. It never will. Make sure that there is an alternative before the present system is given up.

One thing that I never understood: there should have been a currency reform to neutralize some of the vast overhangs of black-market currency that were available. This was something we took for granted as necessary in France and Germany after World War II, and it was a very important step toward the return of those economies to normal operation.

KARIER: *With regard to corporations, you once talked about the countervailing power of unions and government regulators. But now we are in a period in which unions have declined to very low levels and government regulators have backed off. Does this leave the corporations unconstrained?*

GALBRAITH: It is 40 years since I invented the phrase "countervailing power." A lot has happened since that time. It is certain that unions have declined in power. There is no doubt about that. I'm also persuaded that there is a less aggressive regulatory mood at the present time. But I don't think either of those enhance corporate power greatly because where one used to worry about corporate power one now worries about corporate incompetence. It is far more serious.

One thing that has weakened the trade union movement has been the weakness of the corporation. In the past 15 or 20 years, the trade union that has had to deal with corporations in the steel industry or the automobile industry has been the victim not of the strength of those organizations but their weakness. Sometime in the last 10 years I stopped worrying about corporate power and started worrying about corporate inadequacy.

KARIER: *Is that inadequacy more prominent because of the international competition?*
GALBRAITH: Oh, sure. You had a marvelous illustration of that when George Bush took those business executives out to Japan and everybody was led to contrast the effectiveness of General Motors, Ford, and Chrysler as compared with the Japanese firms. I was down testifying in the Congress a few days after that and made the point which I would still stand on—that trip was the most disastrous single overseas operation since, let us say, the Fourth Crusade.

KARIER: *Speaking of corporate incompetence reminds me of bank failures. Banks seem to have done very poorly in their investments in the last 10 years, requiring a flood of government money to bail them out. Do you have any comments on that?*
GALBRAITH: This was one of the anomalies of the '80s. There was strengthened government participation in the S&Ls and continued—and similarly very lush—insurance of commercial bank deposits. At the same time, there was a weakening of their regulation. So you put in government money but didn't regulate the use of government money, potential government money. This was one of the more disastrous economic exercises of modern times. S&Ls in particular were allowed to make insane and larcenous use of what was essentially government money.

KARIER: *Did the government learn anything from this, or do you think it is set to repeat these mistakes?*

GALBRAITH: I think there has been some recognition. I think there is now some feeling that those bank regulations and regulation of the S&Ls has to be more stringent. But you can still have people of vacuous mood talking about the desirability of diminishing regulation in order that the banks can lend more and so get out of the recession.

KARIER: *It seems they have been encouraged to merge and form combinations of even larger banks.*

GALBRAITH: I don't worry about that. There are big banks and small banks, and if you have bigger and slightly less small ones, I don't bother about it.

KARIER: *Wall Street was another area of great corporate incompetence. After the crash in 1987, many people anticipated the beginning of a long decline for the stock market, but instead it expanded for the next five years. What happened? Don't stock crashes have the same effect they used to?*

GALBRAITH: It didn't have the same effect as it did after 1929. There is no question about that. This is partly because a good deal of resilience has been built into the economy since then—Social Security, trade unions, farm price supports (in 1929, the U.S. was still essentially an agricultural country), the deposit insurance we've just been talking about—so that you didn't have as immediate an aftermath, as disastrous an aftermath, as you did after the crash of 1929. But on the other hand, there is no question that we've been in these last years suffering from the extravagant boom of the '80s, and the recession is the other side of that looking glass.

KARIER: *In your new book,* The Culture of Contentment, *you start with the idea of a voting majority reaching a point of contentment and standing in opposition to any improvement in the condition of the underclass. What is the primary source of that contentment?*

GALBRAITH: Money, income, and wealth, no question about that. For the first time in history perhaps, we have a *voting* majority of people who are well off and contented with their situation. That is the case I make in the book. That this is something new.

KARIER: *It describes a society without compassion.*

GALBRAITH: There are a lot of people who agree with me on this point; but they are a minority of those who vote. I'm not suggesting Americans have all become indifferent and uncompassionate. But I am suggesting of those that vote a majority vote their self-interest. Persuasive philosophy says they should.

KARIER: *A philosophy of acting in their self-interest. A philosophy taught in every introductory economics class.*

GALBRAITH: Absolutely. Sure. No one imagines that Ronald Reagan or George Bush would be surprised if they were told that was the nature of motivation.

KARIER: *Certainly some of the middle class may be relatively content, but there is no comparison to the contentment of the rich.*

GALBRAITH: That's right. I argue in the book that a bargain has been struck on the whole between the upper middle class and the rich by which the upper middle class, in order to protect its own tax situation, doesn't talk much about the taxes of the upper 1 percent or even the upper 10 percent. There is a general or implicit agreement there that you don't raise taxes on the rich as a protection of the position, the tax position, of the upper middle class.

KARIER: *You paint a pretty grim future for the underclass. Is there any reason for hope or any avenues for change?*

GALBRAITH: I don't see why any book should have a happy ending if you don't believe in it. This will be the point that will be most criticized in this book—that I don't see a bright future. The fact is I don't, but I'm not predicting the future. I am describing the present.

KARIER: *Is there a culture of contentment on a global scale in the developed countries: the U.S., Europe, and Japan?*

GALBRAITH: That is a good point. I think there is. Yes, I think we are going to see in the next decade or so much less concern for the poor countries than we have had in the past.

In the past, it was always possible to supplement compassion for the poor countries with an appeal to the fear of communism. Now, with the collapse of the Soviet Union and the end of the Cold War, it is not going to be possible to go to Capitol Hill and say, "Well, if you don't come across with this economic aid [then] this country, this country and this country are going to be in danger of going communist."

This is something where I have had a wealth of experience. I used to be ambassador to India. Part of the case for aid to India, which in those days was very substantial, was compassionate. I hope and think part of it was, but conservatives in the Congress could be aroused by the thought that India might go communist. I never believed the danger was serious, but if somebody was voting aid for that reason I never told them not to.

KARIER: *So you think, despite the ill intentions, economic aid did contribute to development in the developing world?*

GALBRAITH: It had a mixed effect. In some cases it was extremely important. It revolutionized Indian agriculture, for example. A country that 30 years ago was heavily dependent on grain imports now has a small export surplus with a population that is twice as big. This has been an incredible thing. Much of it was associated with support to fertilizer production, to grain hybrids and to irrigation.

KARIER: *The abandonment of developing countries, as you describe it, reminds me of what happened in Nicaragua. The U.S. spent a lot of money to overthrow the government there, but once a government was in power friendly to the U.S., the amount of funds to support development dried up.*

GALBRAITH: That's right. That's a very good point. A certain part of our economic aid was related to anti-communist paranoia, and in a world where the communists weren't even a threat. Communism or socialism has never been an effective alternative in the primitive economy. It has been in the poor countries, on the whole, a disaster. Socialism is never a relevant alternative before you have capitalism.

KARIER: *When will there be more discontentment?*

GALBRAITH: If the recession continues and gets worse. If the centers of our cities get worse, or if we get involved in some foolish war, there is no question that the discontent will be much greater. Vietnam was an example. The Great Depression was an example. In the '60s, we had serious outbreaks of violence in the central cities. These can shock the mood. There is no question of that.

KARIER: *What about the role of the media in all of this? Don't they foster contentment while denigrating and ignoring the poor?*

GALBRAITH: I think there is a tendency for the media, particularly television, to be fixed on its natural market, which is the high consumer society. I think that is natural. I don't criticize it. I take it as inevitable. If you're advertising expensive cars on network television, you are going in some measure to be concerned in your programming with the customers. Doesn't that make sense?

KARIER: *Are you saying it's just a business operation, you can't expect much more?*
GALBRAITH: I take the world as it comes.

Conversation with John Kenneth Galbraith

Robert Macneil / 1992

With Judy Woodruff. From the
MacNeil/Lehrer NewsHour, 1 July 1992,
transcript #4368, p. 12–16. Reprinted
with permission of MacNeil-Lehrer
Productions.

MR. MACNEIL: *Next tonight, the second in a series of occasional conversations with people who've been thinking and writing recently about the United States and its position in the new world economic order. That position was underscored by today's White House meeting between President Bush and Japanese Prime Minister Kiichi Miyazawa. The President said the meeting was about creating jobs for Americans by allowing more U.S. exports to Japan. Tonight we get the views of John Keeneth Galbraith, professor of economics emeritus at Harvard University, theorist, social critic, and adviser to policy makers throughout the postwar period. Earlier this week, I spoke with Galbraith about his latest book,* The Culture of Contentment. *Prof. Galbraith, thank you for joining us. Could you just restate briefly your thesis of* The Culture of Contentment.

PROF. GALBRAITH: Well, you know, I'm a professor and I can expand any idea to 55 minutes, but contracting it, essentially I am arguing that where once we had a few fortunate people who were very contented with their position and looked upon their position as distilled virtue, now we have something close to a majority of those who vote who are in that happy, in that contented position, and they have come to dominate our politics in these

169

recent times so that—and the Democrats have imitated the Republicans in
the search for that clientele, that voting support—so, over half of our population doesn't vote, is left outside. This in turn means that the claims of our
cities, the claims of our central cities, which are at third-world levels, the
claims of our schools, the claims for people who desperately need welfare
support—we just can't conceal that—the claims of action against the recession, all get bypassed, because they're not in the interest of what I call the
"contented majority." How's that for a summary?

MR. MACNEIL: *Having read the book, that's pretty good. How is the culture of contentment
responsible, or to what extent is it responsible for the present economic situation in this country, would you say?*
PROF. GALBRAITH: Oh, there's no question about that. If we weren't contented, we would have had a year ago, maybe a year and a half ago, a strong
action against the recession. We would have employed people building
the infrastructure, the roads, the bridges, the hospitals, all the things that
have gone to pieces, gone downhill. And we would have had, of course, a
much stronger position on interest rates. People who are comfortable like
high interest rates. And we would have had strong support to states and
localities which are all struggling with the problems of their budgets and
cutting their budgets and adding to the depth of the recession by the alarm
they create.

MS. WOODRUFF: *Did the culture of contentment create the recession, or help to create the
recession?*
PROF. GALBRAITH: No question about that. We had years of the '80s when we
had a wild speculation and merges and acquisitions. We loaded our corporations with debt. We had a great flow of income from the poor to the very
rich, income that you cannot reliably count on being spent. And we had a
general cutback on our public services, including our support to the inner
cities, which I regard as being the worst problem that we have.

MR. MACNEIL: *Let's look at the outside world. How has the culture of contentment, as
you call it, affected the U.S. position in the new world order, as Mr. Bush calls it?*

PROF. GALBRAITH: Well, the counterpart of the big federal deficit and our unwillingness of the majority to respond with higher taxes because expenditures, except for defense perhaps, could not be cut—the counterpart of that was our big trade deficit. So we passed in the decade of the '80s, from being the world's largest creditor to being the world's largest debtor. And so now when something comes up like the Gulf War, we have to go around begging for help, which isn't the source of prestige and power that we had 10 years ago. And this can only be related, as I say, to the 1980s, and to the policies of that unfortunate period.

MR. MACNEIL: *Some who disagree with you, politically or theoretically, would say that with the—*
PROF. GALBRAITH: I don't countenance disagreement, as you know.

MR. MACNEIL: *—would say that the enormous size and weight of the American military presence and the sheer size of the American economy, even when depressed, as it is now, still gives this country unique prestige and influence in the world.*
PROF. GALBRAITH: Well, people salvage the best view from the situation. There's no question that the United States is still the largest economic force in the world, even with the severe competition that we now face from Japan and from Germany. I don't doubt that for a moment. It is simply that I don't countenance also the fact that we are losing our position relative to what it was in the past, and that we're suffering intense domestic problems.

MR. MACNEIL: *What should the United States be doing to maintain world leadership?*
PROF. GALBRAITH: Well, I would get our own house in order. I would have a strong attack on the recession along the lines that I have mentioned. I would move to increase tax revenues on the upper income brackets, includ-ing maybe even yours. I can see how sad that makes you. And I would move very large substantial resources for the military, including these exotic weapons, which are built not with the idea that they will ever be used, over into the support of our cities, the support of our states, and also the infra-structure development that I mentioned, and then a very orthodox point, I would have much lower interest rates. Our interest rates are still too high.

MR. MACNEIL: *Still too high, even after—*
PROF. GALBRAITH: Still too high.

MR. MACNEIL: *What will happen to the U.S. position of competitiveness in the global economy if the country remains, as you see it, in the grip of this culture of contentment and unwilling politically to do the things you think should be done?*
PROF. GALBRAITH: Well, we have already seen that. We have already lost a relative competitive position to Japan and to Germany, and one of the reasons, of course, is that we've had this enormous military budget which has sucked a lot of our engineering talent and maybe as much as a third of our scientific and engineering talent, into relatively sterile military development where the Germans and the Japanese have had that talent, those resources, for their civilian economy. Also, there's a deeper factor which we should always have in mind. We ended the war with a sense of our enormous success, World War II. The Germans and the Japanese ended the war with a sense of defeat and a sense of determination and a sense of high aspiration. This has certainly been a psychological factor that has weakened us. But I would see as the major factor strong support to our educational system which at university level is still the best, but still it is very bad and getting worse at state and local level. We should restore the prestige of the teacher in the community, which is a matter of pay. There should be no ducking that. We hear a lot of talk about the administrative structure of our schools. And no doubt it can be improved, but there's nothing that could be done without more money; and then a strong program of worker training for the unemployed, a strong program of drug rehabilitation, so we bring back into the society those people who are lost, and, again, this is something that can only be accomplished—we mustn't avoid it for a moment—it's not going to be accomplished by enterprise zones. It's not going to be accomplished even by prayer. It is only going to be accomplished by strong, affirmative government action. One's hope is that the promise of that action will be to bring the people who need that support, need that effort, back into the political process. It's a terrible thing, you know, that half of our people don't think it worthwhile to vote. That's a story in itself on the nature of our government process.

MR. MACNEIL: *The end of your book you are not hopeful for change. You predict what you call more "stasis" and an economic performance that is sadly deficient and erratic. Now, since you finished the book and published it a few months ago, we've had a number of things happen in this country. We've had the Los Angeles riots. One of the things you say might change things is if the underclass rises up. We've had considerable evidence of people being discontent with the present political system, at least in the polls. Are you now more hopeful, a few months after you published the book, than you were, that it's going to change?*

PROF. GALBRAITH: I must say I'm not. It's very hard to write a book like this and not say, well, I have to have a happy ending, but honesty does have its controlling force. And I'm not terribly optimistic. I think that there's real danger that if we have any more eruptions as in Los Angeles, the answer will be not to correct the conditions which lead to that despair, lead to that violence, but to say, well, we'll improve our police forces and we'll have the National Guard standing by and we'll have a little more facilities for confining people, and sort of bury our heads.

MR. MACNEIL: *Well, if you're right to be pessimistic about it, 10 years from now, where is the United States as a world power?*

PROF. GALBRAITH: Well, certainly as a world power we will have continued to diminish and I would rather picture the problem than I would say, well, as the result of reading Galbraith, wonderful as that is, everybody is going to respond and do better.

MR. MACNEIL: *You said in the book that communism, which we've been all gratified to see collapse, might have been saved by a timely injection of a little capitalism, namely in goods and services, maybe in agriculture. And you say, "The same is now true of modern capitalism."*

PROF. GALBRAITH: No. I didn't go quite that far.

MR. MACNEIL: *I was quoting your words.*

PROF. GALBRAITH: This system could not see its faults, could not see the extraordinary faults that it had in agriculture, food production, and particularly in a great range of consumers groups. It was a system in which building basic industry and creating an enormous war machine was quite effective. But the weaknesses could not be seen by those who were involved and what I do say is that this should be a lesson, that we have weaknesses that we should see, and I hope we might see, in spite of my pessimism.

MR. MACNEIL: *Prof. Galbraith, thank you for joining us.*
PROF. GALBRAITH: It's a great pleasure being here.

The Lion in Winter: The Harvard Prof's Latest Lesson: How to Age Wisely

William A. Davis / 1995

From the *Boston Globe*, City Edition, Living,
24 October 1995, p. 55. Reprinted by
permission of Copyright Clearance
Center, Inc.

John Kenneth Galbraith has long gloried in his image as the growling old lion of American liberalism. The role of geriatric guru, however, is one the retired Harvard economist assumed only recently—and rather reluctantly.

"I'm deeply conscious of getting older but also aware that there is no escape from it and see no sense in dwelling on it," says Galbraith, who turned 87 this month. "The end is here but not yet in sight."

His end may not be in sight, but Galbraith himself is certainly highly visible and has recently become something of a star on the senior-citizen lecture circuit. For instance, when organizers of last week's conference on changing perceptions of aging, held at the Harvard Graduate School of Education, were looking for a keynote speaker, they turned to Galbraith.

The conference theme was "Aging Intelligently," a subject Galbraith can expound on with just as much authority as he brings to economics and politics. "It's mainly a matter of staying engaged with life as long as

175

you can," he says. "The one thing to worry about is boredom: If I'm not reading, writing, or talking, the hours pass with infinite slowness."

Galbraith says he started speaking publicly about aging largely because of the response to an essay, based on remarks he made at his 85th-birthday celebration, that ran on the op-ed page of the *Globe*. In the essay, he urged an end to the common but insensitive practice of lightheartedly calling attention to the physical and mental condition of the elderly, who are usually only too aware of their own declining powers.

In his case, he noted, this often took the form of comments preceded by the word "still," as in: "still getting that exercise" when he went for a walk; "still imbibing" when he had a drink; and "still that way" when his eyes lit up on encountering a beautiful woman.

"The physical and mental deterioration that go with age are an undoubted fact. They cannot be avoided or their evidence wholly concealed," Galbraith declared in the essay. "But none of this justifies the uncontrollable tendency on the part of others to proclaim the fact, to tell the victim how certain, assured, and even obvious will be his decline. . . . Let all join with me in condemning the Still Syndrome, as I urge it now be called."

Many older people, it seems, feel just as strongly about the Still Syndrome as Galbraith, who says nothing he has written since *The Affluent Society* (the 1958 book that made his reputation as insightful economist and witty social critic) has elicited such a response. "I got a good many letters, and people—usually people over 70—were stopping me on the street to say how much they agreed with me."

Galbraith is, well, "still" doing a lot of things, including daily physical exercise and maintaining a work schedule that would tire out many younger men. And, yes, he still imbibes.

"I try to swim three times a week and walk a mile or so on other days," he says. He usually swims at Harvard's Olympic-class Blodgett Pool, named for a wealthy alumnus, for 25 minutes at a time. No more and no less—regardless.

"One time I had just started swimming when a man came over and told me the pool was closing and I had to get out," Galbraith recalls. "I asked him if he knew who I was, and when he said no, I said, 'My name, sir, is Blodgett!'" The pool attendant took a second look at the irate and imposing Galbraith—whose craggy features, booming voice and flashing eyes have intimidated generations of Harvard undergraduates—spluttered an apology and fled. Galbraith finished his swim.

Age has had little effect on Galbraith's great height, just over 6 feet 8 inches. So there's still no mistaking him on his walks: stately perambulations around the neighborhood where he has lived for 45 years, an academic residential enclave behind Harvard Divinity School. "The neighbors all know me and say, 'There goes Galbraith again,'" he says.

Long an enthusiastic, but by his own admission notably ungraceful, skier, Galbraith reluctantly gave up the sport a few years ago. "I take medicine to thin my blood and improve the circulation, and the doctors thought skiing was a bad idea," he says. The circulation problem is related to his height, Galbraith says, and runs in his family.

However, his wife, Catherine, still skis at 82. "Although since Kitty broke her hip she takes it easier than she used to," he says. Married for 58 years, the couple have three sons and six grandchildren.

The Galbraiths' favorite ski resort, which they visit annually, is in Gstaad, Switzerland. Among their Gstaad neighbors is conservative pundit William F. Buckley Jr., a fellow indefatigable intellectual warrior and senior citizen (he will be 70 next month) and Galbraith's frequent sparring partner in televised political debates. "Bill's a good neighbor and a good friend," Galbraith says, "just as long as he stays off politics."

For Galbraith, who grew up in a Scottish farming community in Ontario, Canada, where the work ethic had near-religious significance, avoiding idleness is fundamental to graceful, intelligent aging. His great-grandfather emigrated from Scotland when he was 50, Galbraith says, became a very successful farmer in Ontario and died at the age of 103.

Continuing to work at what you do best is the ideal way to stave off boredom, Galbraith says, but he acknowledges that this isn't something every older person can do—or wants to. "The farmers I knew growing up in Ontario were usually glad to end their agricultural labors," he says.

"But farm work is hard and boring, and what a Harvard professor does is interesting and not physically demanding, and most professors try to keep working.

"I keep the same writing schedule that I did before I retired from Harvard," he says. "I start at 9 a.m. and write until around noontime." He is just finishing a book, his 29th, which will be published next year. Called *The Good Society*, it is a summing up of his deeply held liberal Democratic belief that government must play a key role in resolving societal problems. "I hope it will annoy a lot of people," he says.

Ever the political activist, Galbraith included in his discussion of intelligent aging at the Harvard conference a plea to his older listeners to become politically active and use their electoral clout to thwart efforts to cut back benefit programs for the elderly and the poor. "Older people are more apt to vote than younger people," he notes. "Politicians should be afraid of them."

He follows no special diet, and can and does eat just about everything, Galbraith says. "My doctors say not to worry about cholesterol; I seem to thrive on it," he says, "and I have all my basic teeth with a few additions."

Dinner is usually accompanied by at least one glass of wine. "That's a health tip I got from the Bible." He also has an occasional shot of whiskey. "I believe in the old Scottish adage that 'some men are born a couple of drinks below par,'" he says, "and need to take a glass or two from time to time for their health's sake."

Once a moderate smoker, Galbraith gave up cigarettes 40 years ago. He says he often wonders what the economic effect of that decision will be on health-care costs. "If I kept on smoking I would have died earlier and cheaper," he says; "now I'm going to live longer and die expensively."

After lunch, Galbraith says, he spends most of the afternoon clearing off his desk. This usually means reading and answering letters and accepting or declining speaking invitations. "I try to speak to community groups in towns around Boston," he says; "I call it my Good Neighbor policy."

He never takes an afternoon nap, he says, and, untroubled by the prostate or bladder problems that often plague older men, he invariably enjoys eight hours or more of sound, uninterrupted sleep. "I go to bed around 11 and usually get up at 7:30," he says. "All my unmentionable parts are in good condition."

Late afternoons are when he often talks to Harvard economics or political-science classes and seminars. Or receives visitors—students, academics, journalists and just plain admirers—in the book-lined front room of his large Victorian house. "I spend much of my time with younger people and enjoy it," he says, "but it's also a matter of necessity, since most of my contemporaries have taken the great leap."

It's an unusual day when at least one visitor isn't from overseas or out of town. "After visiting Concord, Lexington, the Old North Church and Harvard, travelers are moved, however oddly, to view Galbraith," he once wrote.

But, Galbraith says, callers are enjoyable—and reassuring. "I wouldn't want to be ignored," he says, smiling at the thought of that unlikely possibility. "At my age you should reflect on the past but live in the moment," says the 87-year-old economist, who still writes and lectures.

John Kenneth Galbraith

David C. Colander and Harry Landreth / 1996

From *The Coming of Keynesianism to America:*
Conversations with the Founders of Keynesian
Economics, edited by David C. Colander
and Harry Landreth, Cheltenham, UK,
and Brookfield, VT: Edward Elgar, 1996,
pp. 131–43.

The interview took place in August 1986 at John Kenneth Galbraith's
summer home in Newfane, Vermont.

When did you become interested in economics?
I started college in the fall of 1926, but I didn't have any thoughts on economic matters until some time in the early 1930s. I was an undergraduate
for five years because I had to make up some high school deficiencies. Along
about 1930, the crunch came in Canada. I was studying agriculture, and the
thought occurred to me that there was very little purpose in achieving more
efficient production of crops and livestock if they couldn't be sold for a fair
price. So I shifted my attention to agricultural economics, which at the time
was a very primitive, neglected, subject at the Agricultural College of
Ontario. I confess I didn't learn very much that satisfied me.

Do you remember anything about what they taught you about why the Depression
occurred?
My memory doesn't go beyond the impression that it was inexplicable—
an act of God, modified possibly by sunspots. It wasn't until I went to the

University of California at Berkeley in 1931 that I began serious study. Berkeley was much more eclectic. The mainstream of the Berkeley department, both in economics and agricultural economics, held that the Depression was an exceptionally severe manifestation of business cycles, which would correct itself in time; and the department certainly believed that what would now be called modern macroeconomic steps would be unsound. You certainly didn't deliberately unbalance the budget as an act of fiscal policy—that was out of the question. There was some debate on whether it made sense to reduce interest rates. Otherwise the mainstream attitude, reflected by people like Carl E. Plehn, who was the dominant figure in the department at that time, was negative as regards any activist policy.

Outside the mainstream, there was a younger, more alert and aggressive group of teachers—one was Leo Rogin—who introduced us to a range of thought, including some of the very early expressions of Keynes, long before *The General Theory* was published. Thorstein Veblen, who had died a couple of years before in Palo Alto, was also still influential in the Berkeley community at that time. This view was that depressions were inherent in the business system, that there was a repressive business hold on production that offset the natural productive tendencies of the engineers. Veblen's views were broadly expressed in *The Theory of Business Enterprise* and *Engineers and the Price System*. We read these with great attention.

A third current of thought was well expressed in Robert Brady's work. It held that big business and the liberal tendencies of the corporation were responsible for the Depression. In terms of policy this view called for— vaguely speaking—enforcement of the antitrust laws and the restructuring of the business corporation.

Finally, there was a strong student commitment to the belief that the system was basically at fault and that only radical—very revolutionary— changes could improve the situation. This was essentially under the influence of Marx, although I've always had some doubt as to how much Marx was actually read. Quite possibly he was more discussed than read at the time.

So all of those currents were in competition at Berkeley. I was not strongly committed to any one of them. I was in the Giannini Foundation of Agricultural Economics, a little outside the mainstream, to some extent a bystander—a very much interested bystander. I involved myself with the particular problems of agriculture. So far as I had an interest in policy it was not in macroeconomic policy but in what might be done to restore agricultural prices and control agricultural production.

I suppose to the extent that I was influenced by anybody, it was by Veblen. Not in terms of specific recommendations but by his general attitude of suspicion of orthodox doctrine and by the notion that orthodoxy, to a substantial extent, is in the service of economic interests.

At Berkeley in the 1930s there was a large and active graduate body and a great reluctance to take one's Ph.D. because then one was unemployed. Better be doing some teaching or working on a thesis. I taught at Davis the beginning course in economics, the basic course in agricultural economics, and a course in farm accounting, and I was the full staff of all those departments. Then, in 1933, the emergency agencies opened up in Washington, particularly the Agricultural Adjustment Administration, but also the National Recovery Act and the relief agencies. All of them had to have economists. There was a rush to turn in long-delayed Ph.D. theses and a further rush to Washington—a reverse gold rush. Or to local branches of the new Federal agencies. I was a part of this reverse gold rush.

In 1934 I took my Ph.D. and went to Washington to work at the Department of Agriculture, where I stayed for the summer and all the following year. At that time the Department was the very heart of the economic discussion. No other part of the New Deal could boast of anything like the intensity of economic and political debate. Unfortunately the people who were engaged in that discussion were at a level above me—Rexford Tugwell, Henry Wallace, Jerome Frank and Adlai Stevenson. I either didn't know them, or saw very little of them. I was assigned responsibility of seeing what could be done with all the tax-reverted land in the country. I traveled around to Michigan and New York, talking to people who had ideas of how the Federal government might be the recipient of all this land that had reverted for tax purposes. If I had had my way, there would have been an enormous increase in the public domain from taking over the land. Among the people who shelved it was Rex Tugwell himself.

How did you, an agricultural economist, come to get an offer from Harvard?
At that time there was a chair at Harvard that was given to agricultural matters, held by John D. Black. He, in turn, had an assistant but his then-assistant received a Social Science Research Fellowship in 1934 / 35 and Black needed a replacement. I was recommended. I also taught in the beginning economics course.

Do you remember what text you taught from at Harvard?
At Harvard there was never any question. One used Taussig's *Principles of Economics.*

At that time, were Keynesian thoughts being discussed at Harvard?
No. The nearest that one came was in John H. Williams's Money and Banking course. To everybody's surprise and slight shock, he repeatedly said there was something in the work of Foster and Catchings and that it could not be dismissed. This precipitated a certain discussion of Foster and Catchings and made respectable what would otherwise at Harvard have been considered an outrageous aberration—slightly respectable, but not fully so.

There was one other development before I got there. Lauchlin Currie had written *The Supply and Control of Money,* which had Keynesian over-tones. At least, it was an activist economic tract. It was considered sus-pect, radical—not so much radical perhaps as irresponsible—and it probably was one of the reasons that Currie was not taken on to the Harvard faculty. Instead he went to the Federal Reserve and, in company with Mariner Eccles, became one of the two leading Keynesian intruders upon Washington. Currie's book was a matter for some comment when I went to Harvard. There was no faculty discussion of Keynes at that time, and very little student discussion.

Do you remember the first time you heard about The General Theory *being written?* I don't know that I heard about it before it was written. I have no recollection that I did. One of the reasons that I didn't hear about it was that I was working on my own explanation of the Depression. Why we had this enduring misery: it was the great transcendent fact of one's life.

I was attracted by the notion that the problem lay in the nature of the price structure, that we had moved from competition to a structure of rigid, restrictive prices with competitive energies going into things like advertising. In this view I was somewhat influenced by Ed Chamberlin and his *The Theory of Monopolistic Competition* and Joan Robinson's *The Economics of Imperfect Competition*. I developed a theory of unemployment and aggregate performance, based on the idea of an imperfect market structure and what should be done about it. I wrote a long paper on this which attracted attention during the summer of 1935 / 36, about the same time that Keynes's *General Theory* came out. I had a temporary assignment to work with a group of New England businessmen who were convinced that something had to be done about unemployment and had broken with the ranks of the conservative business apparatus and were supporting Roosevelt.

The leader of the group was Henry Dennison of the Dennison Manufacturing Company. Dennison was an instinctive Keynesian, who had the view that all flows of income were on the way to saving, which didn't get spent, or on the way to consumption, which did get spent, and that one could do something for unemployment by taxing savings and releasing consumer expenditure. I came up with the notion that the problem was in the price structure, and persuaded Dennison sufficiently so that the two of us wrote a book, which I've always recommended that people not read (I don't know that I have a copy of it left). It was called *Modern Competition and Business Policy*, published by the Oxford University Press, which must have been hard up for material at the time.

While that book was going through final revisions I read *The General Theory*. The terrible thought developed in my mind that I had been wrong in persuading Dennison as I did, that he was instinctively right, and I told him so. I got the disconcerting answer that, "Indeed, I always thought that among economists Keynes made more sense than most." Unfortunately, the book had gone so far it couldn't be stopped. It was well received by some of the orthodox of the profession.

I then wrote another book for the three businessmen of this same group. It was called *Toward Full Employment*, and it embraced Keynesian ideas to a much larger measure. One of the businessmen was Ralph Flanders, who was later Senator from Vermont; one was Lincoln Filene of Filene's in Boston; and the third was a manufacturer from Philadelphia, a good Quaker, Morris Leeds. I put together their ideas with, as I say, a heavy Keynesian overtone. My name doesn't appear on the title page. It had no effect. But that was the process by which I became attracted to Keynesian ideas.

Enthusiasm for *The General Theory* at Harvard was prompt and very great. Copies of the book were actually shipped over from England before it came out in the United States. We younger economists were, as I've said, all looking for an escape from the commanding horror of the times. We were comfortable, and we believed others should be too.

Robert Bryce played an important role in bringing Keynesian ideas to Harvard. He came for the academic year of either 1935 / 36 or 1936 / 37, fresh from Keynes's seminars and willing to resolve all of the ambiguities of *The General Theory*, of which there were many. Joseph Schumpeter once said in a half serious manner, perhaps more in amusement than anything else—he wasn't capable of anger—that at Harvard, "Keynes was Allah and Bryce was his Prophet." But Schumpeter, while he didn't like Keynes and deplored Keynesian economics, also could not disassociate himself in the discussion as some of the others did. The younger people, many of whom had been moving to the left, moving toward Marx, found Keynes a very agreeable alternative to the protection of a system which, as I've noted, we all, personally, enjoyed.

Alvin Hansen came on the faculty a year or so later, in one of Harvard's more unexpected steps. He had achieved his reputation as an exponent of liberal trade and what we now would call neoclassical economics. He had co-authored an impeccably liberal orthodox book, sympathetic to needed government intervention but basically a mainstream volume. Hansen had had a dispute with Keynes over a set of equations in *A Treatise on Money*, Keynes's set of equations, and had corrected them—Keynes had admitted the correction. Hansen's first review of *The General Theory* was far from favorable. But in the process of reviewing it and defending it he had, like others (myself included), the same tendency to move to acceptance. Presently his seminar was the official, as distinct from the unofficial, center of Keynesian discussion.

There were lots of unofficial centers. Two or three of us ran a seminar in the evenings on Keynes. By the autumn of 1936 the Tricentennial Celebration, the 300th anniversary of the University, was in prospect and, in a tolerant mood, the professors in the government department asked the young government teachers for their suggestions as to honorary degrees. They considered the names that would be most embarrassing and came up with Leon Trotsky. We were similarly asked, and came up with the name that we thought would be most embarrassing, which was John Maynard Keynes. Both names were righteously rejected; instead in economics they honored Dennis Robertson, a critic of Keynes, who would not now be thought to rank with the master.

In 1937 I received a Social Science Research Fellowship to study abroad. It would have been eccentric to go any place but Cambridge, where I stayed through 1938. My time there was fascinating. That was the year that Keynes had his first heart attack, so he didn't show up at the University at all that year. The Keynes seminar was not held, but that didn't make much difference because R. F. Kahn, Joan Robinson, Michal Kalecki, and Piero Sraffa were all there. We met in the afternoons in the Marshall Library and held a discussion, almost always on Keynes. The intensity of this discussion with my contemporaries was the reward of that year. I can't think that there were many ideas of Keynes that weren't discussed at length at one time or another. All the ambiguities of *The General Theory* were also resolved.

When I finished my year there, I came back to Harvard and then in 1938 / 39 went to Princeton. Princeton was an unsatisfactory place at that particular time for economists of my generation. There was, first, the fact that the war was coming—and had come in Europe. This made study anywhere difficult. Second, at Princeton I felt that I was living in an academic backwater. Harvard, by this time, had very close associations with Washington and in 1938 / 39 you could have held a Harvard faculty meeting on the Federal Express going from Boston to the capital. There was nothing like that at Princeton. Most of all, Keynes had never come to Princeton. There were open-minded figures, like Frank Graham and Ray Whittlesey, but they hadn't embraced Keynes. For others, Adam Smith was still a mentor figure.

In the spring of 1940, I was asked to go out to Chicago and organize a research department for the Farm Bureau Federation, which I did. Then after the fall of France things began to look serious in Washington, and an Office of Price Control was organized under Leon Henderson. Henderson's reputation at the time was that of one of the old New Deal trust-busting types. The New Deal always was split between those who thought that a restoration of competitive markets would be the salvation (going back to my earlier position) and the Keynesians. Lauchlin Currie called me from Washington to say they had to have a Keynesian with Henderson. I got the train the next night. Initially, there wasn't much to do on price stabilization, and I worked for much of the rest of that year (commuting back to Chicago at times) on some matters having to do with plant location. This work was very interesting and very important. We had a plan, more than a little successful, for getting the defense plants out of the Northeast and into the South and West. Then, in the spring of 1941, I went back to Henderson and was put in charge of price control.

Was the theory of price control a Keynesian idea or was it a general economists' idea?
There is always the danger of exaggerating one's particular role. I think it is probably fair to say, though, that I was more a source of the ruling ideas there than anybody else. It would perhaps have been agreed at the time. I wrote a paper in late 1940 / early 1941, setting out the basic changes for price stabilization. At or approaching full employment you stabilized

the economy by controlling the flow of aggregate demand. And you identified and acted on shortage areas with price control and perhaps rationing. I wasn't this precise but such was the general scheme. The paper had a large and interested reception in Washington. It probably led to my appointment to head price control operations.

I was basically responsible for guiding the operation from the spring of 1941 to the summer of 1943. Unfortunately, when I took charge, I discovered that picking out and acting on the individual areas of short-age and price inflation was not practical. Indeed it was administratively impossible. So that plan was set aside. Instead, we placed a ceiling over all prices, and then released or adjusted those that were too low under price regulation.

My design was the right one; however, my political management of the situation, particularly my relations with Congress, was less than perfect. The only real applause I had from the Congress was when I left in 1943.

In 1951 you wrote A Theory of Price Control. *As you reflect back, would price control have been needed at full employment if Keynesian economics was valid?*
This was the beginning of something which I have argued and I have since argued. One must not separate macroeconomic and microeconomic effects. In the absence of price control and wage restraint, there would have been a microeconomic dynamic that would have been disastrous even though one had managed to have some kind of an equilibrium, some kind of macroeconomic equilibrium of full employment.

Going back to 1937, the inflation of 1937, how did Keynesian economists explain the inflation that occurred in 1937, and then the recession again?
Well, there was no real inflation. The movement of prices was to some extent a recovery from the extreme deflationary pressure of those years. The signal feature of that time was the paranoia about inflation. In World War I prices about doubled, and this left a grave fear of inflation in the minds of the older generation of economists and businessmen. They believed that if somehow inflation became ingrained in the system it couldn't be ameliorated or stopped. This attitude was responsible for the restrictive

steps that had already been taken in 1936 and 1937. When the economy was expanding you had the fully unjustified fear that there was going to be some great inflationary surge.

As you look back, what was the thinking of the business writers of the time? Were they influenced much by Keynes? Were they Keynesians?
When I left the Office of Price Administration in 1943 I went to *Fortune* magazine, and the first piece I did was on the establishment of the National Accounts system. No history of Keynesian economics should ever be written without giving nearly equal credit to the scholars who took Keynes out of the realm of theory and into the real world. The numbers in the National Accounts made it impossible for the practical man to deny the validity of Keynesian thinking. In this article I set up a model, it would now be called, of the economy for the post-war years, showing what would be required in production, investment, wage income and so forth—the whole Gross National Product and National Income—and it showed very cautiously that a deficit would be required to maintain full employment.

The January 1944 issue of *Fortune* was just about going to press when this manuscript came along. It was halted; the lead article was torn out, and this article was put in and featured on the cover.

Was that at Fortune *or was that more in general? I guess I've heard a lot of stories about Alvin Hansen going around, and any time he mentioned "deficit," he almost got thrown out. This seems to contradict your story.*
Fortune at that time was way ahead of the crowd, there's no question. Harry Luce had had the idea in the 1930s that it was far better to have a readable journal published by liberals and socialists who could write, than a nonliberal one published by less literate conservatives. He had brought in a whole range of people—Archibald MacLeish, Dwight Macdonald, James Agee—and put them to work on business stories, sometimes with disastrous effect. There was an open mind there that caused me to be taken on.

I do think you are right—and it's an important point—that the wave of business opinion, the respectable corporate opinion and the establishment, was still strongly anti-Keynesian. So too was the establishment position in the academic world, but that was a diminishing sector of that world. The Keynesian community was year by year getting a much larger foothold. In the department of economics at Harvard, by 1948 the Keynesian structure was accepted with few exceptions. On the other hand, there was a very adverse reaction from Harvard graduates. The Veritas Foundation was organized to oppose Keynesian economics. And the Board of Overseers held my appointment up for a year partly because I was thought to be too Keynesian.

Who called you too Keynesian?
The Veritas Foundation. There were also other factors holding up my appointment. I had had a terrific row with the Air Force over a report of the U.S. Strategic Bombing Survey, which demonstrated beyond the shadow of a doubt that the Air Force had greatly overclaimed what it had accomplished in World War II. That report struck at the very heart of the establishment. But my Keynesian reputation was a primary factor. There was, to repeat, a split between the academic community where Keynes was acceptable and the larger business establishment. This split, I think, partly disappeared with the Eisenhower Administration, which in a backhanded way accepted the overall management of the economy.

When did you see Keynes?
I first met Keynes in the summer of 1941 after I'd been put in charge of price control, and I was still deep in the job of getting the basic organization established. On a really hectic day my secretary came in and said, "There's a Mr. Kines who would like to see you." I told her I couldn't see him, but she responded, "He gave me the impression that he expects to see you— and asked if you had received this." She then handed me a paper; it was by John Maynard Keynes on the pricing of hogs. The title is vague in my memory, but it was something like "The Pig/Pig-Fodder Relationship." Keynes had a pig farm in the south of England, as you know. That was

my first encounter with Keynes. It was the Holy Father dropping in on the parish priest!

Keynes was quite frequently in Washington during the war on some negotiating mission. Anybody who's had experience with diplomatic negotiating matters knows that it's an exercise in idleness. You're waiting for instructions from your government, you're waiting for the others to be instructed; you're waiting for a meeting. Keynes filled in those times by moving into the American government. By this time there was a sizable group of younger people, of whom I was one, who were devoted to his ideas—a much larger group, as he has said, in Washington than he had in London. His vanity was not above being touched by this effect, so he brought around him a group of younger Washington people for discussion of wartime policy, and I was naturally in that group. The person who saw most of him, and with whom he communicated most, was Walter Salant. I was less involved, because I was much more actively engaged in creating the whole price control operation. I started with seven or eight people, something like that (including the rationing and rent control staff) and finished with around seventeen thousand.

A Conversation with John Kenneth Galbraith

Kimberly Blanton / 1996

From the *Boston Globe*, City Edition,
28 April 1996, p. A97.
Reprinted by permission of
Copyright Clearance Center, Inc.

John Kenneth Galbraith holds open the porch door for a visitor to his cottage and chats about the daffodils popping in the yard. Even then, this confidant of U.S. presidents and Harvard professor of nearly half a century does not lose the bearing of a man who has wielded much influence in his 87 years. And considerable charm.

Compared with such literary achievements as his controversial 1950s bestseller, *The Affluent Society*, and two clever novels of political and financial intrigue, Galbraith's new book seems tiny. But in its 152 pages he has laid out a big agenda.

"Everybody says what is wrong with the world. I thought it was time to say what would be right," Galbraith explains, after settling his angular frame into a broad wooden chair in his living room. "I found it was a more compelling job than I imagined. It took me a couple years to write it."

The book, his 31st, is *The Good Society: The Humane Agenda*. And he describes his agenda this way: Everyone—regardless of race, gender or ethnicity—has "the basic necessities of life and a chance for an upward movement to improve his or her situation, with a larger consequence of a peaceful and enjoyable life."

His arguments in *The Good Society* are familiar coming from the eminent economist whose views were shaped in the era of John Maynard Keynes and the New Deal: Government has a role in helping the less fortunate, through the provision of health care, environmental protection, basic shelter, education.

But readers may be skeptical that a traditional liberal agenda can be revived at a time when the political tone is set by red-hot rhetoric about a fat, failing federal bureaucracy that should be dismantled. The *Washington Post*, in an unfavorable review last week, called the book "disappointing" and full of "generalizations," its author "content to recycle old arguments."

In fact, many of Galbraith's proposals mirror policies of the Roosevelt administration he joined during World War II as "price czar novitiate" for scarce goods. For example, the federal government should spend money on public projects to create jobs, just as the Works Progress Administration did in the '30s.

The problem with his agenda, according to the *Post* review, is that it "assumes a responsible and responsive governmental machinery that does not in fact exist."

Galbraith does not believe his ideas are popular. But he waves away the doubters.

Take the federal deficit. Individuals borrow money to buy houses and corporations borrow to invest in plants. So, too, should the U.S. government borrow for programs to benefit society and future generations. "This argument indeed is considered eccentric. But on examination, it appears very sensible," he writes.

Years removed from his days in Washington, Galbraith is keenly aware of the current political environment that has put a centrist Democrat in office as president. President Clinton "doesn't go as far as I do on many matters" of policy, Galbraith says. "On the other hand, he's president, and I am only a college professor."

Galbraith's views may be familiar; he insists his inspirations are new.

"During part of my writing I was impelled by the Newt Gingrich revolt, which I didn't think was permanent," he says. "We've now had two years of the revolt and no really important legislation has passed to date.

"Also, I was influenced by the fact that much of what we call liberal legis-lation is really a response to the thrust of history," he says. Just as the New Deal legislation was a response to the Depression, the conservative tide led by the House speaker has ebbed, in Galbraith's eyes, because Gingrich and his followers were "in conflict with the great thrust of history."

Other things also have "come into the picture" since his days in Washington, especially urban poverty.

Poverty is an issue "with which a compassionate society must deal," he says. He believes that "those of us in the fortunate world" do not appreciate the poor. "We'd have no fruits, no vegetables, no canned goods if it weren't for the impoverished workers who do farm work in the absence of" better jobs, he says. "All of us in some measure live on the backs of the poor."

Galbraith may be the Lion of the Left. But as one of the country's most respected economists, he uses the arguments of his trade to make the case for a kinder capitalism. Inflation must be controlled, though this goal should not be adhered to at all costs (high unemployment). Immigrants perform essential work, though their numbers can be limited by the amount of jobs available to the newly arrived. Because the poor and middle class spend a larger share of their incomes on consumer goods than do the sated rich, putting money in their pockets can spur growth.

"There is a strong chance that the more unequal the distribution of income, the more dysfunctional" the economy, he writes.

In a time of rising discontent about ruthless layoffs and firings, Galbraith has no use for spiraling executive pay, and he favors raising the minimum wage. He dismisses those who say raising the minimum wage would interfere with the market.

Galbraith suggests the conservative and liberal ideologies—which some say were carved deep in the political landscape during the New Deal—are today "irrelevant" and a handy "escape from thought." Education, for one, is a key issue for a democracy of informed citizens. "A case could be made," he writes, "that the best in education should be for those in the worst of social situations. They are most in need of the means for escape."

After rattling off a few more opinions—about President Clinton, privatization, public health care—he abruptly ends the interview. "OK, you've got enough." On cue, Kitty, his wife of 58 years, emerges from the back of their house on Cambridge's Francis Street.

Galbraith graciously escorts his interviewer to the door. Stooping his 6-foot-8½-inch frame to open it, he includes an invitation with his sendoff. "Come back when the flowers are out."

The Ken Galbraith (and Bill Buckley) Show

Lorie Conway / 1997

From *Nieman Reports*, vol. 51, no. 4
(Winter 1997), pp. 53–55. Copyright ©
President & Fellows of Harvard College.
Reprinted with permission.

My interview with John Kenneth Galbraith began with his asking me a question. Peering down from his 6 feet 8 inches, the 88-year-old Galbraith inquired, "Just how many hours do you plan this series to be on my life?"

Standing tall at 5 feet 4 inches, I sheepishly replied "Well, just one hour," knowing that, at the time, funding for only a half-hour television documentary was available.

Over the next three days last March the Paul M. Warburg Professor of Economics, Emeritus, B.S.A., S.M., Ph.D., A.M., LL.D., LL.D., Litt.D., Litt.D., L.H.D., S.D., held court, remembering detail after detail of his life, relating historical anecdotes and offering incisive analyses. The result was a compelling, first-person account of much of the last 60 years of American history.

For me, as the producer/interviewer, it was an extraordinary experience. Having William F. Buckley, Jr., the narrator and host of the program, edit my script increased the tension but helped make the story a success. The documentary, titled *Thus Galbraith . . . The Life and Times of John Kenneth Galbraith*, will be aired on PBS early in the new year.

Galbraith wove a tapestry of history seated comfortably in the study of his home off Harvard Square, surrounded by ceiling-high bookshelves and photographs of himself with various heads of state and newsmakers. (A needlepoint in the parlor says "Galbraith's first law: Modesty is a vastly overrated virtue.")

With little help from my one course in undergraduate economics and much more help from some willing Kennedy School professors, I began the interview. What unfolded over the course of three days of filming was a description of many of the pivotal events Galbraith was witness to or architect of since 1933.

The first thing that became apparent was the value of Galbraith's storytelling, something I enjoyed when he visited Lippmann house during my year as a Nieman Fellow, 1993–94. Galbraith doesn't just tell you about the events he witnessed, he places you in the room where history was occurring. He remembers where people were seated, the size and shape of the table on which they leaned, even the color of their ties. Galbraith's uncanny ability to recall even the smallest detail makes you feel the presence of Franklin D. Roosevelt, Lyndon B. Johnson, or even "Cotton" Ed Smith, Chairman of the Senate Agricultural Committee in the 1940s.

"Cotton Ed would sit down at the end of the table and he would take a plug of tobacco out of his pocket, and we always said he'd put the plug in his mouth and the bite back in his pocket. He'd sit up and look for the spittoons and they had been removed so the brown streak would go down on the floor and come closer to your shoes and you'd keep moving your feet around and this was a supreme achievement of Cotton Ed Smith."

He vividly recalled scenes from early in the century—he was born in Ontario on October 5, 1908—to this year. The one person most influential in his life was his father, Archie, a school teacher turned farmer. "He was head of the Liberal party in that part of Canada . . . he was known as a famous figure; he was in the best sense of the word, a community leader."

When Galbraith's mother died of a heart attack he was just 14 years old. Being left under the influence of his strong-willed father guaranteed his leaving the farm and going off to college. "I've often thought that if my mother had lived I would have been kept there on the farm, because she regarded that as the ultimate way in which one served oneself and one served the community. . . . She was much more committed to that than my father was. He was more inclined to encourage me to go off to college."

With $500 dollars borrowed from his sister, Galbraith attended the Ontario Agricultural College, 85 miles away. His major? Animal husbandry. "One of the few economic insights of impeccable character that I had at that time was why worry about producing more and better cattle if you couldn't sell the damn things. So the real problem was the economic rather than the technical aspects of efficient production. So I shifted in the final year from the study of animal husbandry to economics."

After graduating in 1931, the "sour point of the Depression," Galbraith moved west to attend the University of California at Berkeley, which was surrounded by Hoovervilles, the makeshift housing of the homeless and unemployed. "There was at Berkeley at that time a very alert and active Communist community and a more cautious group to which I belonged, which had as its major commitment improving the economy."

From Berkeley, Galbraith received a fellowship to the "other Cambridge," Cambridge University in England, to study at the feet, so to speak, of economic revolutionary John Maynard Keynes. By 1934, during the depths of the Depression, Galbraith was a devoted Keynesian, believing in government-funded programs to increase employment and stimulate business. He began testing the theory working in the Roosevelt administration. "FDR was conveniently exempt from ideology. He was responsive to what you needed to do. His only ideology was to action."

But action aside, given the media scrutiny of candidates, let alone one with a physical disability, I asked Galbraith, "Could Roosevelt be elected today?"

"Whether FDR could be elected today would depend on the economic situation more than a little bit. FDR was the product of the Great Depression . . . but there was the Roosevelt personality. He couldn't walk without crutches. Nonetheless he had the impression of strength. . . . [His election] would not be possible today, because Roosevelt was a cripple and he had to be helped, moved, supported and that would be featured on television.

This would be a great disadvantage without a doubt but he did not suffer at the time."

From setting prices as the chief inflation fighter during World War II to writing speeches for Adlai Stevenson's presidential campaigns in 1952 and 1956, Galbraith witnessed the power elite and industry lobbyists on Capitol Hill. He sees a more informed Congress today. "There are reasons to criticize the Congress today and it is the subject of great criticism, but on the whole, the level of intelligence has improved very much since those days of Cotton Ed. He would be a figure of fun today, which he wasn't at the time."

During Galbraith's five years at *Fortune* magazine, from 1943 to 1948, under *Time/Life* founder, Henry Luce, he learned to cultivate the style and expression that define his 30 books and countless articles.

Learning how to inject life and clarity into writing on the so-called dismal science—economics—brought special insight into his job as a writer. About those years he has written, "No economist ever had the slightest influence who wrote only for economists."

During my interview he explained more: "Henry Luce discovered he had a choice, between conservatives who couldn't write and liberals [who could but] he couldn't print. He chose the liberals on the whole because that was at least a start. That was the role I found myself in there."

Galbraith still writes every day, from after breakfast until noon. If he doesn't, he says he is "psychiatrically disturbed."

After *Fortune*, Galbraith would "enter into one of the most interesting jobs" he ever had, the Strategic Bombing Survey. Reporting on the United States bombing of German munitions factories during World War II, the findings concluded, "the air raids had no appreciable effect on production."

The results did not make him too popular with the Air Force or another member of the survey, Charles Cabot, who came to different conclusions. Since Cabot also served as an overseer at Harvard, his opposition toward the young Keynesian was voiced during Galbraith's nomination for a full professorship. There was a standoff until Harvard's president, James Bryant Conant, threatened to resign if Galbraith's nomination was denied. Shortly after Conant's threat it was approved.

The 1950s brought the publishing of Galbraith's epochal book, *The Affluent Society*, making him close to a household name. Millions of copies were sold worldwide. Ten years later, by the time of the United States involvement in Vietnam, his name would also be known as an ardent opponent of the war. As ambassador to India under President Kennedy, Galbraith admitted to "interfering with all manner of things, but mostly Vietnam." He believes that, if he had lived, Kennedy would have limited United States involvement in Vietnam. "I was always under the impression—the valid impression—that he wanted himself to limit his commitment there and was subject to the pressures of the generals and the Cold War liberals who wanted to go on with the war and that he was grateful for, indeed welcomed, those of us in opposition."

In 1964, Galbraith's opposition to the war meant breaking with his friend, President Johnson, whom he respected. When Johnson ordered an escalation of the war, Galbraith made his move. He accepted every proffered speaking engagement in Texas, knowing the president was an avid reader of his home state's newspapers. "I went to him several times to tell him my opposition and his answer, which was not wholly unpersuasive, was always the same. He said, 'Ken, if I weren't here, you would be in much worse condition for what the generals want to do. You should be glad that I'm keeping this thing under control.'"

By 1968, Galbraith gave up on his persuasive efforts and increased his political efforts. At the Democratic convention in Chicago, he seconded Eugene McCarthy's name in nomination for the presidency. "I was more strongly moved by the need for opposition to Vietnam than any other major issue of my lifetime."

Galbraith has always worn his liberalism on his sleeve, proud and not afraid of the label. Today, he explains the shift towards conservatism in terms of economics and what the media, he claims, has made "fashionable." "I think that when people are happy, comfortable, they tend to be more conservative . . . but I am prepared to argue that the next time there is a slump, liberals will be back and it will be conservatism that is unfashionable."

I chose the conservative Buckley as narrator of the program because of his stature on the opposite end of the political spectrum, for his 30-year

history of debating Galbraith worldwide and, most importantly, for his pro-
found respect of Galbraith. "But don't expect me to suppress my differences,"
Buckley warned me back in May when I approached him with the idea of
hosting the program. I assured him that was part of the charm.

As agreed, I wrote the script, then Buckley worked on it. My nerves were
more than a bit frayed waiting to hear back from him. What he delivered
three days later was a producer's dream, a narrative deftly weaving both the
unique Buckley-esque style and nuance with his differences, political and
economic. I was thrilled and awed by the clarity of his writing. Best of all,
the main structure and content of the script were still intact.

While Buckley was recording the material to camera in New York, I
watched his presentation on a monitor. It became clear why he and Galbraith
have remained respected friends so long. Both possess a passion for their
beliefs and convictions based on intellectual brilliance and integrity. Their
differences only livened the discussion.

Buckley wrote this ending standup:

> John Kenneth Galbraith is celebrated *not for formal economic explorations
> but because of his resonance as a political moralist.* The Affluent Society
> *isn't about economic policy, it is about social priorities.*

Or, as Galbraith himself said:

> *I would like to be remembered as somebody who wanted to go beyond
> analysis, beyond explanation and to the social action. I spent a certain
> amount of my life in practical politics and I would like to see that as proof
> that I wanted to go beyond pure economics, pure description, pure analysis
> to practical action.*

A Gentler, Kinder Approach—
the Galbraith Way

Hardev Kaur / 1998

From *Business Times*, vol. 12, no. 51
(16 March 1998). Reprinted with
permission of *Business Times*.

Lunch with Professor John Kenneth Galbraith is an illuminating, exhilarating, and above all, educational experience. The global economics icon physically towers above everyone around him and obliges all requests for autographs and photographs.

He has some very strong words for "market speculators" but has great sympathy and a strong sense of compassion for the poor. He speaks volubly of double standards for the rich and poor: "Leisure and consumption is tolerated for the affluent but not for the poor." He is greatly concerned by the inherent weaknesses within the capitalist system and the way it can inflict pain upon the poor in society.

Galbraith is the celebrated author of numerous economic books, many of which are compulsory reading for students of economics. "My book on marketing in Puerto Rico is the least read," he remarks with a wry smile and goes on to talk about the virtues of education for economic development.

The name John Kenneth Galbraith is instantly recognised by economists and just about everyone else in the academic world as well. It is a fitting tribute for a man who regularly stresses the importance of education in economic development. According to Galbraith, there is no "literate population that is poor" since literacy allows people to improve their living standards.

He readily admits that "over the years, my own thinking has changed very substantially" adding that economic development is almost always associated with stable, effective government. "The most traumatic cases involving economic development have occurred where there is no stable and honest government."

"I don't like the word globalisation, don't ever use it," he categorically states. With rapid international development, he sees a diminishing role for the "diplomat" and advises those in the diplomatic service that "you may be able to serve it out, but get your children out of it."

Galbraith, who served as the U.S. Ambassador to India during the Kennedy Administration, says that the role of diplomacy is changing and with international development the problems have become increasingly severe and urgent. "I could ignore a telegraph, but not a telephone call," he says.

He conceded that during his tenure as ambassador to India, the different time zones between New Delhi and Washington D.C. gave him more time to think about any problem before responding. However, he notes that with today's technological advances, this is no longer possible.

Galbraith would like to see a world where suffering and events like those unfolding in Bosnia, Nigeria, and Kosovo "simply do not happen." He calls for a larger global role for the United Nations and not the U.S. "Incidentally, I think we should pay our dues to the UN," he adds. He does not want to see "the U.S. doing it" but prefers to have an orderly international power doing what needs to be done. Galbraith feels that "the nature of conflict in the world today demands for an international and independent body and this is the one situation where the UN would be appropriate."

He is disturbed by the "horrors of human suffering that have gone on for so long in countries like Rwanda . . . these are things that should be the heaviest on our minds. I would like to see the intelligent and well-controlled development of poor countries."

The U.S. is definitely a developed country, and Galbraith concedes that "on the whole, the U.S. is a happy place and I want to see it continue this way." However, he would not like to prescribe the U.S. market formula to Europe.

In an interview with the *Financial Times* he had urged Europe "to reject the U.S. market formula in favour of a gentler, kinder approach."

When I asked him to elaborate upon what he meant by "a kinder, gentler approach" Galbraith said: "A rich civilised society should not accept poverty in its midst . . . there should be a safety net" that keeps citizens above the poverty level, and he added that "I would want to see in the U.S. a stronger, more deliberate welfare programme than the one we now have."

In this respect at least, he does not think that the U.S. is a good example to follow. "A rich civilised society such as the U.S. should not accept a situation where some of its citizens live in dire poverty." Galbraith wants to see in the U.S. "a stronger, more deliberate welfare programme" to help the poor.

He would also like to see a larger political process where the UN provides for sovereignty and where people can live in security with economic development being carried out by "simple, honest and effective governments."

Galbraith does not directly say it, but he appears to have a strong dislike for "market speculators." He points out that the stock market levels in the U.S. are "overwhelmingly motivated by speculative buying." Speculators generally have high expectations and always feel that the market should trend upwards. They will therefore move in and keep pushing it up further and this will continue until a new cycle begins.

The frenzy of speculators pushes the market up, and when they move out, the market promptly crashes. "We now face the danger of a stock market crash even though no one wants to talk about it," he warns.

Not hiding his dislike for speculators, he says that "When you think of financial minds, think of a vacuum." He then goes on to relate the events before the market crash of 1929, which he says was predicted by Paul Warburg, one of the founders of the Federal Reserve. When the crash then became a reality, Warburg was severely criticised.

Since Galbraith is now the Paul M. Warburg Professor of Economics, he loudly warns himself not to talk about "a market crash" for fear that it might actually come true. Among his more than 30 celebrated books is the 1955 *The Great Crash* which describes the run up to the 1929 market crash.

Galbraith, the economist, says, "My feeling is that, in the world as a whole, economic development has passed away from economics to politics and public administration."

He associates economic development with "stable, effective government" and in his view the worst case scenario would be one where "there is no stable, honest government." He adds that an "honest government is one that performs its task effectively, efficiently and does not steal."

Galbraith Fears Recession to Trample Poor

Leslie Gevirtz / 1998

14 October 1998. Copyright © Reuters
Limited 2002. Reprinted with
permission.

John Kenneth Galbraith, the "people's economist" who has advised Democratic presidents starting with Franklin Roosevelt, foresees a recession and worries "the innocent" will suffer.

Galbraith turns 90 Thursday—an event that will be celebrated at Harvard University where he has taught for half a century as well as with a new edition of *The Affluent Society*, his seminal work first published 40 years ago.

Guests for Galbraith's gala are expected to include Arthur Schlesinger, Jr., Gloria Steinem and William F. Buckley.

In the beamed-ceiling living room of his Cambridge home near Harvard Yard, the man who wrote the definitive study of the 1929 financial crash said in an interview this week: "You see a speculative bubble and there's always a recession behind it."

U.S. markets are "very vulnerable right now. Not just the stock market, but also these hedge funds and mutual funds. . . . This is invariably a cyclical tendency built into the markets, "he explained in the fading light of an October afternoon.

"After a certain period of speculative mania and a departure from reality, there's what very polite people call a correction," he said.

"I'm not averse to a correction, so long as it punishes the people most responsible for the preceding idiocy. The important thing is that the innocent people not be punished."

The Canadian-born Galbraith acted as price czar under Roosevelt in the 1930s and helped craft the New Deal, which aimed to bridge the gap between rich and poor. That gap has widened in recent years.

"Unquestionably, 50 years ago people were more generous because there were more people who were in need themselves. As people have escaped personal need, they have escaped the problems of those who are still in it," he said.

He urged that the estimated $70 billion U.S. budget surplus—the first federal surplus in almost 30 years—be used not to cut taxes or shore up Social Security, but to strengthen the "social safety net for everyone."

"I would like to be sure that everybody has a good income base. A rich country like the United States can afford to have a good safety net. . . . That means a look at unemployment compensation," he said.

The thought of retiring has not crossed his mind. His as yet untitled political memoir is due out in the spring of 1999, according to his publisher Houghton Mifflin.

Asked about his thoughts on turning 90, Galbraith picked up a thick wooden cane and as he headed out for his evening walk, replied: "Well, in the opening of my speech that I will give at the party, I do say that it's better than the alternative."

Galbraith Says Capitalism Will Prevail

Toru Kunimatsu / 1999

From the *Yomiuri Shimbun* and the *Daily Yomiuri* (Tokyo), 10 January 1999. Reprinted with permission of John Kenneth Galbraith.

In the sixth installment in a series of interviews with world leaders and prominent figures, we talk to U.S. economist John Kenneth Galbraith, renowned for his astute analysis of the capitalistic economy that he presented in such books as *The Affluent Society*, *The New Industrial State*, and *The Age of Uncertainty*.

Born in Canada in 1908, Galbraith served as U.S. ambassador to India from 1961 to 1963 during President John F. Kennedy's administration. He is a professor emeritus at Harvard University.

In an interview with *Yomiuri Shimbun* Washington correspondent Toru Kunimatsu, Galbraith gives his views on capitalism, which he says is the only viable economic system for the next century, but warns it is not perfect.

KUNIMATSU: *Capitalism is not perfect. Do we need another theory for the 21st century?*
GALBRAITH: No sensible person ever assumed that the market system was perfect. I notice, for example, the references to the market system. That is a subtle way of disguising the role of capital as a commanding force and separating the system a little bit from Marxism. That's why we now call it

the market system. It's an innocent form of disguise. But nobody should assume that it has escaped from its past faults, and the most notable one is, of course, the tendency to periods of speculation, foolish optimism, and then the correction, the recession, or the depression. This has been the ancient characteristic of capitalism, the market system, and it is still true. It is still true for Japan and no one should doubt that it could still be true of the U.S.

KUNIMATSU: *So basically, capitalism—the market mechanism—should continue and we ought to develop that basic philosophy?*
GALBRAITH: It's quite true that there's no alternative now to the market system—to capitalism. But there is a major need for recognizing the shortcomings of capitalism. One of them—which requires no explanation in Japan—is its previous position to the speculative bubble. In these last years, we have seen that speculative bubble move in a very substantial way to Wall Street. No one should assume that the American system is free from the danger of speculation.

KUNIMATSU: *The United States had something like a bubble economy in the late '80s. Are you talking about the current situation?*
GALBRAITH: I've been talking about the last couple of years. We had recognition of that in August and early September, a major flushing out of some of the more speculative funds, a notable case being Long Term Capital Management (LTCM), but also difficulties for some of the banks. While there has been some recovery since, I wouldn't say that the speculative mood here was the same in the past. I repeat again, that is a feature of capitalism. When you hear, whether in Japan or the U.S., that we have entered a new era as regards the economic system, then you should immediately take cover and be worried because that has been the statement over the last 200 years whenever there was a speculative boom.

KUNIMATSU: *So you expect speculation in the U.S. economy to continue. And then?*
GALBRAITH: And then the corrective process, that is something which, looking at Japan, has been going on these past years. The corrective

process eliminates incompetent bankers. The corrective process eliminates incompetent and reckless industrial managers. And one hopes that
the corrective process stirs new government action, including a more
effective bureaucratic establishment. All this is what my old colleague
Joseph Schumpeter called creative destruction. Looking at Japan in these
last years, my optimistic note is that I think that process has been continuing and will have an eventually useful effect on the Japanese economy.

KUNIMATSU: *Alan Greenspan tried to moderate the downslide by decreasing the interest*
rate three times in two months. Is it possible for monetary policy, or financial policy, to
stop a recession, to force a correction?

GALBRAITH: One must distinguish here carefully between truth and fashionable belief. Fashionable belief holds that the Federal Reserve system, or
any country's central bank, has some magic power and that a small adjustment in interest rates will create a splendid response. This eliminates the
whole question of other government policy, it eliminates the question of
unemployment. It puts magic in the hands of the Federal Reserve. Those
that think that my old friend Alan Greenspan, all by himself, has power to
rescue the American economy are making fools of themselves. It's the sub-
stitution of hope for reality. Nothing could be so convenient as to believe
that the Federal Reserve or the central bank in any country has all powerful influence. It's a small factor in a much larger situation.

KUNIMATSU: *Japan practiced a policy of correction in the late '80s. At that time the*
Asian way of doing business—Japanese business style—was lauded. However, the U.S.
market economy is currently the best. Do you think that the Asian way has failed and
that the U.S. market economy has prevailed?

GALBRAITH: By no means. As anyone who knows Japan will agree, there is
still basic strength in the Japanese economic and structural situation. Japan
has a literate well-educated population of people who work intelligently, a
big cadre of educated people ready for business or for the government, and
a world of practical experience. These are all the basic strengths of Japan.
And what happened was the classic repeat, the classic speculative bubble
and the need to eliminate incompetent executives from the business firms

and incompetent bankers from the banking community. That's what happens when a speculative bubble bursts. But that doesn't affect the underly-
ing strengths of the country. That is particularly true in Japan. The basic
circumstances, the basic qualifications that made Japan the second largest
economy in the world from a very small country, still exist.

KUNIMATSU: *So after the reform, after removing the incompetent managers, will Japan
grow again in the 21st century?*
GALBRAITH: I am confident about that. Because the basic strengths as I
have just emphasized are still there.

KUNIMATSU: *Is there a need to change anything? Should the basic methods remain the
same?*
GALBRAITH: There are short-run steps that one urges. I am obviously not
in favor of bailing out incompetent banks. I am not in favor of bailing out
incompetent industry. But I want to see the depositors in the banks protected. I want to see the workers in industrial firms protected. This is
important for the economy, because that is what keeps spending flowing.
And any steps that the government takes to expand demand through public projects or through public payments to the unemployed, I strongly
favor. I look with approval that that is the direction in which Japan is
moving. I have always had very, very severe doubts—not referring specifically to Japan—of the International Monetary Fund. It bails out the wrong
people and punishes the people who most need help. It calls for government restraints on welfare payments, on the payments of people who are
suffering most. I want to see recovery action going to the people who
most need help, who will most likely spend their support, and I don't want
to see it giving life, I repeat, to the people who cause the trouble.

KUNIMATSU: *Do you think the IMF should be abolished? Or reformed?*
GALBRAITH: I would reform the IMF so that when a country is in trouble—
as in the case of the Southeast Asian countries—it helps the people who
suffer, but it doesn't help the people who are responsible for the trouble,
namely the bankers and the corporate executives.

KUNIMATSU: *Any opinion on the Federal Reserve's involvement with the LTCM?*
GALBRAITH: We must always be aware in Tokyo and in New York of the danger of speaking of financial genius. A financial genius, as I have often said, is a rising market. Long Term Capital Management was sensible as long as things were normal on Wall Street. But once the correction started on the past speculation, it was heavily mortgaged and completely vulnerable and therefore a financial disaster. I don't think I would have bailed it out. I would say that anybody that is foolish on that scale, should suffer.

KUNIMATSU: *But what about the role of the Federal Reserve?*
GALBRAITH: It was the Federal Reserve that took the action to bail out LTCM. I think this was a questionable action of the Federal Reserve, that it would have been better to have accepted the lesson of that kind of financial foolishness.

KUNIMATSU: *The Japanese government is trying to infuse public funds into major banks. Is this a bailout, or a necessary step?*
GALBRAITH: I strongly endorse that. This is in accordance with what I've long been recommending. I would be repeating what I said before. Instead of putting money in the hands of the people responsible for the bubble, this puts money in the hands of the people who are giving support to aggregate demand and giving support to the economy. And that's what I want to do.

KUNIMATSU: *Since you are saying that cyclical change is inevitable, you must be skeptical of the term "new economy." Some people are saying the U.S. economy will continue to grow forever.*
GALBRAITH: This has been said of every economic boom since 1637. Anybody who hears a reference to a "new economy" should immediately take cover. You're in the company of somebody who is susceptible to speculative insanity.

KUNIMATSU: *We heard the phrase "new economy" about 20 years ago, right?*
GALBRAITH: As I said, hear the words "new economy" and take cover.

KUNIMATSU: How about the words "virtuous cycle" and the phrase, "fundamentals are good"?

GALBRAITH: In 1929, which I have studied at some length, after the stock market crash of that autumn, everyone in Washington and everyone in New York rushed to say, "the fundamentals are sound." It became a cliché. Now when you hear somebody say "the fundamentals are sound," you know that you're in the hands of somebody who doesn't know what he or she is talking about. Because it is when you have a speculative crash, when the bubble breaks, that has an adverse effect on the fundamentals immediately. And the fundamentals are affected, the first casualty of the crash.

KUNIMATSU: *The computer is supporting the U.S. economy now—the Internet— everybody is using it. I didn't see that coming six or seven years ago. How do you think the computer age will develop in the 21st century?*

GALBRAITH: I don't think we should exaggerate that. If one dropped back to my youth, one might have said the world is going to be totally changed by the automobile, which it was, but we accommodated. The world was changed by the telephone, but we accommodated. The world will be changed by computers, the Internet, but we'll accommodate. It is a person of simple mind that states that some technological change is decisive in its economic effect. The only technological change that I worry about, and this is something that will not be news in Japan, is atomic energy and the atomic bomb and nuclear destruction. I worry about that as a technological change which could have disastrous effects. But I'm not going to spend any time worrying about the economic and social effects of the computer.

KUNIMATSU: *The automobile, the telephone, the computer—if it's just a process of technology development, what will come after the computer?*

GALBRAITH: If we have peace in the world, to which I attribute great importance, we will continue to have economic well-being in the rich countries and a terrible problem of poverty in the poor countries. But we will not have any economic problem that we cannot contain. In his book, *Economics for Our Grandchildren,* John Maynard Keynes said that the economic problem, he was talking about the rich countries, would, he said, one day be solved. And economists will be considered interesting people, useful in the same way as dentists. That, I think, is a little optimistic, but I do not see for Japan, the U.S., Europe, the fortunate countries, any insuperable economic problems. I am much more concerned with political problems, keeping the peace and, of course, the terrible problems of the poor countries. I have spent a good certain part of my life in India, and I am much more concerned with the poverty there than I am with the problems of economics in the U.S., although we still have a very serious poverty problem in our great cities.

KUNIMATSU: *Why can't we solve the problem of poverty? The World Bank and developed countries have spent a lot of money.*
GALBRAITH: I have long been an advocate, and I have recently been writing again about the obvious solution. The fact of poverty is the absence of money, and I would provide a certain amount of money to every family to bring every family to a minimum level of well-being. As a rich country, that is something we can afford, something Japan can afford. This, I believe, is going to be the most essential step to be taken in the next century. The guarantee of minimum living standards for the countries that can afford it and a guarantee of help to the poor countries that cannot afford it.

KUNIMATSU: *How? Through official development assistance? The World Bank? NGOs?*
GALBRAITH: I would keep the World Bank in on this, but this is going to take many steps beyond anything we have done now. We must recognize that human beings are human beings and suffer disease and hunger whether they're in Africa or in Japan or in the U.S.

KUNIMATSU: *Will poverty be one of the major problems in the 21st century?*
GALBRAITH: I'm very much afraid so. It has a stubborn quality about it that causes poverty to continue, even in a rich city like New York.

KUNIMATSU: *In some of your books you've written about the environment.*
GALBRAITH: I am much more concerned about the environment because that has a sweeping effect that nobody can control. So when it comes to

global warming or atmospheric pollution or the loss of scenic quality, I do worry. I was first in Japan in 1945 and traveled over some part of Japan at that time, and it was a beautiful rural country. A great spread of grassland, rice, rural beauty. In modern times, I have gone to Japan, traveled between Tokyo and other cities, and it is much less beautiful than it was 50 years ago. And I regret that. The last time I went to Japan, I made a trip to the other side of the country, which is still rural, and it was a great relief to get away from the ugly pressures of suburban and urban environmental effect.

KUNIMATSU: *Facing the Sea of Japan?*
GALBRAITH: Yes, much more beautiful. And I am strongly in favor of preserving the countryside, preventing commercial advertising, commercial activity, keeping the countryside as it should be.

KUNIMATSU: *Yes, we have sacrificed some of our environment.*
GALBRAITH: No question about it, Japan is not nearly as beautiful a country as it was 50 years ago.

KUNIMATSU: *Do you think it's possible to have economic growth, especially in developing countries such as China and Southeast Asian countries, while at the same time preserving the environment and preventing pollution?*
GALBRAITH: Oh, sure. There's already indication that that's possible. I had part of my education in England, and my family came ultimately from Scotland, and these are countries—this is a part of the world—where the environmental beauty has been preserved. It has taken rigorous zoning, rigorous protection, but on the whole, the British have done it. It shows it can be done.

KUNIMATSU: *But in some respects, England has had prolonged gradual growth, whereas Southeast Asian countries have experienced rapid growth in which protecting the environment comes at a great cost to economic development.*
GALBRAITH: Absolutely, and I am prepared to pay that cost. I hope Japan will too.

KUNIMATSU: *How will poorer countries bear the cost?*
GALBRAITH: The techniques are well established. Zoning, control of land use, prevention of advertising and billboards, all that is possible.... I served on a commission in the state of Vermont which abolished all roadside advertising and I consider it one of the most important things with which I was ever involved. It hurts my feelings to go to Japan now and see that beautiful country given over to mindless urbanization. We should pay the cost.

KUNIMATSU: *Karl Marx wanted an equal society and you have suggested a progressive tax system. Some Scandinavian countries tried to be welfare societies, but haven't managed it 100 percent. What's the solution?*
GALBRAITH: I would not agree with that, I have been closely in touch with the Scandinavian countries all my life. I had part of my education in Sweden, I have been close to the Swedish economists, and the Scandinavian countries including Finland are to this day, the most successful example showing that an intelligent and civilized solution is possible. I regard that as one of the optimistic aspects of the current situation. So I wouldn't dismiss that part of the world as a failure. I consider it to be a major success.

KUNIMATSU: *So you suggest the United States and Japan should do the same?*
GALBRAITH: Absolutely. When I talk about a basic income for everybody, I'm talking about the Scandinavian model. When I talk about a larger, better role for our public services, our schools, our environment, I'm to some extent talking about the Scandinavian model.

KUNIMATSU: *Is that the model economy for the 21st century?*
GALBRAITH: I wouldn't reduce it to figures. This is a social and not a statistical problem.

The Origins of the Galbraithian System: Stephen P. Dunn in Conversation with J. K. Galbraith

Stephen P. Dunn / 2001

A large part of J. K. Galbraith's professional career has been devoted to examining modern industrial society and the large firms that dominate it. Nevertheless, the distinctiveness of his contribution appears to be slipping from view. Although theorists like Coase (1937), Penrose (1959), Richardson (1960, 1972), Williamson (1971, 1975, 1985), and Hymer (1970, 1976) have seen an explosion of interest in their particular contributions to the theory of the firm, Galbraith's contribution is largely ignored.[1] Similarly, the origins of Galbraith's contribution to the theory of the firm and nexus to Post Keynesianism have been largely unexplored. On June 22, 2001, I talked at length with Professor J. K. Galbraith and his wife, Kitty—who has been a constant companion and co-organizer throughout his career—about his intellectual history, the origins of his contribution to the theory of the firm, and his relationships and experiences with both the two Cambridges and Post Keynesianism. However, in order to provide a backdrop to the discussion it is worth briefly recalling Galbraith's overlooked contribution.

Galbraith's (1967) thesis is that the centrality and impact of advanced technology calls for organization. Modern technology inevitably necessitates detailed specialized knowledge, effective group decision-making, and the need for large capital commitments to be conducted and coordinated in terms of money-denominated contracts for long periods of time. Planning enables the mitigation of the impact of unforeseen events and the successful organization of production. Planning is an inescapable consequence of advanced technology and the extended, highly specialized, division of labor that is called forth to manage it.

Galbraith contends that modern technology requires extensive planning because such large investments of time, money, specialized knowledge, and organization cannot be left to whim, chance, and the vagaries of the market.[2] The costs of failure are great and must be avoided. Modern technology requires highly specialized investment in capital and labor over a long period of time. Moreover, it is the strategic decision-makers, which Galbraith locates within the technostructure, that are involved and responsible for such investments and are of necessity highly committed to ensuring its success.

The view of the firm that emerges from Galbraith accords with the Post Keynesian view of the business enterprise and is one of a strategic planning organization that coordinates production and shelters it from the inherent uncertainties that are endemic to the market. Planning, in the Galbraithian system, which embodies both conscious decision and human agency, represents an important means of allocating resources that replaces the market. Planning, unlike in the more orthodox conceptualizations of the firm, entails not just coordination, it is also about preparing for, and attempting to control, unforeseen events.[3]

Planning and the organization of production are linked in essence due to the unreliable nature of the market system and the complex, uncertain nature of modern technology. If the uncertainties that surround large commitments of time and money are to be mitigated, then the firm must either supersede the market or subordinate it to the requirements of planning. In the Galbraithian view, the firm emerges in response to the increasingly treacherous and uncertain nature of markets. Rather than viewing the firm as resulting from a purely *instrumental* choice of economizing on transaction costs between alternative modes of contracting, the corporation is a strategic "institution" for coping with, or getting rid of, market uncertainties. Moreover, the size of the modern corporation impinges on the ability of the technostructure to engage in more effective planning and to cope with, and mitigate, uncertainty. The larger the firm is the more likely it will be able to mold the future and absorb unanticipated events. This, according to Galbraith, is a primary reason for the observed growth of the large firm and its nexus to the political apparatus—to emancipate it from the uncertainties of the market.

Moreover, whereas Galbraith recognizes that vertical integration offers the prospect of controlling the price and supply of strategic factors under condition of uncertainty, he also recognizes the role of long-term, money-denominated contracts. The firm can enter into large, long-term contracts as a strategic response to uncertainty. Contracts and their enforceability are a major source of stability and security for the modern corporation. Money-denominated contracts occupy a pivotal role in protecting the prices and costs and safeguarding the sales and supplies at these prices and costs. Galbraith argues that as production takes *time and planning*, money-denominated contracts represent the means by which uncertainties about the future may be mitigated. A large and extensive web of money-denominated contracts cascaded downward, greatly facilitating the future planning and stability necessitated by advanced technology.

Overall, Galbraith advances a view of the business enterprise that is utterly Post-Keynesian–Institutionalist and links technology, capital, money contracts, power, and planning to the concern of uncertainty. Galbraith's corporation represents an *enduring* institutional response to an uncertain future specifically designed to mitigate its impact. Nevertheless, the origins of the distinctive view of the modern corporation have not been widely considered. With this in mind I ventured to Harvard to discuss such matters with Professor Galbraith.

DR. DUNN: *How would you describe the Galbraithian system and where do you see its origins? Would it be correct to view it as a reconstruction of economics after the dissolution of the Marshallian system, ushered in by Sraffa (1926), Chamberlin (1933), and Robinson (1933) and their recognition of the rise of the modern, large corporation? Or would it be more appropriate to view it as part of the old Institutionalist literature and embedded very much in Veblen's (1904)* Theory of the Business Enterprise?

PROFESSOR GALBRAITH: One of the things about your question that interests me is that I never thought there was a Galbraith system. And in some ways it is a rather new question to me because what I've done all my life is start from the usual starting point, which was a thorough and complete grounding in Alfred Marshall. The first, main course I had in economics was at Berkeley; that was after I left Canada where the economics instruction was very poor. E. T. Grether was the dominant economics teacher (not the dominant figure, but the dominant teacher at Berkeley) and I spent the better part of a year going chapter-by-chapter through Alfred Marshall. There are others too who had a strong influence on me, including Thorstein Veblen, but what I did for years to come was to start with Marshall, see the world as it is, and make the requisite modifications until there wasn't much of Marshall left, mostly modifications. But that was the process, and the modifications I made were piece-by-piece, chapter-by-chapter, corporation-by-corporation, if you will, always from that base until the base disappeared.[4]

My thinking was all in modifications. First of all, Keynes, the overwhelming impact of Keynes. I spent one year in Cambridge from 1937 to 1938, and that was the most intense economic instruction I ever had. You talked about economics, and particularly about Keynes, all day and all night. There was the inevitable conflict between Keynes and Dennis Robertson and the ultimate Keynesians, Richard Kahn and Joan Robinson. Sraffa, who you mentioned, wasn't nearly so important. Sraffa was so hard to understand that people thought Pierro had depths of knowledge that they never quite got; and there was that incredible preoccupation of his with Ricardo, which lasted year after year, almost decade after decade. But the effect of both Joan and Kahn and Denis Robertson as a counter-figure was just enormous. I suppose we talked about that everyday, and that meant that I came back to Harvard with all the distinction of having been at the center of the Keynesian discussion, even though during that year I never met Keynes; that was the year he had his first heart attack.

So rather than a system, I've never thought of that, I've always thought of the process by which I learn myself and the conclusions I came to. There are a certain number of people who associate themselves with my ideas, but that isn't a large group. People got particular ideas that I urge rather than any comprehensive system. That would be my judgment at least. I've never heard anybody describe himself as a Galbraithian.

DR. DUNN: *How did your visit to Cambridge influence your economics and the development of the Galbraithian system?*
PROFESSOR GALBRAITH: Kitty was with me in 1937 on our great introduction to Keynesian economics.
KITTY: It was pretty awful because, before we got to Cambridge, England, I had never heard of John Maynard Keynes, and *The General Theory* had just been published, and all I met were his economist friends. So you know I was quite quiet and so I decided one day after we were talking about *The General Theory*, given I was supposed to be fairly intelligent, to pick it up. I started with the introduction, but early on in the book he explains that he hasn't quite thought through all his ideas. So I thought, I'll wait until he writes his next book and that's where my economics rested. There was a lecture "Is There a Rate of Interest?" and I thought that if these people don't know there is a rate of interest, why do they talk about it? And 40 years later that same lecture was on the bulletin board in Cambridge because in a lecture someone asked a lecturer, "Is there a rate of interest?"
PROFESSOR GALBRAITH: I went down to LSE [London School of Economics] every few weeks to go to Hayek's seminar, which was one of the great

centers of discussion at that time. Hayek would come in very tidy and well mannered, sit down at a small desk, and there would be 30 or 40 economists there, all of whom disagreed with him. And there was one great day when he came in and said, "Now, as I indicated last time, we will today discuss the rate of interest," and Nicky Kaldor said, "Professor Hayek, there's no such thing," and that was the last word Hayek got in that day as everybody turned to find out from Nicky why there could be no rate of interest.

I knew Hayek well and saw a lot of him over the years. I sent my son to visit him in Austria once, and shared with him a memorable day in Kirkcaldy recalling Adam Smith.[5] As an aside, I always thought Adam Smith's *Wealth of Nations* was one of the most wonderful books of all time. I was giving a lecture three or four years ago in Pennsylvania and tried an experiment to see how a crowd would accept a quotation from Adam Smith: "The Quakers of Pennsylvania have recently freed their Negro slaves by which we may judge the slaves were not numerous." But it didn't go over at all well. The Quaker faith is still too strong for a joke like that.

DR. DUNN: *Can you describe your process of "conversion" from orthodoxy and to what extent have Veblen, Commons, Mitchell, and Myrdal, the Berkeley Institutionalists, and the Cambridge Keynesians influenced you? What works of theirs had the most influence on you? And who else influenced your intellectual development?*
PROFESSOR GALBRAITH: There are three other influences that were extremely important in my life other than that year in Cambridge. There was first a major job I did in the White House in the late 1930s. The economic policies, the Keynesian policies, of the New Deal. I think, remembering the controversy, that I was the first to admit that these were Keynesian, and a major piece of work came out of that on the Keynesian programs, the PWA—the Public Works Administration—and the WPA—the Work Progress Administration. PWA had as its objective what you got built at the end—the Triboro Bridge or something of that sort. The WPA had its focus purely on the number of jobs that it created. This was a source of great conflict in Washington. And I presided over the study of those

two programs under the auspices of the National Planning Association, and that major study came out just as the war started and got almost no attention because national attention and economic attention had all passed to the problems of the war. And that was the second thing that was very influential in my life because, at a relatively early age, I had what probably could have been the most important of all wartime jobs in economics—I was the price czar. I was second in the order of command to Leon Henderson, but I had an enormous delegation. I started with a staff of seven and ended with thousands.[6] You could lower a price without my permission but you couldn't raise one. General maximum price regulation covered all prices and this had another effect; it was an intimate introduction to the corporate structure of the United States and the discovery, still not fully appreciated, of the extent to which the corporate structure is not capitalist, it is experienced bureaucratic power and intelligence. That's why the word capitalism has to some extent disappeared. It evokes Carnegie, it evokes Rockefeller, it evokes the other wicked capitalists of the past that have been buried, and now the innocent reference is to the market system. That is bland and doesn't specify anything as evil as the old capitalist, and it shouldn't probably because the old-fashioned capitalists couldn't possibly run a modern corporation. That takes a huge bureaucracy and a lot of experience and survival with that. And this was an idea that started to become evident to me when I was running price control. Every afternoon I met with some complaining group of businessmen; business leaders who, making more money than they'd ever made before, were pleading their poverty. It was an introduction to the business community such as very few economists have ever had and that was part of the structure of ideas that became part of my thinking at a relatively early stage.

Then in later years I was editor of *Fortune* magazine. In those days, the subject matter of *Fortune* was the anatomy of the big corporations, and that was a marvelous introduction to the corporate mind such as it is. Not marvelous, but privileged. It reflected a continuing curiosity about the economic process related to that fact that I never had a degree in economics, only in agricultural economics. But that is a detail. I was, at Berkeley, subject to a good economics department at that time and, as I say, the early influence of Keynes before *The General Theory* and the other economists of the time; I've mentioned Marshall, and Veblen. Veblen was the most exciting figure at that time, but he had nothing to do with agricultural economics!

DR. DUNN: *In one sense, I find that quite surprising, as it only seems that somewhat later that the Veblenian influence becomes more prominent in your writing.*
PROFESSOR GALBRAITH: This was a process I began with Marshall. Further discussion and further writing elaborated and modified, and one of the modifying influences was Veblen. And the great modifying influence was of course John Maynard Keynes. Kyle Bruce, from Queensland, Australia, is publishing a book next year on an episode in the 1930s.[7] One of the most distinguished businessmen in the United States was Henry Dennison, the manufacturer of paper products. He invited me to join him for a book and I did, coming out at that time still with the basic Marshallian-Taussig view of the world. He was of the impression that a main line of attack in the great depression (he was very close to FDR) should be through taxation, the remitting of taxation, adding to purchasing power. And I talked him out of that to the argument that the depression was caused by the prevalence of monopoly power and the restrictions on output that that imposed. I persuaded him and when I had finished the persuasion that year *The General Theory* came out and I read that and discovered that Dennison was right and I was wrong so I took steps immediately to halt the book, but it was already in print, *Modern Competition and Business Policy*, and I, with some thought, dropped that out of my list of books.[8]

DR. DUNN: *Both Dr. Bruce (2001, p. 26) and I concur in our view that you have long mused on the role and salience of the firm and the large corporation in advanced industrialized economies.*
PROFESSOR GALBRAITH: I would argue, but I could be wrong, against the influence of the theory of the firm on my thinking, but I never had any doubt on its salience, and this is something that one should cite today as a major shortcoming of economic instruction: the concentration on market behavior which still continues and the neglect of the influence of the firm.

The United States economy has been dominated, not unsuccessfully in these last years, by the great corporations. If you want to find out what is happening in the country you must look into the decision-making process of the great corporations and how united together they can bring influence to bear on government and the extent to which somebody like George Bush is their unknowing captive. Not knowing any of this George Bush is in some ways their ideal instrument.

DR. DUNN: *Your son, Jamie, wrote a provocative and distinctly Galbraithian newspaper article on how the election of President Bush epitomized* The New Industrial State, *with the Supreme Court as the perfidious expression of the corporate structure.*[9]
PROFESSOR GALBRAITH: Jamie wrote in a small Texas publication, called the *Texas Observer*, a few days after the election, and it was picked up by Internet and attributed to me. I had a lot of correspondence on it, which I had to ship off to my son. Jamie once made a birthday speech here at Harvard in which he said it was his ambition in life, hope in life, that I would be seen to have the same stature as John Neville Keynes and he would then be John Maynard.[10] I recall he also mentioned the Mill father and son; he hoped I would be remembered as James Mill. There's no question about that, he's a very good economist.

DR. DUNN: *You write in* A Life in Our Times *that "an enduring reward from my year at Cambridge [1937–1938] was friendship with Michal Kalecki ... the most innovative figure in economics I have known, not excluding Keynes" (1981, p. 75). How did Kalecki influence the evolution of your thought?*
PROFESSOR GALBRAITH: Well, Kalecki, of course, was a socialist, verging on communism, and he was very important to all of us as a continuing critic of the accepted economics. That interposed a much larger role for collective action and the state. It was an escape from the closed apparatus even of Keynesian economics. In Kalecki's thinking, social action intervened much more strongly than it did in Keynes's system, and so likewise in his conversation, likewise in his writing. I was impressed by that in Cambridge, and years later, just before I published *The Affluent Society*, I made a visit to

Poland and Yugoslavia and spent a lot of time there with Kalecki, who was out of favor. He lived out of favor wherever he was.

DR. DUNN: *Did Kalecki influence your bimodal view (Galbraith, 1977) of the economy?*
PROFESSOR GALBRAITH: I don't think so. I think that was from my own observations, but I'm not sure. As a footnote, when he died he was out of favor in Poland; he lived out of favor with the established view. I wrote a letter to his wife on these matters and she was so grateful; I have somewhere in my files the letter she sent back. So grateful that someone was supporting Kalecki and his somewhat inconvenient behavior. He had gone back to Poland in the hope of a system of economic thought influencing policy, which would be more than he encountered in Britain or the United States, only to discover there was another one that was equally rigorous.

DR. DUNN: *One of the salient contributions you identify with Kalecki was his discussion of the nexus between affluence and attitudes to risk (Galbraith, 1981, p. 75). Did Kalecki's principle of increasing risk influence your discussion of the modern corporation and its nexus to uncertainty?*
PROFESSOR GALBRAITH: I suppose so, but it's not a connection that I ever made anything from. I've never been sure where ideas came from and that might well have come from Kalecki, but I couldn't say yes or no.

DR. DUNN: *What was your relationship with Nicholas Kaldor and his influence on your thinking?*
PROFESSOR GALBRAITH: I wrote one part of *The Affluent Society* in Nicky's house in Cambridge, in his library. But I would have to say generally, that through much of my life, I have had debt to an enormous number of contemporaries; Nicky was one, Tommy Balogh was one, Paul Samuelson here was one, various others here, but I have never, perhaps this is a very defective behavior, spent a great deal of time identifying those who contributed to my thought. They all did. I have a debt to them all. What I have written has been in some considerable measure the product of my life and association, but I've never mapped it out in detail. I'm sure that

any one of my friends reading this would conclude that he had some sort of contribution, and he would be quite right.

DR. DUNN: *In many respects, the Galbraithian system and view of the large corporation has several similarities with that of Joseph Schumpeter. What was the influence of Schumpeter on your own intellectual development, and how do you think his vision compares with your own?*

PROFESSOR GALBRAITH: The difference was that I tried to struggle with the reality, however dull, and Schumpeter sought the spectacular, however irrelevant. I learned a lot from Schumpeter, he was a force on all my generation, but he wasn't in any sense a guide to policy. My generation studied economics with a view ultimately to change the economic world, economic policy in Washington, or overwhelmingly, the move to Keynesian macroeconomic policy. Schumpeter had no such interest. He had presided in Austria over an inflation and that was enough public life for him. He was a very popular figure here, we all loved Schumpy. He met at a local teahouse every afternoon with a group of students, anybody who wanted to come, and it was a wonderful session, but it was theatrical rather than real.

DR. DUNN: *Schumpeter's vision is dominated by large oligopolistic innovating firms that make substantial investments over long periods of time under conditions of uncertainty. This appears to accord well with elements of the vision laid out in* The New Industrial State.

PROFESSOR GALBRAITH: He stood above all this. He would not discuss price theory and policy at all. I don't think he ever made anything, so to speak, of imperfect competition, or what was here called monopolistic competition following Chamberlin (1933). On something like creative destruction, he could be quite eloquent. He was a man of driving ideas, rather than of great systems.

DR. DUNN: *In Richard Swedberg's (1991) biography of Schumpeter, he is portrayed as very much an outsider at Harvard, especially in the later years. Was that true?*

PROFESSOR GALBRAITH: Well, everybody tried to be an outsider. He was here during the New Deal years and he wasn't part of the New Deal discussion, the people that went to Washington once a week for some role there, he never dreamed of that, but he was, I would say, the supreme insider. He loved the academic community. He loved the discussions. He loved the audience to which he returned. The audience sought him out. He wasn't an outsider in any sense. There was a dinner in those days, of some of the senior faculty, once every fortnight. This was a special dinner in Boston to which people went overwhelmingly to hear Schumpeter talk. Seymour Harris would come back from those dinners to tell me what particularly fantastic topic had been under discussion the night before.

DR. DUNN: *Did the Oxford challenge to marginalism reach the United States, and what was its reception? Did it have any impact at Harvard in the 1940s, or at the Office of Price Administration?*
PROFESSOR GALBRAITH: I don't think so, it didn't have any particular influence on me certainly.

DR. DUNN: *Where do you see the origins of* The New Industrial State?
PROFESSOR GALBRAITH: That was quite clear. When I finished *The Affluent Society*, and it had gone to press and been a major big-seller, I was faced with the extremely inconvenient thought that I had published the wrong book, or published only half the book. And the half I hadn't published had to do with the structural behavior of the corporation and including the great corporation as distinct from its purely monopolistic ambitions, which was not something that I emphasized before, and this also included the invasion into the modern corporation structure of science and technology, the technostructure. And so I set about writing that book to correct what I saw as a major gap in *The Affluent Society*. I had completed a first draft and then the opportunity, the rather agreeable opportunity, of going to India came along, and so I put it away in a safe-deposit box for two-and-a-half years. I came back and then finished it. As I worked on it I became more and more involved with the structure of the corporation and the technostructure and its aspirations, and that of course became the book.

DR. DUNN: *Does the first draft of the manuscript still survive?*

PROFESSOR GALBRAITH: I doubt it. If it does, it's over at the Kennedy Library, but I wouldn't place any emphasis on it. The first draft is the first flow of ideas and thought, and it can be extremely imperfect.

DR. DUNN: *Would you agree with the assessment of your son, Jamie (Galbraith, 1984), who has suggested that the origins of* The New Industrial State *are to be found in the German historical school and organizational theory rather than more ortho-dox managerial theorists of the firm?*[11]
PROFESSOR GALBRAITH: No, I wouldn't. I was certainly influenced all my life by German thought from Marx over and on, but the major mental incentive on *The New Industrial State* was the actual study of American cor-porations and their behaviors, including my years at *Fortune* magazine. It was one of the rewards of my time at *Fortune* to discover how important were the objectives of the management of the firm, how complex the bureaucracy, and the enormous role of an increasingly deep technology and scientific base and how important that was. Indeed, you saw in the case of something like the steel industry, the hopeless inadequacy of a corporate management that had no understanding of these matters and didn't even know they existed in some cases.

DR. DUNN: *Uncertainty occupies the pivotal role in* The New Industrial State *and underscores the need for the great corporations to plan. How did that arise and come into view?*
PROFESSOR GALBRAITH: I didn't regard that as anything particularly novel. I think that dealing with economic institutions one must always assume uncertainty because there are enough factors that may, by their change or by their interplay, be unpredictable, and I just took that for granted. I simply assumed uncertainty in all major decision-making and just let it go at that.

DR. DUNN: *Were you influenced at all by Keynes's or Shackle's view of uncertainty?*
PROFESSOR GALBRAITH: Oh, Keynes I might have been, but again I get back to the problem that I'm never quite sure where my ideas came from. But Shackle certainly wasn't a major factor in my life.

DR. DUNN: *Why did you not return to* The New Industrial State *and undertake further work on it?*
PROFESSOR GALBRAITH: No question about that. I put everything I write, as I've often said, through four or five revisions, adding the note of spontaneity only in the fifth revision, and by that time boredom has set in, to the point that I don't go back to the topic—I just can't. Not long after I finished *The New Industrial State* I was invited by Rab Butler to spend another year in Cambridge.[12] There I was scheduled to give a term lecture on *The New Industrial State* in the huge new lecture hall where my most important recollection is of Joan sitting in the front seat. Lecturing on that book was so boring that through the year I wrote another book called *Economics and the Public Purpose,* which by and large was something of a major mistake because it retraced ground that I had already covered in substantial parts. It reflected only the escape from the boredom of lecturing on *The New Industrial State,* which was, I thought, an important book, possibly my most important. It has a certain distinction now as one of the first works in economics to deal with the uncertainties of technology although I never had the expectation of technology being the whole basis of entrepreneurship and its disastrous effect.

As an aside, my most precious recollection of Joan was going back to Cambridge at the end of the war in the late 1940s or 1950s. I met Joan and we went across the river and sat down for lunch and I opened the conversation by saying, "Joan, I've been out of touch due to the war, I've been out of touch with my colleagues in this profession. Who are the good people of the new generation?" And Joan's answer was, "Ken, we were the last good generation." She was very firm on that point.

DR. DUNN: *You were one of the first Keynesians to be aware of the potentially inflationary consequence of the Keynesian system and to advocate a variety of incomes policies. Why do you think other Keynesians failed to recognize this?*
PROFESSOR GALBRAITH: To begin with, I'm not sure of the point. I think there was a quite general recognition as time passed, in the later years of the New Deal, and under Kennedy for example. But I suppose, looking

back on it, I was somewhat influenced by the enormous concern for inflation in World War II and my responsibilities there went very deep into
my thinking and so I was more alert to the problem of inflation than not
most, but many of my colleagues. I'd spent the most intense years of my
life dealing with inflation.

DR. DUNN: *You say in your memoirs (Galbraith, 1981, pp. 170–71) that throughout
your time at the Office of Price Administration you managed to keep inflation below
2 percent, which was quite an achievement at that time, and subsequently, inflation started
to increase when the OPA was dismantled.*
PROFESSOR GALBRAITH: Broadly speaking, there is no memory of inflation
in World War II. There was a strong memory of it in the United States in
World War I when prices doubled in a matter of two years. When World
War II came there was a strong feeling of the danger of inflation and one
of the first appointments to the first organizations to deal with the problems of World War II was that dealing with prices, Leon Henderson. It
was that tension, that concern, that policy was motivated by in those
days. With a strong macroeconomic policy under Morganthau and Harry
Dexter White and a strong, very strong, microeconomic policy effectively
under me. The tendency, for two or three years during the war, was for
me to blame any price increase on the macroeconomic policy, and for
them to blame any increase on Galbraith. This was a convenient escape,
but in fact there is no memory of inflation now in World War II. That
problem was solved. It was solved by a strong microeconomic policy, the
general maximum price regulation in the spring of 1942, and by a strong
tax policy, and to some extent also by a public attitude, which restrained
price increases even if they might be possible—you didn't want to be a
war profiteer!

DR. DUNN: *Many economists preserve their ideas via their students—indeed the
Cambridge "circus" that surrounded the development of Keynes's General Theory served
to defend Keynes's ideas from the subsequent orthodox bastardization. Has one of the
unintended consequences of your political activities been that you have been unable to*

devote enough time to teaching and doctoral supervision and create an intellectual vanguard for the Galbraithian system?
PROFESSOR GALBRAITH: Well, one has to make choices in life. I devoted a lot of time to my lectures, which tended to be also what I was writing about. They were, I think, safe to say, rather well attended. I did not spend a great deal of my time tutoring disciples. I saw a lot of them, but I never saw my main function as having a cadre of students taking my ideas to Washington. That was not a clear decision, it was the way things work out.

DR. DUNN: *Would that be a regret?*
PROFESSOR GALBRAITH: One has to make choices. I couldn't have written *The Affluent Society* if I spent ten hours a day teaching, tutoring, and cultivating.

DR. DUNN: *Do you think that the fact that you have not explicitly associated yourself with a school of thought has damaged your intellectual legacy?*
PROFESSOR GALBRAITH: Well, there is a problem of having a legacy, having a Galbraithian view—which is a word that I've taken over from you—if that view changes as the world changes and as your thinking changes. Anybody who wanted to be a student of my views would have had the problem that my views change, as I think an economist must. Most economists having got to a system, got to an idea, stick with it for much of their life—"If you're going to have a view, you'd better keep it even if circumstances change or your view changes." And my basic belief is that I always had to be ready to accommodate myself to two things: the changing of past error, and the appreciation of new events and new knowledge.

DR. DUNN: *I would argue that this implies a pragmatic historical approach and as such, you could say that the Galbraithian system was very much an appreciation of the evolving processes of capitalism over the twentieth century that would constitute a foundation for building new insights over time and adding to it and subtracting from it in the face of new circumstance, novelty, and emerging process.*
PROFESSOR GALBRAITH: I agree with that—if I understand it. It's my view that the only valid economics is a dynamic economics because one lives in a world where two things are urgent, one is change and one is the correction of past misapprehension. A good example of this is the two people that

were associated with the monopolistic flaws in the market. Joan Robinson wrote *Economics of Imperfect Competition* (1933) and then went on to problems of economic development, problems of the labor left in Britain, a whole range of questions, and maintained her role as one of the distinguished figures in the economic profession. My colleague, Ed Chamberlin—a very good man—wrote his book on *Monopolistic Competition* (1933), which appeared almost the same day as Joan's and stayed with that for the rest of his life. Joan remained at the center of the profession, Ed went gradually to one side. And eventually a very unhappy man came to realize this in the later years of his life.

DR. DUNN: *I think it relates to the style of your generation. Geoff Harcourt recalls that a characteristic of people like Nicky Kaldor, Joan Robinson, and yourself, was the agility of mind to turn it to a host of new interesting problems and sit down, not with the literature, but a pen and one's ideas.*
PROFESSOR GALBRAITH: Sit down with the pen and the problem. That would be Nicky's approach. Not sit down with a camera. Do you remember that, Kitty? We were in India together. Nicky went out to get a pictorial record of the whole Indian society, and after he came back I was talking to his daughter. I said, "How did Nicky's pictures go?" And she said, "Not good." And I said, "Why not?" "Well," she said, "There was one problem. He could never remember to take the cover off the lens."
One terrific night Nicky had something that we all yearned to have. This was in Calcutta at the headquarters of the Institute. We had a big farewell dinner because he had a passport and visa for China along with his wife, and we all celebrated their departure, told of our own sorrow that he had got a visa and we hadn't, or had no hope of it evidently. But around midnight they came back, they'd forgotten their passports. They didn't get to China, they had to show their passports to get out of India and discovered they didn't have them. They got in the next day or so later.

DR. DUNN: *When did you first meet Paul Davidson and get involved in the founding of the* Journal of Post Keynesian Economics? *What influence did he have on the evolution of your thought?*

PROFESSOR GALBRAITH: Paul Davidson and his wife, Louise, were formerly in New Jersey and moved out to Knoxville with the journal. He was at Rutgers for many years and there were no known economists at that time in Tennessee, so he was brought out to teach there. And that brought the journal to Knoxville. Professor Davidson is a long-standing friend of mine, and we certainly had long discussions, but that's always been a problem in my life. I have discussions, I come away with some new thought, which I should possibly attribute to the discussion, but it disappears in my memory. Nevertheless, Paul's a very important figure in the history of economics, no question about that. The *Journal of Post Keynesian Economics* is very well edited and very perceptive in its choice of articles and gets away from extreme mathematics, which is very good from my point of view because that's my singular weakness. Moreover, mathematics, with respect to the theory of the firm, excludes that as a subject to some extent because for the great structure of economics the firm becomes a dot on the chart and the separate influence of the structure of the firm and the ambitions within the firm and the bureaucratic apparatus has been very largely excluded from professional economic thought. Here at Harvard it is the main subject of the business school across the river, but it isn't here.

DR. DUNN: *In a recent article in the* Journal of Post Keynesian Economics *(Dunn, 2000a), I argued that part of the future of Post Keynesian economics may lie in business schools and schools of public policy, which is not to denigrate Post Keynesian economics, but to suggest that some of the more salient and insightful contributions to economics that engage the real world are occurring there and that Post Keynesians may find a more receptive audience for some of their ideas in such Schools.*
PROFESSOR GALBRAITH: I agree with that completely. I would only add more emphasis on bureaucratic skills, and give a large place to the particular form of political expression that is sought, which, among other things, includes a large political support for the revenues of the business structure. We are seeing this in very visible form in the Bush administration but all of the things of influence in the American economy in these last

months, in these last years, have been outside of the range of mathematical or technical economics. As I say, they come down to a single figure on
the chart, or a single item, a single letter in the equation.

DR. DUNN: *Thank you very much.*
PROFESSOR GALBRAITH: Very good. This is very nice, I enjoyed that.

Notes

The author is a policy adviser in the Strategy Unit, Department of Health, Whitehall, an economic adviser in Her Majesty's Treasury, Whitehall, and a senior research fellow at Staffordshire
University. He thanks Charley Clark, Geoff Harcourt, Geoff Hodgson, John King, Fred Lee,
Stephen Nash, Klaus Nielson, Malcolm Sawyer, and Nick York for their preparatory discussions
and reflections of the economic contributions of J. K. Galbraith. The kind support of the
Cambridge Political Economy Society Trust and the Royal Economic Society that facilitated
this research is also acknowledged.

1. In a recent series of articles I have drawn attention to Galbraith's contribution in beginning to
explore a conceptualization of the theory of the firm that embeds uncertainty into microeconomic thinking and is distinctly Post Keynesian–Institutionalist in its flavor (see Dunn, 2000b,
2001a, 2001b, 2002a, 2002b).
2. As argued in Dunn (2001b), Galbraith's discussion of the relationship between technology and
organization clearly predates and has many parallels with Williamson's (1975, 1985) recognition
of the importance of asset specificity in the study of organizations. According to Williamson,
asset specificity is critical in that once an investment has been undertaken the buyer and seller
become locked in a transaction for a considerable period thereafter referred to as ex post bilateral
dependence. Conversely, Galbraith's argument is that the imperatives of modern technology and
the associated commitments of time, capital, and specialized labor in an uncertain environment
entail that planning supersedes the market. "Planning exists because this (market) process has
ceased to be reliable ... (the firm) must replace the market with planning" (Galbraith, 1967, p. 41).
Galbraith moves beyond the limiting view of "in the beginning there were markets," toward a
view that "in the beginning there was an absence of a need for extensive planning as technology
was not that sophisticated!"
3. Indeed, as I have argued elsewhere (Dunn, 2000b, 2001a, 2001b, 2001c), although some theorists
of the firm invoke the rhetoric of (fundamental) uncertainty, they typically do not explicitly define
what they mean by such terms such that their substantive discussion implies the reverse or they end
up conflating it with the concepts of opportunism and bounded rationality.
4. Galbraith (1981, pp. 28–29) has remarked, "The Marshallian world is a tidy thing without
unemployment, inflation or depression or anyhow not much. Not surprisingly, many who studied
Marshall found it pleasant to live in his world forever."
5. See Galbraith (1974) on "Scotland's Greatest Son."
6. As Galbraith has remarked elsewhere, "Later the Office of Price Administration would employ
64,000 across the country, along with numerous volunteer workers. However, most of those would

administer rationing and rent control. The prices staff nationwide was much smaller—about 4,300" (1981, pp. 125–26).

7. See Galbraith (1981, pp. 57–70). Bruce (2000, 2001) further elaborates on the intellectual impact of Henry Dennison on J. K. Galbraith's theorizing. Bruce draws our attention to two monographs written with Dennison (one as a ghostwriter), both of which examine the role and relevance of big business for practical policy (see Dennison and Galbraith, 1938; Dennison et al., 1938).

8. Historians of Post Keynesian thought should be made aware of the fact that George Shackle (1939, p. 100) composed a positive and complementary review of Dennison et al.'s (1938) *Toward Full Employment*, noting, "In a field where useful thinking is strenuous, the several authors of this book have earned admiration and gratitude. Their thinking is almost everywhere rigorous and clear, and the evidence of care and enthusiasm lavished on the book is unmistakable."

9. See James K. Galbraith, "Our New Corporate Republic" (2001). A version of this column appeared earlier in the *Texas Observer*.

10. For the text of the speech see utip.gov.utexas.edu/web/JGarchive/1998/jkg_90th_birthday_party.htm.

11. Elsewhere Galbraith has noted, "In the Berkeley years I was also introduced to Adam Smith, David Ricardo, Karl Marx, the early John Maynard Keynes and the great German economists who sought truth in history and of whom only Werner Sombart seriously entered my consciousness. ... However, after Marshall the major influence on me from those [pre–*General Theory*] years was Thorstein Veblen" (1981, p. 29).

12. Rab Butler was at a certain point a Chancellor of the Exchequer and was, at that time, Master of Trinity College, Cambridge (see Galbraith, 1981, pp. 525–28).

REFERENCES

Bruce, K. "Conflict and Conversion: Henry S. Dennison and the Shaping of John Kenneth Galbraith's Economic Thought." *Journal of Economic Issues*, 2000, 36 (4), 949–67.

———. "The Making of a Heterodox Economist: The Impact of Henry S. Dennison on the Economic Thought of John Kenneth Galbraith." In M. Keaney (ed.), *Economist with a Public Purpose: Essays in Honour of John Kenneth Galbraith*. London: Routledge, 2001, pp. 25–50.

Chamberlin, E. H. *Theory of Monopolistic Competition: A Re-Orientation of the Theory of Value*. Cambridge: Harvard University Press, 1933. [8th ed., 1962.]

Coase, R. H. "The Nature of the Firm." *Economica*, 1937, 4 (new series), 386–405.

Dennison, H. S., and Galbraith, J. K. *Modern Competition and Business Policy*. New York: Oxford University Press, 1938.

Dennison, H. S., Filene, L. A., Flanders, R. E., and Leeds, M. *Toward Full Employment*. New York: Whittlesley House, 1938.

Dunn, S. P. "Wither Post Keynesianism?" *Journal of Post Keynesian Economics*, Spring 2000a, 22 (3), 343–64.

———. "'Fundamental' Uncertainty and the Firm in the Long Run." *Review of Political Economy*, 2000b, 12 (4), 419–33.

———. "Uncertainty, Strategic Decision-Making and the Essence of the Modern Corporation: Extending Cowling and Sugden." *The Manchester School*, 2001a, 69 (1), 31–41.

————. "Galbraith, Uncertainty and the Modern Corporation." In M. Keaney (ed.), *Economist with a Public Purpose: Essays in Honour of John Kenneth Galbraith*. London: Routledge, 2001b, pp. 157–82.

————. "Bounded Rationality Is Not Fundamental Uncertainty: A Post Keynesian Perspective." *Journal of Post Keynesian Economics*, Summer 2001c, 23 (4), 567–88.

————. "A Post Keynesian Approach to the Theory of the Firm." In S. C. Dow and J. Hillard (eds.), *Post Keynesian Econometrics and the Theory of the Firm: Beyond Keynes, Volume One*. Cheltenham, UK: Edward Elgar, 2002a, forthcoming.

————. "Towards a Post Keynesian Theory of the Multinational Corporation: Some Galbraithian Insights." In K. Nielson (ed.), *Uncertainty and Economic Decision-Making: Ambiguity, Mental Models and Institutions*. Cheltenham, UK: Edward Elgar, 2002b, forthcoming.

Galbraith, J. K. *The New Industrial State*. London: Hamish Hamilton, 1967. [2d ed. Harmondsworth, UK: Penguin, 1974.]

————. "Scotland's Greatest Son." *Horizon*, Summer 1974. [Reprinted as "The Founding Faith: Adam Smith's *Wealth of Nations*." *Annals of an Abiding Liberal*, J. K. Galbraith. London: Andre Deutsch, 1979.]

————. "The Bimodal Image of the Modern Economy: Remarks Upon Receipt of the Veblen-Common's Award." *Journal of Economic Issues*, June 1977. [Reprinted as "The Valid Image of the Modern Economy." *Annals of an Abiding Liberal*, J. K. Galbraith. London: Andre Deutsch, 1979.]

————. *A Life in Our Times: Memoirs*. Boston: Houghton Mifflin, 1981.

Galbraith, J. K., Jr. "Galbraith and the Theory of the Corporation." *Journal of Post Keynesian Economics*, Fall 1984, 7 (1), 43–60.

————. "Our New Corporate Republic." *Boston Globe*, January 7, 2001.

Hymer, S. H. "The Efficiency (Contradictions) of Multinational Corporations." *American Economic Review, Papers and Proceedings*, May 1970, 60 (2), 441–48.

————. *The International Operations of National Firms*. Cambridge, MA: MIT Press, 1976.

Penrose, E. T. *The Theory of the Growth of the Firm*. Oxford: Basil Blackwell, 1959.

Richardson, G. B. *Information and Investment*. Oxford: Clarendon Press, 1960.

————. "The Organisation of Industry." *Economic Journal*, September 1972, 82, 883–96.

Robinson, J. *Economics of Imperfect Competition*. London: Macmillan, 1933.

Shackle, G. L. S. "Review of H. S. Dennison and Others, Toward Full Employment." *Economic Journal*, 1939, 49 (193), 100–02.

Sraffa, P. "The Laws of Return Under Competitive Conditions." *Economic Journal*, December 1926, 36, 535–50.

Swedberg, R. *Schumpeter: A Biography*. Princeton: Princeton University Press, 1991. Veblen, T. *The Theory of the Business Enterprise*. New York: Charles Scribner's Sons, 1904.

Williamson, O. E. "The Vertical Integration of Production: Market Failure Considerations." *American Economic Review*, May 1971, 61, 112–23.

————. *Markets and Hierarchies: Analysis and Antitrust Implications*. New York: Free Press, 1975.

————. *The Economic Institutions of Capitalism*. London: Macmillan, 1985.

On Bush, Greed, and God's Ministers: John Kenneth Galbraith Speaks Out

Sharon Basco / 2003

From TomPaine.com, 4 April 2003.

Unsettling times call for comfort from those experienced in coping with challenges. Throughout World War II, John Kenneth Galbraith helped Franklin D. Roosevelt run the economy. Now 95, this venerable veteran of troubled times, former presidential advisor and speech-writer, ambassador and longtime Harvard professor, shared his thoughts on the economy and more with TomPaine.com's Sharon Basco.

TOMPAINE.COM: *Professor Galbraith, does the current economic situation have parallels in any other era, or is the misery of a bad economic situation unique unto itself?*
JOHN KENNETH GALBRAITH: No, it's not unique. The basic characteristic of the modern economy goes from boom to recession. And we had a period of rather wild boom and speculation, and now as in the normal course of events, we're having a recession. And the recession is made worse by somewhat perverse economic policy. I say somewhat perverse; quite perverse.

TP.C: *What perversion are you referring to? The Bush administration's tax cuts?*
GALBRAITH: I wouldn't attribute it to George Bush any more than I would to the established view of the industrial community, of the corporate elite,

which urges action—as we all do—for their own financial benefit. As, for example, in the proposal to cut taxes on dividends. That is a benefit for people who don't need the money and may not spend.

And then we will have partly as a result of the war, a substantial budget deficit, and that will lead to pressure to control social spending, help for the poor. And they are the people who are reliable spenders. If you have no money and get some money you're a favorable force on the economy because you have to spend it. So we have a policy which is bad for—excepting recession—for the speculation that leads to it and a policy that is bad, or at least inadequate, for doing anything about it. We rely on the Federal Reserve, but it has had years of demonstration as to how little effect it has.

TP.COM: *Why would a president lead an economy down this path unless he had great faith in a supply-side, trickle-down approach?*
GALBRAITH: Well I would respond with two observations. First, I don't believe that President Bush has economic judgment of any great depth, and second, he relies on what one would call the corporate elite, which automatically and reliably comes in for any action which seems to be in its own interest, which seems to support earnings and dividends, and not the reliable expenditure of the masses of the people and the poor. We have economy there, and a liberal policy of tax-cutting for the rich.

TP.C: *When you speak of rich corporate types wanting even more money, it brings to mind the greed you described in a book you wrote almost 50 years ago,* The Great Crash: 1929. *Have we seen all this before? Is there anything new about today's greed?*
GALBRAITH: I would have to make a personal apology because you ask me a question about a book that is just going to press. I will even give you the title. It's called *The Economics of Innocent Fraud*, and there is a misguidance—perhaps I shouldn't say fraud—in the way that the great corporations respond to their power that they now have. They have replaced the old-fashioned capitalists as the influence in the modern economy.

We see one effect of the corporate management in the way in which they have, on occasion, rewarded themselves. They have used their power for their own extreme enrichment, the so-called corporate scandals. But they have also been strongly in support of a policy which is good for corporate earnings—as you would expect—and they have been on the general side of conservative social policy, where money gets reliably spent.

I don't attribute that to George Bush. I attribute it to the larger community which has come into power with him.

T.P.C: *I think some of us puzzle over why it is that the very greedy CEOs aren't concerned about the long run, about the harm they're wreaking on their organizations?*
GALBRAITH: They're not doing anything illegal. They're taking advantage of a power that corporate management endows them with. And this is a very great power that is passed from stockholders, shareholders to management. And that is an opportunity that exists—I think it's fair to say that most corporate managements are respectful of it, do not carry it to excess, although they're likely to be fairly generous—and that some have carried it to excess and provided in the last year or two for a great deal of newspaper comment. And the invention—which I must say I never expected—an invention of the word "corporate scandal" which is now in common use.

T.P.C: *How do you see the proposed tax cuts playing out in years to come?*
GALBRAITH: It will reward basically people who already have a very good flow of income. And will not greatly increase their spending, certainly for consumer's goods, and maybe not for any useful investment, times being bad. And it will lead to pressure for economy, along with the war debt, that is the result of the large public deficits. So that, on the whole, it will lead to a policy which doesn't have any regenerative, any good effect, and has some possibility of making things worse.

I would like to be optimistic, that's my basic tendency in life, always to assume the best will happen. But I don't think anybody, given the present situation of the economy, can be wholly optimistic about the future of the economy.

TP.C: *Do you see the Bush policies creating economic problems that will last a long time? Could a new economic approach, or let's say a different administration, improve the economic picture in a few years?*

GALBRAITH: Oh sure. I'm not that pessimistic. There's always the possibility that we will have a situation, an economic situation which all but forces a turn-around. That's possibility we must keep in mind.

Could I conclude with something that I've encountered in the last few days from my own history? It was the day after Pearl Harbor, when we had a situation in Washington that could have been crucifying as regards our entry and our participation in the war. It became evident that the Japanese were going south, and we would have no more natural rubber from the southern part of the continent. And the responsibility came to me, because I was in charge of both price control and rationing, to do what needed to be done.

And with the support of the governors of the various states, who gave us some help from the highway patrol, I put into effect—we put into effect, I should say, but I was the person responsible, and it was done from our house in Washington—a rigorous prohibition of the sale of rubber tires except for a few absolutely essential people, which included doctors. It included people with a key role in the defense program—there were perhaps half a dozen altogether. And that, I say, was on a Sunday night. On Monday, it was big news. And on Tuesday I got the message of my life from Franklin D. Roosevelt. It commented on the action and said: "What congenital idiot thought that you could say that ministers of the gospel were not essential?" Franklin D. Roosevelt.

TP.C: *So did you make an exception for ministers of the gospel?*
GALBRAITH: Early the next morning!

TP.C: *Well, speaking of presidents who claim a close partnership with God, is it possible that Bush's economic policies will work?*
GALBRAITH: I don't think so. If you're poor or in the middle-income brackets and you get more money, you will most likely spend it. And those who are very rich—in the multiple thousands and millions brackets—getting

more money are not reliable spenders. They don't have a sense of urgency. They've already satisfied their basic aspirations and wants.

TP.C: *Thank you, Professor Galbraith.*
GALBRAITH: It was a great pleasure.

TP.C: *Professor John Kenneth Galbraith, speaking from his home in Cambridge, Massachusetts.*

Index

Acheson, Dean, 12
Ackley, Gardner, 18
Affluent Society, The, xiii, xv, 3, 16, 49, 60,
   83, 95, 104, 106, 116, 142, 153, 161,
   176, 192, 200, 206, 208
Age of Uncertainty, The, xv, 208
Agee, James, 189
aggregate demand policy, xiii, xv,
   22–23, 51–52, 133–34, 141–43, 162,
   171, 183, 193. *See also* economic
   stabilization policy
aging, xvii, 175–76
Agriculture, Department of, xii, 182
American Capitalism, 121
American Economic Association, 146
American establishment, 47–48
Americans for Democratic Action
   (ADA), xii, 30, 44–45
Anatomy of Power, The, 116
Atlantic Monthly, 130

Baruch, Bernard, 46
BBC-TV, 105
Berkeley, University of California at, xi,
   181, 198, 220
Black, John D., 183
Black Thursday, 21
Brady, Robert, xi, 181
Brezhnev, L., 93
Britain, 3

British economy, 3, 4
Bruce, K., 224
Bryce, Robert, 185
bubble economy, 209, 212
Buckley, William F., Jr., 107, 177, 200–1,
   205
Bundy, McGeorge, 48
Burma, 42
Bush, George H., 142, 151, 164, 170,
   225
Bush, George W., 234, 238–39, 241
Butler, Rab, 230

Cabot, Charles, 199
Capitalism, Communism and Co-Existence, 147
Central Europe. *See* East-Central Europe
Challenge Magazine, xv, xvi
Chamberlin, Ed, 184, 220, 227, 233
Chayes, Abe, 39
China Passage, A, xvii
CIA, 41
Clay, General Lucius, 64
Clinton, William J., 193
Cohen, Wilbur, 47
Colander, David C., xvii
Common Market, 13
communism, 13, 43, 67, 173
comparative economics, xvii
Conant, James B., 199
Congress, 89th, 19

convenient social virtue, xiv, 84, 85
conventional wisdom, xi, 47, 50
countervailing power, xi, xiv, 164
Cox, Archibald, 39
creative destruction, 210
Culture of Contentment, The, 165–66, 169
Currie, Lauchlin, 183, 187

Davidson, Paul, 234
Davis, William, xvii
De Gaulle, Charles, 109
Democratic Party, 45
Dennison, Henry, 184, 224
Department of State, 12, 33, 38–39,
    41–42, 70
devaluation of the dollar, 58
dual economy, xv, 6, 76–81, 83, 86, 89,
    95–98, 101–2, 104, 121, 126–27,
    135, 208–9, 218, 223
Dunn, Stephen P., xii

East-Central Europe, xii, 13, 148, 149,
    163, 226
Eastern Economic Journal, xv
economic development, xvii, 132, 153,
    156, 158–59
economic stabilization policy, xiii, xvi,
    17, 21, 99, 104, 107, 111, 114, 121,
    123, 131, 133–35, 137, 141–42, 145,
    164, 187, 210–11
Economics and the Public Purpose, xiii, xiv,
    75, 84, 91, 95, 106, 116, 121, 142,
    153, 230
Economics for Our Grandchildren, 213
Economics in Perspective, 132, 144
Economics of Imperfect Competition, 233
Economics of Innocent Fraud, The, 239
education, 7, 172, 202
Eisenhower, Dwight, 20, 27, 64, 190
Engineers and the Price System, The, 181
environment, 214–15

Farm Bureau Federation, 187
Fay, Paul, 40
Filene, Lincoln, 185

fiscal policy. *See also* aggregate demand
    policy
Fisher, Irving, 20
Fleming, Ian, 40
Fortune Magazine, 130, 189, 199, 223,
    229
France, 6
Frank, Jerome, 182
Friedman, Milton, 134

Galbraith, Catherine, 177, 217, 221
Galbraith, Jamie, 225
Galbraithian System, 220, 227, 232
General Theory, The, 141, 181, 184, 186,
    221, 224
Germany, xii, 6, 14
Giannini Foundation of Agricultural
    Economics, 182
Gingrich, Newt, 194
Goldwater, Barry, 27
Good Society, The, 178, 192
Gordon, Myron, 128
Graham, Frank, 187
Great Crash, The, xv, 57, 106, 108, 205,
    239
Great Society, 17, 19, 20
Greenspan, Alan, 210
Grether, Ewaldt, 140, 220
Gruening, Ernest, 73
guaranteed minimum income, 9, 59, 87,
    89, 92, 97, 102, 207, 214
Gulf War, 171

Halberstam, David, 39
Hansen, Alvin, 185, 189
Harriman, Averell, 12
Harvard University, xii
Hayek, F. A., 49, 221
Hazlitt, Henry, 52
Head Start, 8, 19
Heller, Walter, 17, 20
Henderson, Leon, 222, 231
Hoffman, Paul, 12
Hoovervilles, 198
Humphrey, Hubert, 45

In These Times, xvii
India, xii, 37, 130, 159, 167, 203
Indochina, 38
industrial policy, xiii, 145, 211
Institutionalist School, xi, xvii, 219
International Monetary Fund, 211
Internet, 213

Japan, 210, 214, 215
Job Corps, 8
Johnson, General Hugh, 64
Johnson, Lyndon, 10, 13, 20, 24, 34, 39, 43, 44, 106, 200
Journal of Post Keynesian Economics, xv, 234
Journey to Poland and Yugoslavia, xvii, 147

Kaldor, Nicholas, 226, 233
Kalecki, Michael, 148, 225
Kennedy, Edward, xii
Kennedy, Jacqueline, 40
Kennedy, John F., xii, 10–11, 20, 27, 35, 37–39, 43, 48, 106, 130, 200
Kennedy, Robert, 40, 43, 68, 108
Keynes, John Maynard, xi, xiii, xvi, xvii, 18, 49, 87, 94, 140–41, 181, 186, 190, 193, 213, 220, 224
Keynesian policy. *See* aggregate demand policy
Keynesianism, 17, 183, 185–86, 189, 221–22. *See also* aggregate demand policy
Killingsworth, Charles, 18
Korea, 65

Landreth, Harry, xvii
Lange, Oskar, 148
Leeds, Morris, 185
Lekachman, Robert, 17
LeMay, Curtis, 63
Lewis, Anthony, xvii
Life in Our Time, A, 225
Lippman, Walter, 12
Loeb, James, Jr., 45
London School of Economics, 221
Long Term Capital Management, 212

Los Angeles riots, 173
Lowenstein, Al, 44
Luce, Henry, 189, 199

Macdonald, Dwight, 189
MacLandress Dimension, 108
MacLeish, Archibald, 189
Manchester, William, 40
Mao Tse-tung, 69
market system. *See* dual economy
Marshall, Alfred, xii, 132, 140, 224
Marshallian System, 220
Martin, William M., 22
Marx, Karl, 101, 141–42, 181
McCarthy, Eugene, xii, 30, 44, 200
McClaughry, John, xv
McCloy, John, 12, 47, 48
McGovern, George, xii, 97
Medicare, 46–47
military establishment, 137, 171
Mill, John Stuart, 141
Modern Competition and Business Policy, 184, 224
monetary policy. *See* aggregate demand policy
Money: Whence It Came and Where It Went, 105
Monopolistic Competition, 233
Morse, Wayne, 73
Moynihan, Patrick, 98

National Planning Association, 222
negative income tax. *See* guaranteed minimum income
Nehru, Prime Minister, 37
neoclassical economics, xii, 75, 78, 82, 93, 95, 128, 140, 185
New Deal, xii, 18, 34, 49, 161, 182, 187, 193, 207, 222
new economy, 212
New Frontier, 16
New Industrial State, The, xiii, xiv, 39, 51, 61, 78, 80, 95, 104, 106, 116–17, 153, 208, 228, 230
new socialism, 88, 91, 95, 103

new socialist imperative, 88
Newark, John, xvii
Nixon, Richard, 27, 93, 96, 98, 131

Office of Price Administration, xii, 189, 231
Office of Price Control, 187
Office of Strategic Services, xii
Ontario Agriculture College, xi

Pell, Claiborne, 147
Pethwick, 42
planning system. *See* dual economy
Playboy, xv, xvii
Plehn, Carl E., 181
Polish economy, problems with, 149–51
political asymmetry, 133–34
Post Keynesianism, 217, 234
poverty, 8–9, 16, 59, 154, 156–57, 194, 202, 214
power, xiii–xiv, xv, 91, 113, 116–20, 122, 124–26, 239–40; theory of countervailing, 120–21, 123, 163
Pressman, Steven, xii, xv
Princeton, 187
Public Broadcasting System, xv
public cognizance, 86, 87
Public Works Administration, 222

Reagan, Ronald, 27, 130
Reaganomics, 142–44, 162
reform, general theory of, 85–89, 101, 124
Reich, Robert, 125–26, 145
Reston, James, 72
Review of Political Economy, xv
Ricardo, David, 142, 221
Robbins, Lionel, 141
Robinson, Joan, 184, 220, 230, 233
Roche, John, 44
Rockefeller, Governor, 28
Rogin, Leo, xi, 181
Rohatyn, Felix, 126
Roosevelt, Franklin D., 198, 207, 241
Rowstow, Walt, 67
Rusk, Dean, 70

Salinger, Pierre, 40
savings and loan crises, 144, 151, 164
Scandinavian model, 216
Schlesinger, Arthur, 10, 33, 39, 43, 45, 70, 205
Schumpeter, Joseph A., 141, 185, 210, 227–28
Scotch, The, 106, 109
Selective Service System, 61
Senate Foreign Relations Committee, xvii
Sexual Revolution, 61
Shriver, Sargent, 8
Simon, Norton, 103
Smith, Adam, 142, 187, 222
Smith, "Cotton" Ed, 197
social (im)balance, theory of, xiv, xv, 83, 84, 102
Social Science Research Fellowship, 186
social security, 59, 130, 162
socialism, 91–93, 103, 163, 167
Somervell, General Brehorn, 64
Sorenson, Theodore, 33, 39
Southeast Asia, 43
Sraffa, P., 220
Stein, Herbert, 96–97, 103
Steinem, Gloria, 205
Stevenson, Adlai, xii, 108, 182
stock market, 22, 130–31, 165, 204, 206
Sweezy, Paul, 99–100

Taussig's *Principles of Economics*, 183
taxes, xvi, 17–18, 53, 56, 144, 161, 171, 238, 240
technostructure, xi, 80, 95, 99–101, 218, 228
Theory of Price Control, The, xii, 50, 188
Theory of the Business Enterprise, 181, 220
Thorson, Thomas, 69
Thurow, Lester, 145
Toward Full Employment, 185
Treatise on Money, A, 186

Triumph, The, 41, 108
Truman, Harry, 46
Tugwell, Rexford, 182
Twining, Nat, 63

Udall, Morris, xii
Ulmer, Melville, 98
United Kingdom, 3–6
United Nations, 203
U.S. Strategic Bombing Survey, 190, 199

Veblen, Thorstein, xii, 128, 140, 181, 182, 220, 224
Veritas Foundation, 190
Vietnam, xii, 8, 9, 14, 18–19, 21, 24, 43–44, 46–47, 53, 66–69, 71–72, 107, 120, 168, 200

wage-price spiral, xv, 71, 121, 134–35, 137–38. *See also* aggregate demand policy; economic stabilization policy
Wall Street, 165, 209
Wallace, George, 29
Wallace, Henry, 182
Wealth of Nations, The, 222
Weber, Max, 116
Weisner, Jerome, 37
Whittlesey, Ray, 187
women, in economic life, 84–85, 141
Works Progress Administration, 222
World Bank, 214
World War I, xiii
World War II, xiii
Wylie, Craig, 107

Youth Corps, 19

CONVERSATIONS WITH PUBLIC INTELLECTUALS SERIES

Douglas Brinkley and David Oshinsky, General Editors
The collected interviews with notable public intellectuals, including

Betty Friedan ~ George F. Kennan ~ Dwight Macdonald ~
Edward W. Said